BESS

BESS

THE LIFE OF LADY RALEGH,
WIFE TO SIR WALTER

ANNA BEER

CONSTABLE · LONDON

Constable & Robinson Ltd
3 The Lanchesters
162 Fulham Palace Road
London W6 9ER
www.constablerobinson.com

First published in the UK by Constable
an imprint of Constable & Robinson Ltd 2004

A copy of the British Library Cataloguing in
Publication Data is available from the British Library

ISBN 1-84119-542-1

Printed and bound in the EU

For Becca and Elise

Contents

———

Acknowledgements		ix
List of Illustrations		xiii
Map		xv
Family tree		xvi
Introduction: 'Wantonness and Wit': The Court of the Virgin Queen		1
1	'My One and Only Daughter': Growing Up Under Elizabeth	13
2	'True Within Ourselves': Bess and Sir Walter	57
3	'Him That I Am': Building a Life at Sherborne	77
4	'A Most Dangerous Woman': The Return to Power	103
5	'My Dead Heart': The Traitor's Wife?	139
6	'Of Liberty Deprived': The Tower Years	159
7	'God In Mercy Look On Us': Journey's End	201
8	'*Generosa Virago*': Creating the Future	223

CONTENTS

Epilogue   255

Notes and References   263

Appendix   269

Note on Methodology   273

Annotated Bibliography   275

Index   281

Acknowledgements

One of the pleasures of writing a book such as this has been to meet and communicate with so many new people, who, in their various capacities, have shared their knowledge with me generously. I am also blessed with some remarkable friends and family, whose expertise and kindness I have drawn on in equal measure.

I am grateful for the help of the staff at the Gloucestershire Records Office, the Surrey History Centre, the Berkshire Records Office, the Sutton History Centre, the Northamptonshire Records Office, the Guildhall, the Bodleian Library, the Public Records Office, the Heinz Archive at the National Portrait Gallery, the British Library, the Folger Shakespeare Library, Angela Max at the Société Jersiase and Mary Robertson at the Huntington Library. The Marquess of Salisbury has kindly given permission to quote from the Cecil Papers. I am especially grateful to the individuals who welcomed me into their homes or into the churches in their care: to the Duchess of Roxburgh at West Horsley; to Mrs Ann Grace, the Church Warden at West Horsley; to Mrs Ann Smith, the archivist at Sherborne, and to the Wingfield Digby family, who generously permitted me access to the room believed to be Ralegh's turret study; and to the kindly Church Warden at Paulerspury, who left her afternoon baking in order to show me Arthur and Anna Throckmorton's remarkable tomb.

ACKNOWLEDGEMENTS

The following experts have offered invaluable advice and information in their particular areas: Karen Hearn on portraiture; Geoffrey Tyack on architectural history; Mark Nicholls on the Main and Bye plots; Stephen Clucas and G. R. Batho on the Earl of Northumberland; Deborah Harkness on medical history; Steven May on the Elizabethan court; and Justin Lewis-Anthony on all matters Anglican. Thank you also to Penny Tyack and to John and Ann Sants for fascinating analyses of Bess's spelling, to David Skinner and Brian Robinson for their translations (Latin and Italian respectively), and to Katrina Crossley for an evocative trip to the Middle Temple. Throughout the writing of the book it has been a pleasure to discuss various issues with another aficionado of Bess, Karen Robertson of Vassar.

A small number of people have been burdened with reading my work in progress, and have proved themselves constructive critics and fine friends: thanks especially to Jim Holstun and Karen Elliott. Jan Fossgard, Martin Gorst, Trevor Aston and Kathryn Morrison deserve particular acknowledgement for encouraging me to write the book in the first place, and other friends have helped me stay the course in different ways. Thanks to Jenny Quayle for the lip-gloss, to Sian Lewis-Anthony for the best (but sadly unused) title, to Paul Schwartfeger for Atlantic, to Roger Harvey for Lady Carbury, to Rebecca Williams for the lack of toffees, and to Chris Insole for the third bottle.

My colleagues at Regent's Park College have provided a valuable sense of community over the last few years, but I am even more grateful to all of my students, both past and present. Each one of them has made me think in new ways, but I would particularly like to thank Sarah Keenan, Kate Arthur, Lesley Wood, Clare Backhouse, Julia Richardson, Paul Whyles, Tony Brignull, the members of the Women's Voices classes in both Oxford and Witney, and the remarkable Merton Shakespeare group.

I have been extremely lucky to have a superb editor in Carol O'Brien. From the very start she has combined rigour with enthusiasm, making my task of writing a real pleasure. Thank you, Carol.

Last thanks need to go to my family, all of whom have had their own challenges to face during the writing of this book, and all of whom have shown incredible willingness nevertheless to provide practical and emotional support. It is not always easy having a writer in the family. Thanks, therefore, to Steve Roberts, to Matt and Ann Beer, to Katey Anderson and, above all, to my mother, Margaret Beer: quite simply, I could not have done it without you. But *Bess* is dedicated, with my love, to my daughters, Becca and Elise.

List of Illustrations

Bess as a young woman (*c.*1591)
Courtesy of the National Portrait Gallery, London

Bess's hand-written letter to Robert Cecil, November 1603
Courtesy of the Marquess of Salisbury, Hatfield House

'Bess as Cleopatra' – a doubtful attribution
Courtesy of the National Portrait Gallery, London

Bess in middle age (*c.*1603)

Bess in widowhood with her son Carew (*c.*1619)
Courtesy of the National Portrait Gallery, London

Nicholas Throckmorton, Bess's father
Courtesy of the National Portrait Gallery, London

Sir Walter as a young man (copy of a miniature by Nicholas Hilliard, *c.*1585)

Sir Walter in 1588

Sir Walter with his son Wat (1602)

Bess's miniature of her son Wat (*c.*1619)

Sir Walter in middle age (*c.*1597)

LIST OF ILLUSTRATIONS

Queen Elizabeth I: the Rainbow Portrait

Queen Anne of Denmark

King James I

Robert Cecil, Earl of Salisbury

Robert Devereux, 2nd Earl of Essex

The Tower of London in Bess's time (from 'A True and Exact Draught of the Tower Liberties, survey'd in the year 1597')

Present day Sherborne Castle

A typical Jacobean interior

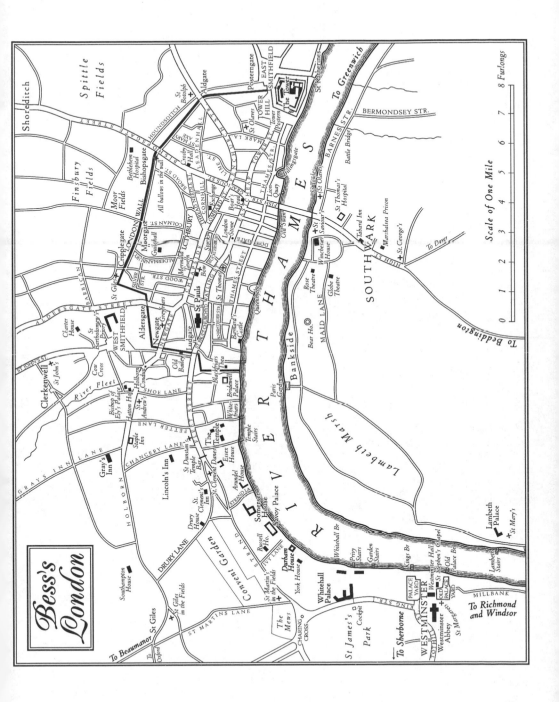

Bess's Family

Sir Walter's Family

Sir Walter's Family:

Katherine Champernoun m.

(1) Otho Gilbert

John Gilbert

Humphrey Gilbert

Adrian Gilbert

(2) Walter Ralegh

Margaret Ralegh

Carew Ralegh

Sir Walter Ralegh ex 1618 m. Bess Throckmorton

Bess's Family:

HENRY VII m. Elizabeth of York

Arthur

HENRY VIII

Margaret Tudor

Mary Tudor d. 1533 m.

(1) Louis XII of France d. 1515

(2) Charles Brandon, Duke of Suffolk d. 1545

Frances Brandon m.

(1) Henry Grey, Duke of Suffolk ex. 1554

(2) Adrian Stokes d.1585

Jane Grey ex. 1554

Catherine Grey d. 1568

Mary Grey d. 1578

Nicholas Carew ex. 1539 m. Elizabeth

Anne Carew d. 1587 m. and 3 daughters

Francis Carew d. 1611 (without heir)

(1) Nicholas Throckmorton d.1571

George Throckmorton m. Katherine Vaux

John

Clement

Francis Throckmorton ex. 1584

Job Throckmorton

and 16 sons and daughters

Arthur d.1626 m. Anna Lucas

and 4 sons

Nicholas d.1643 m. Mary More

Bess d.1647 m. Walter Ralegh

Damerei d. 1592

Walter d. 1618

Carew d. 1666 m. Philippa Ashley

Introduction: Wantonness and Wit: The Court of the Virgin Queen

October 1591

It is a misty autumn morning and the air off the nearby Thames is chill. A woman of twenty-six wakes early, and, although she feels tired and sick, she rises nevertheless, because she must be ready to attend on her mistress. Beside her, on a straw-covered bed, lies her own woman servant, who will prepare her for the day. After washing her face and hands in a bowl of water, she dresses. Over her underclothes and smock she puts on a corset ('a pair of bodies') made stiff with whalebone. The bodies flatten her rounded stomach and push her breasts high, to fill the low square neckline of her heavy dress. The dress is a valuable gift from her mistress; the headdress she places on her dark hair is perhaps a gift from a suitor, courting her influence. Then from her closet she takes some jewels from a case. She decides to wear her mother's pearls, bequeathed to her four years earlier. The long string is looped around her neck three, four times and still hangs down to her waist. Purse, handkerchief and fan are taken up, and then, on a girdle fastened around her waist, she hangs her scissors and penknife, her bodkin and her seal. Bess Throckmorton, Gentlewoman of the Privy Chamber, is now ready for her day's work, her body's

1

secret concealed beneath her clothes. She walks from her own bed-chamber to that of her mistress, under the gilt ceiling of the Privy Chamber, past the eyes of King Henry VIII gazing out of a mural of the Tudor dynasty painted by the master himself, Hans Holbein.

In the bed of state lies 'the most high, mighty and magnificent empress, by grace of God Queen of England, France and Ireland, and of Virginia, Defender of the Faith', Elizabeth I.

The Queen is not, and never has been, a morning person, and her Gentlewomen know to tread carefully this early in the day. Today, Elizabeth breaks her fast, sharing her food with her women, and then walks, still in her nightclothes, in the Privy Garden. Later, her women help dress the Queen in her sumptuous robes, make up her face with the white lead that worked its poison into the skin, and adorn her hair and body with the richest jewels in the land. At fifty-eight years of age, the ageing Queen has her own secrets to hide. Only now would men be allowed into this morning world of women.

First to enter is the Queen's Captain of the Guard, her personal bodyguard, a post entailing close attendance upon the monarch, a post which sanctions the Captain's access to his mistress in her Privy Chamber. The possessor of this coveted position is Sir Walter Ralegh: he is in his mid-thirties, strikingly handsome, with thick, dark, curly hair and knowing brown eyes. Ralegh has done very well for himself from relatively humble beginnings, and he knows it, boasting to his friends of his 'nearness' to the Queen. Others were less charitable: the man who represented himself as the ocean, punning on his own Devonshire pronunciation of his first name, was to his enemies 'filthy puddle water'. How could the Queen stoop to his level? But Ralegh, undeterred, carries his sword with the confidence of the seasoned soldier and adventurer, yet is also dressed magnificently, even by the standards of this rich court. Two pearls the size of quails' eggs hang from one of his ears, while even the shoes on his feet are encrusted with jewels 'worth more than six thousand, six hundred gold pieces', or so people said. He wears the monarch's colours, black and white, the fabric studded with pearls, a further symbol of his devotion to his Virgin Queen's inviolable chastity. Sir Walter's eloquent poetry – for he is a man of many talents – is known for its passionate celebration of Elizabeth's eternal power. The Queen is the moon goddess

Cynthia, and he is the sea, the 'water', whose every movement is governed by her power, the depth of his love mirroring the depth of the waters: 'Ocean's Love to Cynthia' would be his greatest work of poetry. To the Queen, her poet is also her 'little pug', the man from whom she cannot bear to be separated for long. Ralegh's very motto, 'amor et vertute' (love and virtue), confirms that he is the Queen's man, her loyal, virtuous lover.

The Queen herself knows the value of maintaining convenient political fictions. These were the years in which all images of Elizabeth that suggested age and thus mortality were suppressed, any realism displaced by a formalized mask of youth. Sir Walter knows this more than anyone since he had helped forge the image of the Virgin Queen.

Today, Elizabeth needs to talk to Sir Walter about an emerging political crisis. News was coming through that English ships had suffered a humiliating defeat at the hands of the enemy, Spain. The very ship that Ralegh was to have sailed in (if only the Queen had permitted him to leave her side) had been taken by the Spanish, the only loss of an English vessel over the many years of war. Could Sir Walter perhaps write something that would turn this actual defeat into a moral victory? Of course he could. Ralegh's 'The Last Fight of the *Revenge*' tells the glorious story of one lone English captain's brave stand against a vast Spanish fleet. Yes, the ship had been lost, yes, the captain had been killed, but all the glory was England's, and that of her Queen. Sir Richard Grenville's foolish, dangerous lone stand is transformed into an act of transcendent heroism. Ralegh's Queen is ordained by God to bring Spanish Catholicism to its knees, and to lead England to further Protestant greatness. Elizabeth 'by the favour of God' will continue to 'resist, repel, and confound all whatsoever attempts against her sacred Person or kingdom. In the meantime, let the Spaniard and traitor vaunt of their success: and we her true and obedient vassals guided by the shining light of her virtues, shall always love her, serve her, and obey her to the end of our lives.'

At least two of her ostensibly true and obedient vassals were having some difficulty with a number of these aims. Bess Throckmorton, Gentlewoman of the Privy Chamber, was five months pregnant. The father of her baby was the Queen's own 'virtuous lover', Sir Walter

3

Ralegh. This autumn they would marry in such secrecy that it is still unclear when the ceremony took place. They were desperate to conceal their long-standing sexual relationship and their recent marriage, which, if exposed, would reveal as a hollow sham both of their public identities. They were not alone in their covert undermining of the Queen's sexualized power games. The gap between the physical reality of the court and the ever more extravagant myth-making was increasingly visible. The atmosphere of deception and lies encouraged cynicism: a few years earlier, Sir Walter had written to his friend and cousin George Carew that 'the Queen thinks that George Carew longs to see her; and therefore see her'. Alongside the cynicism, frustration with the rule of the Virgin Queen led to frequent eruptions of distinctly unchaste behaviour. The year 1591 was a particularly fruitful one for sex scandals, ranging from the banishment of Mr Dudley for kissing Mistress Cavendish, to Sir Francis Darcy being sent to the Tower 'about Mistress Lee who was brought abed in the court'. Others, such as Sir Walter Ralegh himself, successfully concealed their own activities. In the summer of 1589, Ralegh, visiting his estates in Ireland, became involved with a young woman, Alice Gould. Alice became pregnant, and Ralegh headed swiftly back to England. When Alice's father wrote to Ralegh in October, his claim that Ralegh had been 'too forward' with his daughter was dismissed. Sir Walter insisted that he had only returned to London because, as he put it, 'my nearness to Her Majesty makes me much business here'. In a postscript of striking insouciance Ralegh writes: 'Commend me to the gentlewoman your daughter.' Ralegh was lying, something he invariably did under pressure. In his will made eight years later, he would acknowledge a daughter born 'upon the body of' young Alice Gould.

Ralegh's disloyalty towards Alice Gould was on a small scale when compared with his and Bess Throckmorton's disloyalty to their Queen. The scale of Bess's and Sir Walter's political betrayal can be understood only in terms of the mechanics of personal monarchy. Outside the Privy Chamber, where Bess and Sir Walter were permitted access, lay the Gallery, the Great Hall, the Great Chamber and the massive Presence Chamber, dominated by the royal throne and its canopy. To get anywhere near this throne, to get anywhere near the

Royal Presence, sometimes took Queen Elizabeth's subjects months of bribes, gifts and letters. Even then, the Queen might not emerge from her guarded and locked private chambers. The wait would be worth it, since this was the only place that counted: all power rested in the will and person of the Queen 'and was quintessentially personal. Access was all'.[1] The Privy Chamber was thus the Queen's main refuge from the constant pressure from those who wanted access to her. Her Gentlewomen shielded her from the demands of her nation. Her Captain of the Guard protected the royal body from the very real threat of assassination. The women who attended her, the men who shielded her, had to be loyal to the Queen and the Queen alone.

Generations of Ralegh biographers have, understandably, focused on his relationship with Bess from their hero's perspective. He invariably emerges as both virile and culpable, Bess as both his sexual victim and his political nemesis. So one of the earliest lives of Sir Walter has him roguishly 'devirginating a Maid of Honour' (deemed 'the worst Action of his whole Life') but nevertheless doing the honourable thing and marrying 'the Object of his Love, the deflowered Lady'. Three hundred years on, Robert Lacey, author of the most readable twentieth-century biography of Ralegh, 'knows' that Bess (how could she not?) 'succumbed' to Ralegh's overflowing passion, but notes that he thus risked 'a substantial loss of income and prestige' for indulging his natural desires.

But what if Bess was not a passive and innocent victim of Sir Walter's skilful seduction techniques? This is not to diminish Ralegh's attractions. His immense wealth and handsome face might well have been enough for many. He was charming, experienced, urbane. He was also suspiciously like Bess's own father in appearance and outlook. Both men were comfortable with Machiavellian politics, with *realpolitik*, both men proponents and practitioners of aggressive foreign policies.[2] A comparison of portraits of the two men even shows the same dark, almost Celtic, good looks.

But there was more to it than this. In an era in which the personal *was* the political, Bess's pregnancy and secret marriage were indicative of her involvement at the highest levels in a challenge to the power, authority and future of the Queen herself. These were the years in which it was clear to her subjects that the Queen would not have an heir from her own body, when aspiring courtiers looked to a brave new political world after Elizabeth's death. If the political vision of what was called, euphemistically, a monarchical republic surfaced repeatedly in the early and middle years of Elizabeth's reign, finding particular voice when the Queen's death seemed possible, and there was still no successor to the throne, then it gathered force in the closing years of her solitary rule. Who would emerge as the leaders of the nation when the old Queen died? Bess had her own political ambitions. They had been nurtured for years by her powerful mother, and now she had manoeuvred herself into a position where she (with a suitable husband and the all-important male offspring) could stake a claim, if not to the throne itself then to a part in a coalition of powerful courtiers on the death of the childless Queen Elizabeth. Bess, whether motivated by ambition or desire, was playing for high stakes by bedding the Queen's political favourite.

In a world 'so interconnected by ties of blood and marriage that very few political relationships could ever be exclusive',[3] it was unlikely that Bess was operating alone. The key players behind the scenes were Robert Devereux and his sister Penelope. Robert, Earl of Essex, had erupted on to the political scene in 1585 as a brilliant and beautiful young seventeen-year-old. It helped that his stepfather was the Earl of Leicester, but Robert was intelligent, accomplished and full of youthful zeal. The Queen liked him, as much if not more than she liked her reigning favourite, Ralegh. It was noted that the Queen was often 'abroad, nobody near her but the Earl of Essex and, at night, my Lord is at cards, or one game or another with her, that he cometh not to his own lodging till birds sing in the morning'. The tensions between Ralegh and Devereux, Earl of Essex, were the stuff of court life. In the dog days of summer 1587, the latter challenged his Queen. She had, according to Essex, tried to exclude one of his sisters from the court. Essex thought he knew who was behind it all: his rival for the Queen's attention, Sir Walter Ralegh, the man he hated for 'what he had been and whose he was': that is, Essex believed that Ralegh had, in his early days, relied on the patronage of the Earl of Leicester but, when success had been thrust upon him, had betrayed his erstwhile patron. Essex was probably right on both counts, although he may have overestimated Ralegh's influence in the case of his sister.

The tension did not abate in the cooler months of the year: in the middle of that winter, the Queen was forced into travelling up the Thames from Greenwich to Richmond to sort out a quarrel between the two rivals.

Biographers have struggled to understand the apparent *rapprochement* between Essex and Ralegh in the early 1590s. It is perhaps no coincidence that this improvement in relations occurred during the time of Bess's illicit involvement with Ralegh. The clue may be Essex's sense of Ralegh as the single, major threat to his own pre-eminence. One way to neutralize him would be to bring his rival within his circle, something Ralegh on his side (with more money than he knew what to do with, but a lurking and unfulfilled aspiration to be accepted into the aristocratic elite of the nation) may have been only too happy to do. Bess was Sir Walter's way into this world. The Earl of Essex did nothing to expose either the affair or the marriage: indeed he may even have encouraged them. And so Ralegh was brought into Essex's sphere, started supporting Essex's causes. Essex was, and Ralegh became, zealous in their support of the more radical Protestant ministers, Bess's cousin Job Throckmorton among them, who were, they believed, being persecuted in England. In 'The Last Fight of the *Revenge*' Ralegh even makes his one-time rival look good, transforming Essex's inept and unwanted participation in a military action two years earlier in Portugal into a masterpiece of martial strategy. Above all, Essex and Ralegh came together in their commitment to war. The latter may have been keen to take up arms against the Spaniards for territorial and economic reasons, the former may have been motivated by his religious ideology and the desire to defend England's fellow Protestants in Europe, but both men were sure of the primary aim: to destroy the power of Catholic Spain. In the spring of 1591, both Essex and Ralegh were delighted by the prospect of a war in France, in support of the Protestant Henry IV. The Earl was desperate to be in command of this expedition and spent two hours on his knees in front of his Queen, begging for the honour. Elizabeth, always her own woman in these matters, gave leadership of the expedition to Sir John Norris. Ralegh's job was to ready the navy for action. As spring turned to summer, he paid out eight thousand pounds for 'sheathing' and victualling the *Garland*, the *Crane*, the *Revenge* and the *Moon*. By early July, Ralegh may have had a point when he complained that he was paying for the war.

The pleasures of warmongering aside, Bess had drawn Sir Walter into a group of young courtiers who knew how to party. Stern commentators looked on at the fashion choices of the elite: 'What should I say of their doublets with pendant codpieces, or the breast full of jags and cuts, and sleeves of sundry colours?' As if pendant codpieces were not enough, sumptuous banquets continued the theme. While the use of coriander and cumin and caraway and cloves to flavour dishes was a relatively subtle way to 'stir up Venus', displays of parsnips and carrots, 'the bigness of a man's finger and very long' and 'great furtherers of Venus her pleasure', left little to the imagination. Both men and women were advised that 'moderate venery' was 'very expedient for the preservation of health'. Immoderate lust, induced perhaps by one display too many of root vegetables, could and should be subdued by Bible reading, meditation, fasting, labour, hard fare and hard lodging. There was little labour, hard fare, and hard lodging for the Earl of Essex and his coterie, and it is perhaps unsurprising that the cult of chastity surrounding the Virgin Queen at her court had its reverse image at Essex House on the Strand.

Essex House was the locus for some of the most interesting sexual politics of this generation of young courtiers, their behaviour making Mr Dudley's kissing of Mistress Cavendish seem rather tame. Through 1591, Robert Devereux, Earl of Essex, was making love to two women, while his sister Penelope was making love to two men. Political, dynastic marriages operated alongside these less legally sanctioned sexual relationships. In the early spring of 1590, Essex had married Frances Walsingham-Sidney, the young widow of the national hero, Sir Philip Sidney. Although the match had its romantic side, his union 'was a matter of politics rather than love'.[4] It was a sign of Essex's commitment to the values espoused by the late, great Sidney, who had died fighting in defence of Protestantism on the battlefields of Europe and had spent the last years of his short life opposing the Queen's final marriage negotiations. Frances was not only Sir Philip Sidney's widow, but she was also Sir Francis Walsingham's daughter, tying Essex still further to the aggressive Protestant cause championed by the Queen's ruthless minister for internal security, a foreign policy that Elizabeth was never willing fully to embrace. The marriage of Robert Devereux and Frances Walsingham-Sidney was conducted in secret, its symbolism hidden carefully from the very person it threatened. When the Queen did find out, months later, Frances was immediately banished from the royal presence 'for her Majesty's better satisfaction' and ordered to 'live very retired in her mother's house'. She had no father to go to: Walsingham had died shortly after the marriage, handing on both his hawk-like foreign policy and his daughter to the young Essex.

Despite or perhaps because of this political alliance, Essex continued to engage in sexual relationships with female courtiers, such as the twenty-one-year-old Elizabeth Southwell who became pregnant by him in 1591. Her baby, christened Walter, was born at the end of the year. Essex took some time to acknowledge little Walter publicly, eventually making provision for him in a financial settlement four years later. At the time, and at court, one Thomas Vavasour was blamed for 'Mistress Southwell's lameness in her leg' (sic), enduring the Queen's anger and a brief spell of imprisonment for his conduct. When the Queen eventually learned about Essex's paternity, she was more than angry: not only had Essex hidden his transgression for four years, but he had caused her to punish an innocent man in his stead. Essex continued to have extra-marital relationships throughout the 1590s, with, among others, the young Countess of Derby in the first couple of years of her own marriage, and with Elizabeth Bridges and Elizabeth Russell, who had their ears boxed by the Queen for making an assignation in the Privy Garden which probably involved Essex. A contemporary commentator pointed out the obvious: 'to fleshly wantonness he was much inclined.'

So, indeed, was his sister, who also had significant, if rather more literary, connections with Sir Philip Sidney. His witty and passionate sonnet sequence, *Astrophel and Stella*, records the poet's love for a married woman, named Stella, but identified within the sequence as Penelope Devereux, wife to Lord Rich (although Astrophel, the star-struck lover, is quite sure that Penelope/Stella's only 'misfortune' is that 'Rich she is'). Penelope/Stella is the teasingly reluctant recipient of sonnet after sonnet of ardent desire. Although there is no evidence that Penelope Devereux ever reciprocated Sir Philip Sidney's passion, and although there is plenty of evidence to suggest that the sonnet sequence is an elaborate fiction based on events that happened many years earlier, it is nevertheless another connection with the Sidney heritage. Penelope herself has been described by her biographer as 'the first of a new kind of woman. A woman of influence at court, a woman of wit and intelligence, a practical and successful woman.'[5] Another historian describes her as 'extremely active on Essex's behalf, despite her absence from court. Men associated with Essex repeatedly praised her hospitality and intelligent conversation.' Intelligent, charming and hospitable she certainly was: and she was also leading two lives with two different men. There was, of course, her husband, Lord Rich. But there was also Charles Blount, and at a spectacular court tournament on 17 November 1590 Blount rode out wearing Penelope Rich's colours, going public about his feelings for her and the status of their relationship. When Penelope had a baby girl, another Penelope, in the spring of 1592, her father was openly acknowledged as Charles Blount. Sexual politics aside, Bess Throck-morton had above all drawn a willing Ralegh towards the heart of a group of courtiers increasingly frustrated with the ageing Queen's apparent political inertia and her unwillingness to confront the vexed problem of the succession. It is perhaps no wonder that in this political and sexual hothouse atmosphere, Bess embarked on her relationship with Sir Walter.

Throughout 1591, Robert Devereux, Earl of Essex, was the leading light in what has been described as the Court's 'rat pack' of young aristocrats.[6] When Devereux and many of his friends departed for the French war in the summer of that year, one of his companions who remained behind in London lamented that 'love here is almost banished'. Love was not entirely banished from the city. Bess and Sir Walter were still there. Ralegh was busy reviewing his previous assessment of love as a dangerous force avoided by all but fools: he added two further lines to an earlier poem reflecting his change of perspective.

> Yet when I saw myself to you was true,
> I loved myself, because my self loved you.

10

Even allowing for poetic licence, there is an element of startled realization in these lines: Ralegh is almost caught out by his own desire to be 'true' to Bess. But the two of them would not have come together in the way they did without a strong measure of attraction on both sides. Ralegh, being Ralegh, wrote erotic poetry on the subject, celebrating his ideal woman:

> A violet breath and lips of jelly
> Her hair not black nor overbright
> And of the softest down her belly
> As for her inside he'd have it
> Only of wantonness and wit.

As that last line of poetry hints, sex was not the only attraction, at least for Ralegh. Bess's 'wantonness', her overt sexuality, is allied firmly to 'wit'. As their baby grew inside Bess, however, it was unclear where her wantonness and wit, her ambition and intelligence, would lead them both.

Generations of Ralegh's biographers have sought to show how much he stood to lose, if and when the relationship and child were exposed. Bess, however, was equally, if not more vulnerable. She was also playing for higher stakes. Hers was a political world in which it was an act of treason for a person of royal blood to marry without the sovereign's consent (according to an act of 1536). Bess's position as trusted Gentlewoman of the Privy Chamber had been achieved despite her numerous familial and social connections to individuals with extremely strong claims to the throne, the most significant being her stepsister, Lady Jane Grey, who had indeed been queen for nine days. Bess may not have had much, if any, royal blood in her veins, but this had not stopped pretenders to the Crown of England in the past, and it would not stop them now.

1

'My One and Only Daughter': Growing Up Under Elizabeth

She had been born in April 1565, a precious daughter to relatively elderly parents who had already produced six sons. Bess's father, Sir Nicholas Throckmorton, fifty at the time of her birth, would live only another six years. It was thus Bess's mother, Anne, and one of her older brothers, Arthur, who were to exert the greatest influence upon her as a young girl. Anne Throckmorton harboured great hopes for her daughter, hopes rooted in her own traumatic childhood experiences, and her intimate and perilous involvement with the power struggles and shifting regimes that characterized the mid-sixteenth century. Historian Alison Plowden, reviewing the early years of the future Queen Elizabeth (her mother, Anne Boleyn, executed before her daughter was three, Jane Seymour dying soon after giving birth to Prince Edward, a third stepmother executed for adultery), argues that 'it would be hardly surprising if by the time she was eight years old, a conviction that for the women in her family there existed an inescapable correlation between sexual intercourse and violent death had taken root in her subconscious'.[1] But this conviction may well have been shared by an entire generation of women, including the young Anne, who suffered, directly or indirectly, from the actions of

13

their king as he slid into unhappy despotism in his search for a male heir and a loyal wife.

Anne's father, Nicholas Carew, had been a loyal follower of Henry VIII and, more problematically, of Henry's first wife, Katharine of Aragon. Carew survived the dangerous years in which Henry abandoned his first wife, Katharine, because of his desire for Anne Boleyn, and then, when convinced of Anne's adultery, swiftly married Jane Seymour, a mere eleven days after his second wife's execution. Throughout this time, Nicholas Carew continued to be one of Henry's closest friends, a 'jolly gentleman' by all accounts. But the King was a dangerous friend, and with a suddenness that by this stage of Henry's despotism probably surprised no one, Nicholas Carew fell from favour. Execution swiftly followed. One of Anne's first, and by definition last, memories of her father would have been a visit to him the night before his death on 3 March 1539 to make her farewells. Her mother, Lady Carew, had done all she could to prevent her husband's fall, exhorting him 'to obey the king in everything', but to no avail. Anne's mother lived on for another seven years. She would be buried with her 'traitor' husband, leaving a few pounds to one daughter, her clothes to another, and nothing to adolescent Anne.

Despite this traumatic start to life, and her lack of dowry, Anne made a respectable marriage, allying herself with another survivor of the troubled closing years of Henry VIII's reign, Nicholas Throckmorton. Her new husband's problem was not that he was one of nineteen children (although this would have minimized his inheritance prospects), but that his family remained loyal to the papacy despite England's move towards reformed religion and eventual Protestantism. Nicholas's father, George Throckmorton, a leading courtier in the early years of Henry's reign, and the pleased recipient of generous gifts of land from his royal master, opposed the King's eventually successful plan to divorce Katharine of Aragon. This was politically unwise, and George was advised by Henry's chief minister, Thomas Cromwell, to 'stay at home and meddle little'. Over the following decades, Throckmortons were to fail, extremely conspicuously, to do just that. Home for the defiantly Catholic Throckmortons was (and still remains) Coughton House in Warwickshire: those nineteen children remain in brass effigy in Coughton Church.

The following lines, from a long, and execrable, poem in which Sir Nicholas looks back over his life (poetic licence being deployed since the protagonist actually dies during the poem), give an impression of a childhood surrounded by anxious women:

> No joys approached near unto Coughton House:
> My sisters they did nothing else but whine;
> My Mother looked much like a drowned Mouse.
> No butter then would stick upon our Bread:
> We all did fear the loss of Father's Head.

Nicholas's father kept his head, just, but his son presumably learned from the experience and turned his back on the dangerous Catholicism of his family and embraced the new reformed state religion. He was therefore eligible to join the household of Henry VIII's sixth and last wife, the staunchly Protestant Catherine Parr, and so began his long career as a courtier in July 1543. In Catherine Parr's house, Nicholas was joined by two young girls, Lady Jane Grey and Anne Boleyn's daughter, the Princess Elizabeth. Their futures would become entangled with his for many years, and both Jane's and Elizabeth's shadows would fall over Bess, Nicholas's only daughter, years after his death.

Through the 1540s, young Nicholas would have witnessed the actions of Lord Thomas Seymour, Catherine Parr's subsequent husband, as he attempted to control Princess Elizabeth both sexually and politically while she was still in her early teens. Historians are divided over the precise nature and extent of the relationship, but it is certain that once Catherine Parr died, Seymour openly courted Elizabeth. Early in 1549, however, the tide turned against him, and his ambition to marry the young princess was construed as treasonous. He was executed in March of that year. Nicholas Throckmorton watched and studied what he saw and continued to rise. Three years later he made the shrewd move of giving up an annuity of a hundred pounds in exchange for the manor of Paulerspury, thus establishing himself as a prominent landowner in Northamptonshire, independent of his Throckmorton relatives in Warwickshire. The same legal document identifies him as a Gentleman of the Privy Chamber, and thus at the

15

heart of the court of the boy king Edward vi, Henry viii's successor, the old king's youngest child and his only son.

Although the precise date of their marriage is unclear, Anne Carew and the upwardly mobile Nicholas Throckmorton were certainly married when the still teenage King Edward recognized that he was dying and made moves to determine his own successor. Edward's choice to follow him, or, more important, that of the Earl of Northumberland, his chief adviser, was the young Lady Jane Grey, daughter of Frances, Duchess of Suffolk. Her tenuous claim to the throne rested on the fact that she was the daughter of the daughter of King Henry viii's sister, Mary. But her real value lay in her Protestantism, and in the fact that Northumberland could marry her to his own son, Guilford Dudley. Edward vi himself encouraged this marriage as part of his continued attempts to set aside the claims of his older sisters, the Princesses Mary and Elizabeth. The accession of the fiercely Catholic Princess Mary Tudor to the throne was a disastrous prospect for Northumberland for good political reasons, and in ideological terms King Edward opposed strongly the idea of a return to Rome. Between them, Edward and Northumberland overturned both Henry viii's will and the Succession Act of 1544, and a rash of dynastic marriages, orchestrated by Northumberland, took place that spring. As the historian Susan Brigden concludes, 'Northumberland was kingmaker'.[2]

The pace of events quickened still further as the young King's health deteriorated. By June, Lady Jane Grey was suffering physically and mentally from the strain of expectation upon her. On 6 July 1553 Edward vi died, but the public announcement of his death was delayed for two days. A further two days later, Lady Jane was brought on a barge from Sion House, the Duke of Northumberland's house, to the Tower of London, pausing at Westminster and Durham House. At the Tower she was proclaimed Queen. Only nine days later, and in the face of a hostile response in London and elsewhere to Queen Jane, Princess Mary Tudor was proclaimed Queen in London: 'a conciliar conspiracy had put Queen Jane on the throne; a popular rising deprived her of it.'[3] It appeared that the issue of legitimacy (Mary was Henry viii's daughter; Jane was only his great-niece) counted with the people, that Northumberland was widely distrusted if not hated, and, perhaps most important, that the reformed religion that Jane represented had not taken as firm a root in the country as its Protestant leaders had thought or hoped. Lady Jane Grey became yet another casualty of the power struggles of the mid-sixteenth century, one of the many tragic ironies of her situation being that her own father rallied support for Queen Mary and renounced the regal claims of his own daughter. Jane's sister Catherine, who had been hastily married to Henry Herbert, was as hastily cast off by her new husband's family, when it became clear that she would not be sister to a queen. The convenient, and possibly valid, excuse was that the marriage had not been consummated.

Jane Grey's father and mother, the Duke and Duchess of Suffolk, were pardoned by the merciful new Queen Mary, but Jane's own fate remained uncertain. Only a few months later, however, in the first winter of Mary's reign, her father was involved in a new rebellion against the Queen's authority. His change of allegiance ensured not only his own execution but that of his daughter, and on 12 February 1554 Lady Jane was beheaded.

Young Anne Throckmorton had backed the wrong queen. She had been dangerously close to the Grey faction, even deputizing for Queen Jane as godmother on the very day, 19 July 1553, that Queen Mary was proclaimed sovereign in London. The accession of Mary, and the subsequent execution of Lady Jane, were politically disastrous for both Anne and for her husband, Sir Nicholas. Only a week after the execution of Lady Jane, Nicholas was imprisoned in the Tower for his part in the Duke of Suffolk's recent conspiracy. Anne was heavily pregnant with her first child at this time, and preparing for her first confinement. Two months later, in April, her husband's case came to trial at the Guildhall, the charge treason. For Anne Throckmorton, daughter of executed 'traitor' Nicholas Carew, this was disturbingly familiar territory.

Astonishingly, Sir Nicholas was acquitted by the jury. Queen Mary was so distraught at the decision, without precedent in a treason trial, that she apparently took to her bed for three days. Once acquitted, Sir Nicholas made moves to ensure that Anne would be provided for, in case of further threats to his life. She, meanwhile, had given birth to a boy, christened William.

Having survived these early months of Queen Mary's reign, Anne and Nicholas maintained a low profile. Anne gave birth, safely, to two further sons, Arthur, born in 1558, and Robert, probably born a year later. The Queen, struggling, but failing, to produce children herself with her husband, King Philip of Spain, was not overly vindictive towards what remained of the family that had attempted to usurp her. She had ordered the execution of the husband, brother-in-law, daughter and son-in-law of Frances Brandon, Duchess of Suffolk, but showed leniency towards the Duchess herself, and her surviving daughters. Frances seemed quite ready to move on in her own life. With something like indecent haste, Lady Jane Grey's mother waited a mere three weeks after her husband's execution before she married again. Her first marriage had been made for her when she was sixteen. This time she appears to have followed her own desires, although whether those desires should be described as personal or political, or a combination of the two, is hard to tell. Her choice was a young – indeed, a very young – man called Adrian Stokes: Frances was thirty-seven, Adrian twenty-one. To make the marriage even more titillating to contemporaries, Stokes had been Frances's secretary and groom of the chamber. Princess Elizabeth, Queen Mary's younger sister, allegedly focused on the class issue rather than the age gap, commenting with horror that 'the woman has so far forgotten herself as to marry [that is, mate with] a common groom!'. Frances may not have 'forgotten herself': indeed, it is quite possible that this was a marriage of political expediency, signalling that the Duchess of Suffolk had no intentions of making another dynastic marriage, and thus no intention of attempting to place another of her offspring on the throne. Queen Mary was generous to Frances and her new husband Adrian, and to Lady Jane's younger sisters, Lady Catherine and Lady Mary Grey, who were allowed to live with the Queen at court although, as with Bess a generation later, there were good political reasons to keep potential pretenders to the Crown where they could be watched.

In 1558 a new dynastic crisis exposed everyone's loyalties to scrutiny again. Catholic Queen Mary died without having a child, and her younger sister, the Protestant Princess Elizabeth, became Queen. Meanwhile, the surviving Grey sisters had not been leading a life of retirement and discretion. Lady Catherine Grey married, secretly, the Earl of Hertford, Edward Seymour. Her mother Frances was already seriously ill during the discreet negotiations and died before the actual marriage, which took place late in 1560, after the accession of Queen Elizabeth. The Earl of Hertford and Adrian Stokes, the Duchess's young husband, disagreed on the political tactics in the case. Stokes wanted to be open with the new Queen about the marriage and thus helped to prepare an explanatory letter. The Earl of Hertford decided that to say nothing would be more tactful. Hertford appears to have forgotten that it was an act of treason for a person of royal blood to marry without the sovereign's consent, and that his prospective wife, Catherine Grey, was certainly 'a person of royal blood'. Indeed, there were others who were interested in marrying her for exemplary dynastic motives. King Philip II of Spain, having just lost one wife, Queen Mary of England, was strongly considering taking on Catherine Grey, since he, for one, adjudged that she had a better claim to the throne than Queen Elizabeth. Certainly, as Queen Elizabeth's subjects considered the ever-present threat of her death, they favoured Catherine as her successor, primarily because of her Protestantism. Indeed, to the House of Commons she was the legitimate heir.

Hertford misjudged the situation, and when the Queen found out she was furious, shouting that it 'was bad enough to have Lady Catherine to deal with, let alone her brats'.* Catherine's life was not an easy one. In the fraught summer of 1561, she was not just married, but pregnant. She and the Earl were sent to the Tower, where she had the temerity to produce three 'brats' over the next three years. There was no hope for her: not only was she producing heirs and spares, but every time her release was discussed some faction or other would revive her claims to the succession, thus condemning her to continued imprisonment, first in the Tower and then later under house arrest in Norfolk. There she would die in January 1568, her ongoing and increasingly forlorn appeals to join her husband ignored by her Queen.

It was not just Catherine Grey who would not fade away. Her

---

* Stokes, on the other hand, did not suffer, and, indeed, after his wife Frances's death in 1559, became a wealthy man. Frances had bequeathed her estate, Beaumanor, in Leicestershire to him (originally a gift of the Crown) and Queen Elizabeth, in 1563, recognizing Stokes's loyalty, authorised his continued ownership of the property, despite his continuing link, as stepfather, to the Grey sisters.

younger sister Mary also made a secret marriage. Even though she did not make a dynastic alliance, her marriage to one Thomas Keyes, a mere Keeper of the Water Gate at Westminster, was nevertheless conducted in secrecy, although it was soon to be exposed. The marriage was the subject of jokes for some: 'Here is an unhappy chance, and monstrous. The Sergeant Porter, being the biggest gentleman in this Court, hath secretly married Lady Mary Grey, the least of all the Court.' But the letter-writer, Queen Elizabeth's chief minister, William Cecil, goes on to comment, more ominously, that Mary and Thomas 'are committed to several prisons. The offence is very great.' As with Catherine Grey, Queen Elizabeth did not relent. Despite the fact that Keyes was a widower with several children, the couple were kept apart until Keyes's death in 1571.

There was little that even their supporters could do for the Grey sisters. Edward, Earl of Hertford, Catherine's husband, wrote forlornly to Sir Nicholas Throckmorton, addressing him as his cousin (there was a tenuous family connection), on 4 February 1565, desperately pleading for his support, especially with the Queen's favourite, Robert Dudley, Earl of Leicester. Hertford acknowledges, pitifully, that Sir Nicholas has been 'in adversity' as well. This was true, but Sir Nicholas was now doing very well out of the new Queen's reign, ironically in part because of his role as manager of the woman who threatened the throne of England even more acutely than the Grey sisters, Mary Queen of Scots. Sir Nicholas was a superb ambassador for Elizabeth, often risking his own political reputation, and indeed life, to give his Queen good advice even when she did not want to hear it. On one occasion the Queen in fury said to Nicholas, 'God's death, Villain, I will have thy head!' Nicholas replied, with a confident assessment of Elizabeth's dependence on his diplomatic abilities, 'In that case, you will do best to consider, madam, how you will keep your own on its shoulders.'

Even in the first hours of her reign, Sir Nicholas was perceived to be a valuable ally by Elizabeth (although the evidence comes in a marginal note added to the execrable poem quoted earlier). 'Upon a rumour of Queen Mary's death, the Princess Elizabeth sent for Sir Nicholas Throckmorton to come to her at Hatfield, & would not stir thence till he did so. After some conference with him, she sent him to view her sister's corpse, & that she might be sure of her Death, ordered him to bring the black enamelled Ring from off her Sister's finger, which her Husband the Infant of Spain gave her on the day he married her.'

The anxiety lurking in this account, Elizabeth's need to be 'sure of' her older sister's death, her fear of making a precipitate move, characterizes these early years of the new Queen's reign. When Elizabeth came close to death in October 1562, having contracted smallpox, the nation was paralysed with indecision, and a terrible vision of chaos loomed ahead. Indeed, as one historian points out, 'the most alarming aspect of this traumatic event was the total inability of the Council to reach agreement on a successor'.[4] Leading the field of rival claimants were Mary Queen of Scots and Lady Catherine Grey. There were also two men to consider: Henry Hastings, the Earl of Huntingdon (married to Catherine Dudley, daughter of the Duke of Northumberland), and Robert Dudley, now Earl of Leicester.

The latter may not have had a dynastic claim to the throne, but he was without doubt the man closest to the young Queen Elizabeth. Brother to Guilford Dudley (the husband of Lady Jane Grey), son to Northumberland, Robert had been Elizabeth's friend since childhood, and was now looking more and more likely to be her husband. There was, however, the small matter that he was already married to Amy Robsart. But on 8 September 1560 Amy was discovered at the bottom of a staircase with her neck broken. Everyone thought they knew why Amy had 'fallen' down stairs and died in the first year of the Queen's reign, and everyone expected the Queen to marry her Robert. Some disapproved, among them Sir Nicholas Throckmorton. His long-time friend, Sir Thomas Killigrew, warned him to keep quiet about it, since it looked as if he opposed the marriage because of his own ambition, rather than his concern for the state. But Elizabeth did not marry Robert Dudley, maintaining her political and social autonomy for the meantime at least.

Sir Nicholas, the trusted confidant of Mary Queen of Scots and called a cousin by Catherine Grey's husband, the Earl of Hertford, was, in addition, closely involved with the aspirations of the other key male player at this time, the Earl of Huntingdon. His descent on his mother's side from Edward iv's brother, George, Duke of Clarence, made him claim that he had the right to succeed Queen Elizabeth, a right that put him ahead of both Lady Catherine Grey and Mary Queen of Scots. It helped, of course, that he was male, and his claims did not fall on deaf ears. Indeed, in 1562 the majority of Protestant nobles supported the claims of Huntingdon to the throne. There was still no escaping the Dudley family's ambitions, however: Huntingdon's wife was Catherine Dudley, daughter to 'kingmaker' Northumberland. Huntingdon and Throckmorton shared a passionate commitment to the cause of the French Protestants, known as the Huguenots. In an extreme reaction to his own family background, Sir Nicholas proved bitterly opposed to Catholicism, persuading his reluctant Queen, in 1562, to give military backing to the Huguenots, and soon after travelling himself to France to fight before helping to broker the Treaty of Troyes, signed on 1 April 1564. For Nicholas, support for fellow Protestants was more than just a holy war; it was vital for England's security as a Protestant nation, since the English might be reliant on the support of others when they were attacked by the forces of popery, as would inevitably happen. As he said to his Queen: 'What shall become of us, when the like professors with us shall be utterly destroyed in Flanders and France?' To this end he spent much of 1563 and 1564 in France, on the battlefield or imprisoned by the Catholic French, all in support of the 'like professors' of the reformed religion.

This was the world into which Bess was born. There was a young unmarried queen on the throne, and confusion and fear about the future: where was England heading in political and religious terms? Who could succeed Elizabeth if she died? Bess's parents' generation had suffered the effects of Henry VIII's desperate quest for a son, a quest that dominated the history of his six marriages, and the effects of the religious and political crises generated by Henry's half-hearted break from Rome, his son's embracing of the reformed religion, his oldest daughter's return to full-blooded Catholicism, and now his middle child's attempt to forge a *via media*, a middle way. Simply to survive in this world was an achievement, to maintain one's principles, as it appears that Sir Nicholas Throckmorton did, was astonishing. For Anne Throckmorton, the issue of political survival was matched by that of physical survival, as in the winter of 1564 she pondered her chances of withstanding the dangers of yet another confinement. The climate that year did not make her life easier. On 21 December an extremely hard frost set in. Amazingly, the Thames itself iced over. Queen Elizabeth, staying at her Palace at Westminster, was able to enjoy the pleasures offered by the freak weather conditions and went on to the ice every day, indulging in various sports including archery. Then, on 3 January, the weather warmed up. By 5 January 'there was no ice to be seen between London Bridge and Lambeth', and the sudden thaw caused 'great floods and high waters' throughout England, causing the 'deaths of many, and the destruction of many houses', as one chronicler expressed it. Sir Nicholas missed the spectacle of the frozen Thames, moving relentlessly between France and Scotland, and Anne, responsible for her five older sons, and nearing her own confinement, went to her brother's house in Beddington, Surrey. Francis Carew, after the execution of his father, had become in effect the head of the family, and not only Anne but her sister, Lady Darcy, spent a lot of time at his estate. Lady Darcy's daughter, another Elizabeth, would be born and christened at Beddington ten years later.

Beddington was a magnificent place to be born in. Built by Nicholas Carew, Anne Throckmorton's father, it was 'a fair house (or palace rather)' which 'by the advantage of the water, is a paradise of pleasure'. The writer of these words, Thomas Fuller, was probably referring to the river, which curved through the park, entering the grounds through a small waterfall and falling into a large lake in the garden and also supplying the moat. This water had practical as well as aesthetic functions. Fresh water was piped from there into the kitchen basement, and it seems that Beddington had the honour of being one of the first houses to have had a 'pretty machine to cleanse the House of Office', known to us as a lavatory.

Through her earliest years, Bess's mother was the most important figure in her life and Beddington the most important location. (Paulerspury in Northamptonshire, her father's estate, had not been developed at this time.) Beddington was a pleasantly furnished house, a place of vibrant colours, warm rooms and all the entertainments and pleasures of a country house. A surviving inventory for the main living area, the parlour, gives a vivid picture of one room. There was

23

a long table covered by a green 'carpet' and ten 'joined Stools' and two leather chairs. There was a square table, also covered in green material, and numerous cushions, some in yellow, some in 'orindge-tauny needelwork [sic]', others in green and red velvet. The walls were covered in wainscoting and hung with painted cloths, and two virginals stood ready for music to be made. The most valuable items in the room were three 'old turkey carpets', and two new ones, valued at nearly seven pounds. This contrasts with the value of the pictures hung on the walls. All eighteen were priced at a mere six shillings and eight pence. Outside the house at Beddington there was an enclosed courtyard, providing further living quarters for servants, a stable for riding horses and a playground for Bess. The limit of her freedom was probably the gatehouse: beyond lay the drawbridge over the moat and beyond that the 'park'.

Her father was away more than not. The political business he dealt with only emphasized the stark and limited options open to women in power. While Queen Elizabeth continued to resist marriage to Robert Dudley, her cousin, Mary Queen of Scots, was planning to ally herself with Lord Darnley. A few weeks after Bess's birth, the records show that Sir Nicholas was up in Scotland, working to prevent the marriage. Nicholas had to deal with an 'elegant, coquettish, literary-minded, slightly cold woman, with her graceful, leaning figure, her red-gold hair, her laughing flirtatious ways, her demand for obeisance to which she had been accustomed from her earliest years' (as her biographer Antonia Fraser describes her), and Nicholas by all accounts relished the task.[5] He could not prevent Mary's marriage to Darnley. The alliance would indeed be disastrous for her, not least because she then only escaped the marriage when Darnley was murdered and promptly married the man who had orchestrated the murder, the Earl of Bothwell. Fraser mentions in passing that one of the three reasons why Mary married her third husband, Bothwell, was that he had raped her: 'the union had already been consummated: it remained to transform it into a legal marriage.'[6]

The Darnley marriage broke Mary. In the spring of 1565, she was 'a young and beautiful woman, healthy and energetic, long widowed, eager to be married'. Two years later she was, in sharp contrast, 'broken in health, distraught, nervously concerned about the future of her government in Scotland'.[7] Another two years on, Sir Nicholas himself would suffer from his commitment to finding diplomatic solutions to the intractable problem of Mary's claim to the throne of England. Despite having travelled relentlessly throughout Bess's early years in the service of his Queen, even as his health began to fail, he was to be imprisoned for his suspected support for a rebellion in the north of England led by Catholics, and in support of a marriage between Mary Queen of Scots and one of the leading noblemen in England, the Duke of Norfolk. It was 1569, and Bess was four years old.

Anne Throckmorton worked successfully, with the help of her old friend Thomas Killigrew, to get her husband released, but the imprisonment broke Sir Nicholas. Early in 1571 he died. The death was sudden: one minute he was eating a salad at the Earl of Leicester's house, the next he was dead: 'he was feeding hard at supper on salads when he was taken as some report with an Impostume of the lungs, as others say, with violent catarrh and died.' There was some speculation about poison: hadn't Throckmorton opposed Leicester's marriage to the Queen? Didn't he perhaps harbour his own ambitions? Others interpreted Nicholas's death as a boon for his family, since it pre-empted any further trouble with the Queen. He died, it was argued by William Camden, 'in good time for himself and his, being in great danger of losing life and estate by his restless spirit'.

Bess, coming up to her seventh birthday, may have sensed some of the unease and speculation surrounding his death when she attended his funeral in St Catherine Cree Church in the City of London. Her eldest brother William was now eighteen, but Arthur, aged fourteen, was already emerging as the head of the family, which suggests that not all was right with William. But despite the powerful presence of her older brothers, and the undoubted stature of her father ('a man of great experience, very ready wit and singular diligence', according to one obituary), Bess's mother remained by far the most significant person in her life. This was in part because Anne was, without doubt, a formidable woman, active both in political and domestic life. Women were often used as political informers, sometimes unwillingly: in Henry viii's reign, one 'Lady Shelton was instructed to report every detail' of a confidential meeting to the King's ruthless chief minister, Thomas Cromwell. Women were also the object of letters from aspiring courtiers, seeking a good word here, a good word there. Men wrote to Anne, asking her to 'advertise' (make known) news, and advising her politically. This was a world in which endorsements mattered. When her husband had been granted land by Queen Elizabeth, Anne was encouraged to thank Her Majesty less for the land than for her 'good words', which were deemed five times more valuable than the land given. Women's words were not their only political tool. Throughout her marriage, but particularly when Sir Nicholas was away, Anne dealt with financial matters on his behalf. She also had strong bonds with her older sons, evident in letters from their tutor to her and their father: the tutor describes her sons as 'those most dear to you', says that they are 'well brought up' (then again, he would say that) and that he hopes and expects them to serve their country as do both their parents. The tutor sees Anne as serving her country quite as much as her husband, Sir Nicholas.

What might Anne have hoped for her Bess, her only daughter? Social and financial independence were rare experiences for women, even if Anne had aspired to this revolutionary ideal. In economic terms, Bess did not inherit very much money from her father, but it would have been enough to keep her if that had been her future. The five hundred pounds she received along with the two youngest sons shows Sir Nicholas being fair to his daughter, which was not always the case at this time. The bequest of five hundred pounds, however, was all very well, but property and land were still by far the most valuable things one could inherit. Girls, on the whole, inherited personal property: clothes, household materials and, if wealthy, jewels. Bess lived in a culture in which power and enfranchisement depended on land ownership, from which women were effectively excluded.

But she would not have her five-hundred-pound legacy for long. On 1 February 1572, in a transaction that would haunt her entire life, the money was lost to Bess. Anne Throckmorton lent Bess's inheritance to Henry Hastings, Earl of Huntingdon. At the time there was nothing underhand about the loan, which was standard practice among the aristocracy of the time, and Huntingdon signed documents to say that he, if he defaulted on repayment of the loan, would be liable to repay a further five hundred pounds. The loan was certainly a sign of continued close involvement between the two families, and might even be an indicator that Bess was going to be educated within the Earl's household. The Earl's wife, Catherine Dudley, 'kept a kind of finishing school for the children of the nobility': she once wrote 'though myself do say it, I think there will be none make questions but I know how to breed and govern young gentlewomen'. Young girls would enter a household such as that at Ashby-de-la-Zouche, where they would receive 'a form of practical education as well as a useful step towards marriage'. The Huntingdon household was, however, a rigorously godly household. The Countess was a powerful woman, 'strong-willed and renowned for her sternness and Puritan bearing'. Little Margaret Hoby, six years Bess's junior, went into the Huntingdon household and spent her formative years learning to 'prepare herself to be a good Christian wife and mother'. Margaret was to be a good Christian wife three times, but never to be a mother.

If Bess was sent to Ashby, she would not only have learned stern lessons about how to lead a godly life but would also have gained an early insight into high politics. Putting aside for a moment the Earl of Huntingdon's claims to the throne, his foreign policy was troublesome enough to his Queen, and echoed – indeed, was formed alongside – that of Bess's father, Sir Nicholas Throckmorton. Bess's father had been, and the Earl continued to be, actively committed to English support for the Protestant cause in mainland Europe. Huntingdon had strong and powerful allies in his beliefs: in these years, his brother-in-law Robert Dudley, Earl of Leicester (still the Queen's favourite), and the young Francis Walsingham, rising fast, and the man who would preside over one of the most powerful spy networks of the era.

But whether she was sent to stay in another aristocratic household, or stayed with her mother, Bess's education would have been 'neither democratizing nor meritocratic'. Education for both girls and boys was designed to reinforce existing social distinctions, with every lesson carefully 'tailored to the individual's future social role'. Bess, however, did learn to read and write, which was more than most female children did: levels of literacy among women were around ten per cent, placing women at the same standard of literacy as the humblest levels of society. At the age of five or six, Bess learned her letters by rote, orally from the 'hornbook' (a hand-held piece of horn with the alphabet inscribed on it). Then she moved on to basic words, learning to recognize them. Reading was important for a godly woman in that a girl could read the Bible for herself, but it carried its dangers, since girls were just as likely to devour romances, ballads, songs, sonnets and ditties of dalliance rather than the word of God. Once the dangerous art of reading was established, a girl might progress to the skill of writing, but at this point they were often discouraged from progressing very far. Since any skill was valuable only in terms of its usefulness to the particular social role of the child, what need was there for girls to learn to write in a complex style? Every decision about a girl's education, even in the most 'modern' and humanist of households, was 'limited in scope because of the prior construction of women's social role – framed by considerations of marital duty, house-hold economy and bringing up children'. Above all, there was a residual tension between the desire to educate women in order to counteract their essential wayward natures (and therefore make them better raisers of children) and a fear that education might 'undermine the strict separation of roles upon which early modern society was based'.[8]

However, in some ways women's education was far less program-matic and prescriptive than men's. It could reflect the interests of their individual families rather than some general cultural norm. For Bess, this meant that her phenomenally wayward spelling was never beaten out of her. She clearly struggled with writing, her lack of education compounded by what we would recognize as some form of dyslexia. The fact that it was a struggle did not stop her writing: when she does not know the conventional spelling for words, she chooses to write phonetically ('necklegans' for 'negligence', 'honnarabell' for 'honour-able'). This tendency extends to words that she presumably would have learned to spell, such as her own husband's first name, but to Bess he is always 'Wattar' her 'hosban'. Thus, it is possible still to hear her accent and catch a glimpse of her emotional reactions from minute to minute, with sentences and ideas flowing into each other, as in this extract from a letter written much later in her life, when she complains that her brother has dealt with her unfairly, refusing to 'put a man to my soone wich I am veri glad you ded not becaus he hath litted onn a veri onnest onn yet hit had bin but a nordenari curtisi [put a man to my son, which I am very glad you did not, because he hath lighted on a very honest one, yet it had been but an ordinary courtesy]'.

In contrast, Bess's older brother Arthur was tutored and coached from an early age. Soon after the visit to London for her father's funeral, he went up to Magdalen College, Oxford. Although he was only fourteen years old, this was the standard age for university education at the time: his departure to university disrupted one of the closest relationships of Bess's early years. Throughout Bess's childhood, Arthur proved himself a loyal and regular correspondent with his little sister, wherever his gentlemanly upbringing took him. Bess and her mother wrote back as often: the impression from his diary, at least, is of a close, caring family.

If not education, let alone financial independence, for women, then there was always marriage. Anne Throckmorton perhaps demonstrated her own commitment to the institution, and what it could do for women, when she made a surprisingly swift marriage, and to a rather surprising second husband, only six months after Sir Nicholas's death. Anne's choice was Adrian Stokes, the secretary, then husband, then widower of Frances Brandon, Duchess of Suffolk, and, significantly, now the stepfather to the one surviving Grey sister. In this second marriage, Anne kept her Throckmorton name and title (as had Adrian's previous wife, Frances, Duchess of Suffolk), maintained the Throckmorton house in London and continued her strong relationship with her brother, Francis Carew, at Beddington. But she now also became mistress of the manor at Beaumanor in Leicestershire, the residence that Stokes had inherited from his first wife, the Duchess.

Beaumanor thus became Bess's main country residence during her later childhood. At Beaumanor, there were visible signs of a fourth career path, and its concomitant dangers, for a few select women: the pursuit of the highest political power in the land. Bess was now stepstepsister (in her time, it was simply 'sister') to the Grey sisters through her mother's remarriage. The household inventory at Beaumanor lists Bess's room, and that of Lady Mary and Lady Catherine, even though by the time of Anne's marriage to Adrian, Catherine was dead. Mary's life by 1571, and little Bess's arrival at Beaumanor, was a grim one. Her husband, Thomas Keyes, died in September: Queen Elizabeth remained hostile, and at first would not even permit Mary to wear mourning. Mary lived on until 20 April 1578, when she died 'in a little house in London'.

Independence, education, marriage, political power: decisions did not need to be made yet. Overall, after the upheavals when she was six and seven, Bess's life settled into a familiar pattern for a daughter of the ruling classes, although the spectre of the Grey sisters' experiences must have haunted her family's life. Her mother and stepfather were important members of the Leicestershire community, involved in a range of activities, from Adrian managing the local military brigades, to setting up a new school in Leicester (specification: 'one substantial school house meet and fit for children to be taught in, made with windows and doors necessary, and covered with slate'), to the welcoming of players from London: the Lord Herbert's players; the Earl of Sussex's players; the Earl of Warwick's players. There was even talk of Queen Elizabeth coming to Leicester, and two of the Queen's men were plied with sweet wine 'when they came to view the town and a place against her coming then supposed'.

Of course, if Bess had been a boy born into the same social world, her options would have included those staples of Renaissance early manhood: exploration, travel and war. Indeed, even a young man from remote Devon, with no money, no great family behind him, but a handsome face and a lot of wit, could pursue these activities with their potential for either great reward or early and violent death. Through these years, young Walter Ralegh made his name doing what he would always do best: putting together a group of ships and going to seek his fortune. When he first came to London from the far west of England, he relied on the support and influence of his half-brothers (the Gilberts), but he was soon captain of the hundred-ton *Falcon*, returning to England more experienced and slightly richer in the spring of 1579. Typically, he found a good motto for his ship and for himself: '*Nec mortem peto, nec finem fugio* [I neither seek out death nor avoid the end]'. He had already been to France as a teenager, fighting in the wars, and by 1577, when Bess was twelve, Walter was living an independent life in Islington, then a village well outside London. Tradition (rather shaky tradition in this case) has it that his home was a building that later became the Old Pied Bull Inn. Apparently, the inn's parlour (according to a historian writing in 1811) was decorated with coats of arms and various 'fragments of heraldry' which contained images of sea-horses, mermaids and parrots, in addition to green leaves supposed to represent the tobacco plant. Quite why the twenty-something Walter would have had his lodgings decorated with tobacco leaves, years before he had anything to do with the Americas, is hard to work out, but it is one of the many myths that would become attached to this charismatic man.

Once in London, Walter Ralegh, still only in his early twenties, fell in quickly with the crowd of ambitious young men who frequented the Inns of Court. In the city, Walter was operating on the edges of Bess's brother's world, the two young men of similar ages although of very different temperaments. While Walter had gone away to fight in his mid-teens, Arthur was twenty-one before he became engaged in his first military campaign in the Low Countries. These months, in the summer of 1578, would be Arthur's first exposure to the grim realities of war. Nevertheless, he reports his experiences in his diary with studied negligence: on 12 August he notes that the English have captured the enemy's 'kine, mares and horses' and then, in passing, that some spies 'are taken and put to death in our camp'.

In December 1578 Arthur began the long journey home, travelling in four days from Antwerp to Dunkirk, then taking a ship to Margate and riding on towards Rochester in Kent to stay with 'my lord Cobham'. From there, Arthur sent his man, Peter, ahead to Beaumanor to bring news of his safe arrival back in England. The head of the family had returned. Arthur did not travel on to his mother and sister at Beaumanor, however, but went straight to the centre of power, the court, then at Richmond Palace on the Thames in Surrey. It appears that while Arthur was away, Anne Throckmorton had decided that her daughter's future lay at the court. Her sustained campaign to put Bess at the locus of power began this year. Bess was just thirteen, and her childhood was over. As a member of the elite class, she had received the care and protection of her family for many years more than children from poorer backgrounds: at age seven, parish officials would place the most impoverished girls in the households of others so that they could work as servants or apprentices, and thus contribute to their own maintenance. Bess, at thirteen, was preparing to enter the domain that had dominated the lives of her parents, the court.

Arthur was already part of this world. Having reached Richmond Palace on 21 December, he spent the Christmas season moving back and forth, up and down the Thames, between the Queen's court and the City of London. This was a fine time of year to be there, the traditional time for masques, entertainments and plays, while throughout the country the Christmas season was spent in mummeries and dancing, in dressing up and feasting. In the coldest and darkest part of the winter, these celebrations were essential to maintain both body and soul. Arthur celebrated Twelfth Night at Richmond Palace on 6 January, before, the Christmas festivities over, he rode north to Barnet to meet his mother on her way from Beaumanor to the city. Together they went to the court, now at Whitehall.

The pattern of visits to court continued over the coming months, Arthur and Anne preparing the ground for Bess, while she remained at Beaumanor. Throughout a cold, snowbound February in London, Anne made sure she was highly visible, in part because she knew there were troubled times ahead. Two days after she went 'to take leave of her majesty', taking Arthur along with her, Arthur's cousin, Anne's nephew, Francis Throckmorton was 'delivered' (arrested) and ordered to appear before the Queen's council. (Arthur notes this in his diary in code, clearly anxious, even in his private diary, about knowing too much.) Francis Throckmorton had been discovered carrying letters for Mary Queen of Scots: this was all too close to home for Anne Throckmorton, no doubt remembering the accusation made about her husband in the last years of his life, that he too had been a secret supporter of the Scottish Queen's claims to the English throne.

Despite having taken leave of her Queen, Anne did not leave London, perhaps anxious to keep an eye on what was happening to her nephew. A few days later she fell sick, and at this troubled time Bess received a letter at Beaumanor suggesting that she come to London and to the court. This was apparently Arthur's initiative, and on 3 March 1579 Arthur wrote in his diary: 'my sister and I went to the court.' For Bess, not quite fourteen, this was her introduction to the complex, exciting, dangerous royal household.

At court, the talk would have been of Throckmorton's fate, and of the ongoing political drama of the winter, the possible marriage of Queen Elizabeth to Francis, Duke of Anjou. Both the Queen and the French Duke were treating the marriage as a serious proposition, for serious political reasons, not least the increasing power of Spain. When Jean de Simier, the Duke's ambassador, arrived in England in January 1579, Queen Elizabeth greeted him 'with a courtesy and coquetry that surprised most contemporaries' since the Queen had been through all this with Francis's older brother, Henry, eight years earlier, in the summer of 1571, and had not had a serious marital negotiation since. Yet, from January, 'for more than two months she held regular, lengthy and intimate interviews with the Frenchman – sometimes three times a week, sometimes every day'. All this Bess would have witnessed on her first trip to court, and she would perhaps have asked the same questions about this late burst of matrimonial activity as everyone else, then and now. Could this indeed be, at last, love? Were the negotiations, as some historians have suggested, precipitated by the onset of menopause in the Queen? Certainly, as ever, the prospective marriage of the Queen was the most 'dominant and often divisive political issue in England', and although we now know that Elizabeth remained single and childless, her contemporaries did not have the benefit of 400 years of hindsight. Indeed, the historian Susan Doran has shown convincingly that there is little evidence to suggest that 'the queen had made a conscious decision to remain unwed either because of her implacable hostility to matrimony or her determination to rule alone'.[9] Although she expressed a preference for a life of celibacy, she also recognized that for the sake of her 'house, the care of her kingdom, and love of posterity' she might need to marry and have children. The Queen was as hemmed in by the options open to her as any other woman.

After two months of intimate conversations between the Queen and Simier, formal negotiations began at the end of March 1579. Elizabeth's main aim was to get Francis himself over to England, in part because he had not shown up seven years earlier when a marriage had briefly been discussed. As Robert Dudley, Earl of Leicester, wrote (reeling from the Queen's hostility to his own recent marriage to Lettice Knollys), 'she will marry if the party like her': Anjou needed to like the Queen, but he also needed to be to the Queen's liking for negotiations to proceed.

But there was bitter opposition to the match, with Sir Francis Walsingham leading the attack. Walsingham disliked the Duke's religion (there was the small matter of his Catholicism) and was uneasy about his being French: a foreign consort for the English Queen might compromise the independence of both Church and state. Walsingham, and others, found many reasons to condemn the prospective union. In the first place, Elizabeth was too old to contemplate marriage. If she did marry, and she conceived a child, she ran the risk of dying in childbirth and, if the child died too, there was the danger of a disputed succession or a French seizure of the English throne, either on Anjou's behalf or that of Mary Queen of Scots. On the other hand, if Elizabeth failed to conceive, her husband might 'seek by treason to be delivered of her' in the hope of having children by another wife.[10] Everyone was forced into taking sides on the issue. Young Walter Ralegh, on the fringes of the court, began by supporting the marriage, primarily because the Earl of Oxford, his patron at this time, supported it. When the Earl changed his mind and began denouncing the alliance and calling its advocates traitors, Walter not only quickly followed his leader but sought out the patronage of even more powerful opponents to the match, the most obvious being Robert Dudley, Earl of Leicester, who feared the potential power of a foreign, Catholic husband for the Queen. Ralegh's move was probably a wise one, since popular opinion also opposed the French marriage: 'indeed, so many London ministers were railing against the match that according to George Talbot, son of the Earl of Shrewsbury, Elizabeth prohibited ministers from preaching on any text that might be construed as relevant to the question.'[11]

Bess's first visit to a royal household gripped by these events was a short one, and it is extremely unlikely that she got anywhere near the Queen herself, let alone be in a position to judge how serious she might have been about the marriage. Bess would, however, have witnessed the frenzied attempts to extricate Francis Throckmorton from the consequences of his treachery. The day after she left the court, these attempts paid off, and Francis was released, but only on condition that he went to his father's house: again a Catholic Throckmorton was advised to 'stay at home and meddle little'.

Short though it was, this visit marked the start of Bess's active involvement in the institution that would dominate her adult life. Commentator after commentator warned of the dangers of the court-ier's life, especially to those who rose too fast, too soon. Writer after writer wrote of the duty of the courtier to offer honest counsel in a personal and absolute monarchy and the hazards that ensued if the advice was too honest. Young Walter Ralegh's first published piece of poetry (written while he attended the Middle Temple law school) commended a work which offered a 'Steel Glass', exposing 'abuses all' to princes and their people. Ralegh warned proleptically:

> For who so heaps renown above the rest
> With heaps of hate, shall surely be oppressed.

But while courtier after courtier indulged in poetic fantasies of retreat from the public world to a safe place in the country, very few actually retired from the struggle for 'renown above the rest', continuing to seek what the greatest courtier-poet of the previous generation, Sir Thomas Wyatt, described as 'the slipper top of court's estates'.

Chaperoned by her mother, Bess would come to court again in April, and she, Arthur and Anne stayed up in London throughout this spring, mixing with their cousins from their mother's side of the family.

This trip may have been Bess's first extended stay in London. There, she would have stayed at the Throckmorton residence in Mile End, where Bess was at the heart of a close-knit network of related families, all linked to her mother. The official records show that Anne's brother, Francis Carew, her brother-in-law, Edward Darcy, and her husband, Adrian Stokes, all owned houses in this area of London. Bess probably slept in a room with her mother, on a makeshift bed, as did Lady Anne Clifford who went to court at Christmas as a girl of nearly thirteen and lay in her aunt's 'Chamber on a Pallet'. Sleeping with friends and family of the same sex, often in the same bed, was completely normal in an age when the notion of privacy was in practical terms unworkable, in ideological terms absurd. Arthur, for one, notes in his diary that when he went to Westminster Hall in May, he 'lay with my cousin FD [Francis Darcy] all that night'.

Like all her contemporaries, Bess would have moved around London predominantly by water, sometimes on foot, very occasionally on horseback or in a carriage. The Thames was the main highway of the city. Roads had no pavements and were at the best of times extremely dirty, at the worst of times a mass of mud and various kinds of waste, human and animal. Pedestrians protected their shoes with pattens, which were then left at the door. To cross to the South Bank of the river there was the renowned London Bridge (which remained the only bridge across the Thames until the eighteenth century), but it was, however, extremely crowded at all times with people, carts and animals, so it was quicker to cross by water. For journeys from the city down to the court at Whitehall, or further west to Richmond, or east to Greenwich, a barge or wherry would be taken.

After her spring in London, Bess returned to a potentially dull Beaumanor. It is to be hoped that Anne Throckmorton ignored the advice of those advocating the 'godly bringing up' of girls, such as Bartholemew Batty, who recommended the following stern maxims:

> Let not her eat openly (that is to say) in the feasts and banquets of her parents, lest she see such meats as she might desire and lust after: let her not learn to drink wine, wherein is all excess and riot.
>
> Let her not delight and take pleasure in the hearing of musical instruments, shawms, zithers, lutes and harps, nor know wherefore they were invented.
>
> Let her not set her mind on silks, as taffeta, damask, satin and velvet.
>
> Let her so eat as that she may be always ahungered, that immediately after the meat she may either read or sing psalms.

Young women's diaries, if not showing 'excess and riot', demonstrate that life in the country did have its pleasures. One unmarried female diarist records (with suitable repentance) 'flirting shamelessly with suitors, running up debts at court, mounting a production of *Il Pastor Fido* with a cast of Lincolnshire yokels, and over-indulging in fruit'. Another remembers that she 'used to wear my Hair color'd velvet every day & learned to sing & play on the Bass Viol of Jack Jenkins my Aunt's Boy'. She and her friends and cousins 'did use to walk much in the Garden & were great one with another'. Travelling players continued to visit Leicester, and Bess, as the daughter of one of the leading families in the county, would have been present at the performances, and perhaps given the gifts of money at the end before the players moved on. And, unlike most of her contemporaries, Bess would not have been hungry. Domestic accounts from the time suggest that an average elite household, perhaps twenty or twenty-five people in all, consumed a barrel of beer each week, twenty loaves of bread and one entire sheep. Mutton or lamb probably dominated the menu, but there was also beef or poultry, and each week several pounds of butter and cheese and four or five eggs. Fish was another staple food, particularly herring, although the amount of fish eaten might depend on the religious beliefs and practices of the house. In theory, fish was to be eaten every Wednesday and Friday, and provisions of salt fish brought in to last the winter. At Beddington, Bess's uncle's house in Surrey, a servant rode off, at the beginning of November, before rains made the roads difficult, taking 'three baskets to London and bringing home a load of fish'.

Servants no doubt brought news as well as produce from the city and the court. While there was still talk of the French marriage as negotiations continued on their fraught way, there was also a new scandal to discuss. The Earl of Leicester, Elizabeth's long-time favourite, the man the nation had believed she would marry on the death of his wife Amy Robsart, had secretly married Lettice Knollys. Mary Queen of Scots, an expert of sorts on the issues of men, marriage and monarchy, reported that Leicester's marriage 'hath so offended this Queen, that it is thought she hath been led, upon such miscontentment, to agree unto the sight of the duke'. After three days of agonizing, 'and many tears', Elizabeth at last gave permission for the Duke of Anjou to come over to England. However keen she may have been to see him, Elizabeth was also aware that popular opinion was against her. Anjou arrived in August, travelling incognito. The news got out, however, 'forcing Elizabeth to forbid all gossip among her ladies and gentlemen and to take measures to prevent attacks on Anjou's person'.[12]

Again, questions were asked about the Queen's motives. Had she been advised that time was running out if she wanted a child? Was she on the rebound from Leicester? Was she worried about the increase in Spanish power? It is most likely that Elizabeth saw sound political reasons for pursuing the negotiations, that she was influenced by her head more than her heart. Those who continued to oppose the relationship were viciously persecuted – one man who wrote a tract against the marriage had his hands cut off – but many still spoke out against the Duke, including the courtier-poet Sir Philip Sidney. While at court the Queen received gifts of frog jewellery, in the wider world 'frogs' and 'toads' were viciously attacked in the political writings of the time, a coded way of demonstrating opposition to the marriage.

Arthur relayed news to Bess, and probably continued to bring her to London to the court during the following winter and spring. Through 1580 Elizabeth still toyed with the idea of the marriage to Anjou, and was still relentlessly opposed by Walsingham and his followers. Meanwhile, there was yet another scandal to intrigue and possibly to ring alarm bells for the young Bess. The shocking story involved a girl of exactly Bess's age. Anne Vavasour had come to court at fifteen as a Maid of Honour. There she was noticed, and desired, by the married Earl of Oxford. Anne and the Earl had a sexual relationship, and the inevitable outcome was that on a 'Tuesday at night Anne Vavasour was brought to bed of a son in the Maiden's Chamber. The Earl of Oxford is avowed to be the father.' Anne 'the selfsame night she was delivered was conveyed out of the house and the next day committed to the Tower'. Others 'party to the cause' were also imprisoned. The Queen would not tolerate this licentious and disrespectful behaviour in her courtiers. Another scandalous example of uncontrolled passions involved violence, rather than sex. One Walter Ralegh was brought before the Lords of the Council, his crime fighting at court, his punishment a week cooling off in a cell in the Fleet Prison. He did not cool off for very long since only a few weeks later he was committed to another London prison, the Marshalsea, for 'a fray beside the tennis-court at Westminster'.

Bess was learning fast about the complex mores of the courtly world, what could be done, what could not be done. Now the Earl of Leicester, recovered from the taint of his marriage to Lettice Knollys, flourished again in the aftermath of Elizabeth's failed attempt to marry the Duke of Anjou. The French delegation were still being treated to magnificent entertainments and festivities, although the talk was no longer of marriage but simply a military alliance between France and England. Indeed, there was to be no more talk of marriage for Queen Elizabeth. Both then and now there have been some quite extraordinary explanations of the Queen's failure to marry, with appeals to mysterious diseases or physiological impediments to intercourse, or to the psychological effects of her early life. In Bess's own time one thing was clear. Elizabeth was now irrevocably the Virgin Queen. She would not marry, and she would not have an heir from her body. The political climate had changed again.

But for the next two or three years Bess's ambitions were put on hold, as Arthur set off in June for a great adventure, a tour of Europe that would last for nearly two years and take him through Central Europe and then down to Italy, a country he would fall in love with. His travels clearly absorbed him, and he wrote less and less to his sister back home, eventually returning to England full of the latest Continental news on meteorology and astrology.

As a young woman Bess was denied the opportunities that her brother had to travel. However ambitious and talented she might have been, she could never hope to engage in the activities that any one of her male contemporaries, or at least those from her class, pursued, nor could she aspire to be independent from her family. In contrast, young Walter Ralegh's military experiences on the front line in Ireland allowed him to become a self-styled adviser on the Irish question, and pushed him into contact with two of the most powerful men in the Elizabethan court, Lord Burghley and Sir Francis Walsingham. To pursue his career, Ralegh put his family in Devon behind him: on the very day, 23 February 1581, that his father was buried in the church of St Mary Major, Exeter, young Walter wrote confidently to Sir Francis Walsingham about matters military from far-distant Cork in Ireland. Later that year, he was sent back to England with dispatches. At court he attracted the attention of the Queen, and once he had her attention there was no stopping him. When, a few months later, he was again posted to Ireland, the Queen insisted that he stayed in England, allegedly for further training. Ralegh, a soldier and sailor for thirteen years, hardly required such training, but his Queen needed him near her, and Ralegh, ever the opportunist, needed no further encouragement. Within a year he could write to his half-brother, Humphrey Gilbert, from the court at 'Richmond this Friday morning' and revel in his intimacy with the Queen. Walter, now a trusted intermediary, enclosed a jewel for Humphrey (embarking on a transatlantic voyage) from the Queen herself: 'a token from Her Majesty, an anchor guided by a Lady as you see.' The token did not do Gilbert much good – he was to die at sea during his return voyage from North America. Ralegh, safely on land in England, began to reap the financial and political rewards of his bond with the Queen, not least by being granted a patent similar to the one that Humphrey Gilbert had been granted: to discover unknown lands, to take possession of them in the Queen's name and to hold them for six years. It was this patent that was the first step towards Ralegh's ambition to set up the first American colony at Roanoke: this ill-fated venture was to absorb much of his energy and money over the following years. He had money to burn, having received from his Queen, among other gifts, the lucrative, and long-term monopoly of wine licences. He was not only rich but powerful, his influence such that long-established members of the nobility were now reliant on his favour with the Queen. Some even saw him as a more profitable intermediary than Elizabeth's chief secretary, William Cecil, Lord Burghley, particularly in those tricky, more personal, matters. Thus, on 13 November 1584 Sir Edward Hoby approached 'Mr Ralegh to be a dealer in his domestic and private troubles, rather than Mr Secretary'. Ralegh himself cultivated the image of a man detached from the romantic pursuits of some of his contemporaries. When the courtier Sir Thomas Heneage wrote a poem welcoming 'love, thou mortal foe to lies', a prize 'of joy for which the wisest run', Ralegh quickly countered his naivety. Love was, instead, 'a way of error, a temple full of treason', 'A quenchless fire, a nurse of trembling fear', 'a path that leads to peril and mishap'. He, of course, was impervious to its power, and thus safe from its dangers:

> False love, desire, and Beauty frail, adieu.
> Dead is the root, from whence such fancies grew.

The only thing Mr Ralegh, in control of his fancies and desires, lacked was a suitably imposing London residence and a title: both were forthcoming from the Queen, and by the end of 1584, Sir Walter Ralegh was master of a palace on the Thames, the magnificent Durham House.

Arthur, having gone to be a soldier, and done his Grand Tour of Europe, returned to England to pursue a more conventional path to financial and domestic security. He led a very good life in London, going to the theatre (two shillings for a night out, but that included paying for two servants to go with him, complete with torches to light his way) and when he did occasionally stay in (on a cold night in winter, the eleventh night of Christmas, for example, perhaps having had one too many revels over the previous days and nights) his diary records the four pence spent on 'a capon and butter to baste it', the three pence for bread and oranges, the five pence for a quart of white wine, and the shilling for faggots for the fire to keep his chamber warm. Arthur may well have also become increasingly familiar with various hangover cures, such as Balls of Violet ('Take the best blue violets you can get . . .' goes the recipe), and scented 'cachous' for clearing the head.[13] Uncle Francis Carew at Beddington occasionally gave generous gifts of money: Arthur spent one New Year's gift on silver lace, silver for his hat, a ring and 'tennis'. Perhaps he needed a new racquet to pursue his interest in one of the court's most fashionable recreations. The rest he lost at dice. In the autumn and winter of 1583, he fell in love, which, from the evidence of the diary, was an expensive business, involving buying paper and ink for the love letters, gifts for his beloved, and a new and particularly ornate codpiece, presumably guaranteed to attract the lady in question. He needed money to pay for this comfortable, independent, city lifestyle – and in his mid-twenties he consolidated his increasingly dominant position within the family through a deed that concentrated all the family's land and property into his hands, and his alone. His older brother William was, at last, completely sidelined. If Arthur died without heirs, the other surviving brothers would inherit. There is no mention of Bess in these documents, a perfect example of her invisibility in the historical record, as traditionally understood.

41

Another document from the time again emphasizes women's marginalized position with regard to property, in this case affecting Bess's mother, Anne. Bess's stepfather, Adrian Stokes, was getting his affairs in order, and, prompted by the knowledge that his own claim on Beaumanor would end the following year, he drew up a document 'devising' the house and lands to Henry Brooke, Lord Cobham, for twenty-one years from the end of his own claim. This same document stipulates that Stokes is the rightful owner at present, and makes arrangements that, if Stokes dies, his brother William Stokes and one Robert Price get the property, and clarifies the list of people they will need to support, which include Adrian Stokes's servants. The men, whether family or servants, get everything except the following fascinating list of items, set aside for Anne Throckmorton:

> . . . all the plate of silver and gilt of the said Adrian; the hangings and furniture of the Duchess' chamber as it standeth; my lady Kathryn her Chamber as it standeth; the Lady Throckmorton's chamber (wife of the said Adrian) with her Closet as they stand; Mistress Elizabeth Throckmorton's chamber as it standeth; the chamber on the gate; the Wardrobe of my lady Mary's chamber as they do stand.

The contents of these chambers, closets and wardrobes were potentially valuable to Anne, but her husband's instructions nevertheless exclude her from the power and income created by property ownership.

Anne may have expected to inherit from her husband, and pass on to her daughter, the contents of the women's closets of Beaumanor, but Bess's future did not lie there. Nor did it lie in a conventional aristocratic marriage: that may have been Arthur's future, but it was not to be Bess's. In the summer of 1582, when Bess was seventeen, well-meaning and well-placed friends, Lord and Lady Drury, had suggested a marriage between Bess and one Bassingbourne Gawdy. Bess had been staying with the Drurys, and herself brought to her mother the letter suggesting the union. Brokered by the Drury family, who had, Anne acknowledged, been very good towards Bess, the marriage would have been a secure and conventional path for Bess to take. All that was needed was Anne's 'resolution for consent'. Consent was, however, not forthcoming. Anne began by stalling. The proposal of marriage was very sudden, and Anne needed more information: she had heard good things about the gentleman, and of his father and mother, 'but he is now known yet to none of my friends'. Moreover, Bassingbourne and Bess were 'both young enough, and especially my daughter', there was no need to rush into things. Above all, she wrote touchingly that Bess is 'my one & only daughter in whom is my hope & comfort'. The Drurys and Gawdys were not to be put off, and the pressure on Anne to give her consent was increased. She wrote again, this time more acerbically. She needed more time 'in so great a matter for two causes'. The first was Bess's 'unmeetness yet to marry: not for her age only but the littleness of growth and the unaptness I do find in her to match with any'. Bess was clearly resisting the idea of an early marriage, even hinting that she would never consider marriage, and her mother fully supported her. The 'littleness of growth' is an intriguing hint as to Bess's physical development and appearance. Whether Anne is referring obliquely to a late onset of puberty in her daughter, or to her lack of height, is impossible to know, but the impression is of a physically immature, possibly small, girl rather than a fully mature young woman. The second 'cause' alleged by Anne in refusing the match was that none of her 'own friends nor of her father's' lived close enough for her to take advice: yet another indication that Bess's stepfather did not become, as it were, a father figure to Bess on his marriage to Anne, but that Anne continued to defer, when necessary, to Sir Nicholas Throckmorton's friends.

Anne ends this second letter with a promise that, when she comes to London as she means to do before Easter, she 'will go through with the matter one way or other'. While Anne stalled for time (her next letter blamed the 'weather and the ways' for her failure to get to London), Arthur's attitude was more ambivalent. Young Bassingbourne Gawdy came to visit him, and clearly the men got on. There was a flurry of letters between brother and sister, attempting to thrash out the issues. Whatever Arthur may have said, Anne and Bess won out, this time at least. There was no marriage for Bess, and instead Anne began to work seriously towards a different long-term ambition. Anne must have believed that her daughter had a future at court. That future may still have involved marriage. The Queen might act *in loco parentis*, bestowing dowries on dutiful (and dowryless) young women. Other mothers, aunts, grandmothers worked just as tirelessly to the same end. Anne Clifford was intensely grateful that her aunt had taken her to court when she was in her early teens, and felt 'much bound for her continual care & love of me'. But Anne Throckmorton was not only aiming to let her daughter be seen in the best marriage market in the country, although that may have been an issue. More important, Anne believed that Queen Elizabeth would 'prefer' Bess 'to be of the Privy Chamber'.

The political opportunities for women when there was a queen on the throne were well known, as one historian explains: 'At court, access to the monarch, in her private apartments, was allowed only to her ladies, whose influence with her was great. [. . .] Men seeking influence with the queen, and information, tried to "fall-a-talking" to them.'[14] Young Bridget Manners was advised by her uncle in 1589 that she should be 'diligent, secret and faithful' in the Queen's service, and thus ensure that her friends and family would get the maximum benefit from her insider position. Even the Queen's most powerful male ministers knew that they had to talk to, and listen to, the Queen's women: they aimed, before actually seeing the Queen, to learn 'her Majesty's disposition by some in the Privy Chamber with whom you must keep credit, for that will stand you in much stead'. Keeping in credit with the Queen's women cost aspiring courtiers money, and thus brought plenty of rewards to the women concerned: they were always open to bribes, either in their own official capacity or as go-betweens with their male relatives, and this was an entirely accepted part of political culture. There were other opportunities to gain wealth. The Queen's women might be granted the control or management of patents and monopolies, and they could and did receive secret pensions from foreign governments in payment for information supplied. It was not the prospect of a salary as such that was tempting, therefore, but the power and wealth that would come to Bess when she had access to patronage and information, both of which she could then, in effect, sell on. Above all, Gentlewomen of the Privy Chamber had access to the intimate space around the monarch and controlled admittance to her person. In a personal monarchy, knowledge of the monarch's disposition and access to that person were both valuable political commodities. The most prestigious position was thus not that of a Maid of Honour (although this suited many young women, who would benefit from the Queen's contribution to their dowry when they stopped being Maids and were appropriately married off), but that of Gentlewoman of the Privy Chamber.

Anne's plans for Bess received a setback, however, when her cousin, Francis Throckmorton, once again made the world a dangerous place for anyone with the Throckmorton name. Francis Walsingham had never stopped suspecting Bess's cousin, and when he was tipped off early in 1583 that Throckmorton was indeed one of 'the chief agents of the Queen of Scots' he went gleefully to work. For six months, spies tracked Throckmorton's every move until Walsingham had what he wanted. Early in November 1583, two gentlemen of 'no mean credit and reputation' were sent to seize him at his house by the Thames in London. Two of his brothers slipped Walsingham's net, both escaping abroad with the help of their mother, but it was too late for Francis. Among his papers was found a list of noblemen sympathetic to his cause, a plan of harbours suitable for the landing of foreign forces, and a number of 'infamous pamphlets against her Majesty printed beyond the seas'. Throckmorton was hauled in front of the Privy Council and charged with treason. He steadfastly refused to answer questions, denying everything. Walsingham knew what was needed, and sent him to the Tower to be racked. Throckmorton endured the torture with astonishing courage, but Walsingham simply sent him back for more, this time to Mr Norton, the notorious 'rackmaster'. The Queen's minister for national security was quite sure that his victim would not hold out again: 'I have seen as resolute men as Throckmorton stoop, notwithstanding the great show he hath made of Roman resolution. I suppose the grief of the last torture will suffice without any extremity of racking to make him more conformable than he hath hitherto shown himself.' Walsingham was right: when Throckmorton was placed on the rack again on 19 November, and 'before he was strained to any purpose', he agreed to confess everything he knew. He exposed plans to murder Elizabeth, plans to seize the throne, plans to invade England, with armies landing from Scotland and from France. Arundel in Sussex was the place chosen for the invading armies to make their assault.

While Francis faced his inquisitors, Anne Throckmorton was going to work. On 22 May 1583 she arrived in London; two days later she was at court. What she would have been pushing for was an audience with the Queen. She was, of course, not alone in this. The French ambassador's efforts to get to see the Queen, and his eventual success, were recorded by him in some detail. Each day he would press for 'an audience'. Eventually, just as he thought he would always be denied and was thus 'resolved' to make his 'complaint', his luck changed. 'About one hour after noon there came a gentleman from the Queen who said to me that her Majesty was much grieved that she had not given me audience sooner, and that she prayed me to come to her that very hour.' Having waited for days, he was expected to leap into activity 'that very hour', and he did. The gentleman 'brought me in a coach to take me down to the river where one of the barges awaited me, and we went thence to the gate of the Queen's palace.' At the landing place, another gentleman welcomed him, and with 'four or five other gentlemen' led him 'across a chamber of moderate size wherein were the guards of the Queen, and thence into the Presence Chamber, as they call it, in which all present, even though the Queen be absent, remain uncovered. He then conducted me to a place on one side, where there was a cushion made ready for me. I waited there some time.' At last, the Lord Chamberlain (who, the ambassador notes in his account, 'has the charge of the Queen's household' and the power 'to arrange audiences and to escort those who demand them') came to find him and led him 'along a passage somewhat dark, into a chamber that they call the Privy Chamber, at the head of which was the Queen seated in a low chair, by herself, and withdrawn from all the Lords and Ladies that were present, they being in one place and she in another. After I had made her my reverence at the entry of the chamber, she rose and came five or six paces towards me, almost into the middle of the chamber. I kissed the fringe of her robe and she embraced me with both hands.'

The French ambassador's efforts had paid off at last, and he had his chance to put his opinions to the Queen in person. This is what Anne, and indeed Arthur, were working towards: a chance to present Bess in person to the Queen. Of course, there was still the problem of their cousin, Francis Throckmorton. He was eventually executed in June

1584, but his terrible fate was not allowed to deflect the campaign to get Bess accepted into the inner circles of the court. During the autumn of that year, Arthur continued to press for his sister. He travelled up to London on 21 September 1584, and after a week of negotiations he noted triumphantly in his diary that 'Mr Vice-Chamberlain delivered my letter to her Majesty' and then wrote to his mother and stepfather with the news. Arthur was extremely excited about the prospects his near success opened up, and immediately went shopping for material for new clothes. His mind turned also to lodgings – he clearly believed he would soon need to arrange for accommodation at the court. Having done so, he wrote to his mother and sister again at Beaumanor, sending his letters 'by Watt to whom I delivered 5 shillings'. This letter must have given instructions as well as cash to the women, because a week later, on 19 October, Arthur rode north out of London in order to meet Anne and Bess at Dunstable two days later. The following day, they were all in London and Arthur headed back to court, this time with Bess. Still there was an agonizing wait to see if the Queen really meant business.

On 8 November 1584 the waiting was over. Bess had made it. Arthur wrote: 'I came and dined at Hampton Court. My sister was sworn of the Privy Chamber.' The very next day, her mother began the journey back to Beaumanor and Bess's independent life at court began in earnest. The family dynamic was completely transformed. Bess was now at the heart of things, Arthur a mere visitor to the court, Anne back in her county base. Although the salary Bess received was the least of the economic benefits inherent in her new position, it was nevertheless hers to keep and to spend. She received a yearly wage of thirty-three pounds, six shillings and eight pence a year, and all her meals (and the meals for three of her servants) were provided at the expense of the Queen. Bess would most likely have had one woman in personal attendance on her, and probably a chambermaid to keep her quarters clean. Both these women would have worn her livery, in part to make sure that 'strangers' did not end up eating a free meal at the court.

Bess, as a Gentlewoman of the Privy Chamber, was now one of perhaps ten or twelve women in personal attendance on the Queen. There were usually twelve Ladies, Gentlewomen and Maids of the

Privy Chamber. She knew that she was supposed to embody all the virtues of the sixteenth-century Gentlewoman: chastity, obedience and silence, allied, of course, to complete loyalty to her mistress, the Virgin Queen. She quickly learned that the reality was more entertaining: plays, masques, music, revels and dancing. An elderly courtier, Sir William Knollys, was not alone in his complaint that he was kept awake at night by the young women of the court who 'frisk and hey about'. Daily life was fuelled with a generous allowance of bread, wine and ale. Bess may not have been a duchess (they received a gallon of ale in the morning, a gallon of ale in the afternoon and a gallon of ale and a pitcher of wine after supper), but she would have received more than enough alcohol each day for herself and her women servants.

There was much to see and enjoy. Within a few days of her appointment, the biggest and best court festival took place, the Accession Day Tilt, held every year on 17 November to celebrate the day on which Elizabeth had become Queen back in 1558. The Accession Day Tilt had grown more and more significant through the 1580s. They were 'annual exercises in arms' (according to a contemporary) 'begun and occasioned' because of a 'great zeal, and earnest desire to eternize the glory of her Majesty's Court'. The tournament was held at least every year from 1581, except 1582, a year of plague, and always in the Whitehall tiltyard, but it was only one part of the extensive celebrations surrounding this extremely popular national holiday. Throughout England, there were sermons and bell-ringing, fireworks, bonfires and gun salutes, the poor were given bread, prisoners were given alms, and the great houses of the land opened their doors to the wider community, who could feast, for once, at the expense of their landlords. All the celebrations were accompanied by particularly virulent anti-papal, and anti-Spanish, propaganda: no one was allowed to forget that Elizabeth was a Protestant Queen, denounced and excommunicated by the Pope of Rome, the prospective target of a Catholic holy war at any time.

The Queen herself clearly enjoyed the occasion, especially when she did not have to pay much for the pleasure. One of her subjects commented tellingly after the following year's tournament: 'These sports were great and done in costly sort, to her Majesty's liking, and their great cost.' In 1584 there was not only the Accession Day Tilt at Whitehall for Bess to enjoy, but a few weeks later, on 6 December, jousts were organized between ten married men and ten bachelors. Bess might have looked carefully at the ten bachelors, wondering which, if any, might be deemed an appropriate husband for her by her Queen.

As the months went by, Bess settled into her new life at court. She witnessed the negotiations and preparations being made for Ralegh's Roanoke voyage, and perhaps watched the fleet set sail in April. She played card games late into the night, retiring to sleep for a few hours as the scavenging dogs sought to pick up the scraps left by the courtiers and their servants. Occasionally, her family's affairs would intrude on her life. In April 1585 came distressing news. Arthur, still in London, heard from the Earl of Leicester that Adrian Stokes was dead. He quickly made plans to ride north, and four days later arrived, with Bess, at Beaumanor. On arrival, however, they found that the rumours of Stokes's death had been greatly exaggerated, and, presumably relieved, brother and sister could return to the real business of their lives, in Bess's case her career at court, in Arthur's case pursuing his cousin Lady Mary Darcy. This relationship was to be a stormy one. Arthur wrote of days of 'disgrace in love and in loss', and, more than once, that 'my L: M: D: and I fell out'. The relationship did not end happily: one night 'Lady Darcy and I fell out at 10 of the clock at night where out grew all the poison her nature could yield me as follows'. Mary Darcy knew exactly what she had to do, and did it. She mentioned to important people that Arthur had slandered the Earl of Leicester. Punishment came quickly. Arthur was sent to the Marshalsea prison, where he would stay for two months.

This imprisonment, throughout the spring of 1585, did not do Arthur much harm (since he not only kept his servants, but entertained a string of male friends in his prison quarters) and would have some interesting repercussions for his sister. Arthur knew that, as the first step towards being released, he had to get a suitably apologetic letter through to the Privy Council, and he knew that the man for the job was Sir Walter Ralegh, as the Earl of Oxford and many others had realized in recent months. So in May 1585 he wrote, asking for Sir Walter's support in his efforts to gain his release, perhaps asking Bess to deliver the letter personally to the great man. At the same time he also asked Bess to be an intermediary between him and the woman who had landed him in prison. In an attempt to regain her favour, he had written some poetry for Lady Mary, but instead of some passionate verse in reply he merely got a letter back from Bess, who was in the process of travelling to Nonsuch Palace with the royal court. The falling out with Lady Mary was starting to look permanent. Finally, on Midsummer's Day, Arthur was released from the Marshalsea prison, his letter-writing campaign finally successful. On 25 June he bathed himself, and on 26 June he wrote to his mother.

Prison cleared Arthur's mind, and on his release he began the courtship of another young woman, Anna Lucas. One of his first actions was the onerous task of buying a 'cod of musks' for thirty shillings. How could Anna resist? The marriage was probably encouraged by the same family who had tried to set up Bess with Bassingbourne Gawdy years earlier and apparently Bess also supported the match. Brother and sister made time to meet in September (shortly after the cod of musks investment) at Epsom, perhaps to talk through the implications of Arthur's promising courtship, and by October 1585 Arthur and Anna were seriously involved. A sign of the gravity of the situation was his decision to have his hair cut 'close'. Their marriage would be the conventional end to a conventional youth: Arthur had been a student, a soldier, a traveller and a courtier, and would now be a married country gentleman. This did not stop him flirting with his prospective wife: on the end pages of Arthur's diary he has written 'Anna Lucas is a naughty girl and a naughty girl is she'. Anna, meanwhile, used the same pages to practise writing her married name, which, after a few attempts, she achieves in a beautiful script.

Arthur still remained close to his sister and his mother, travelling with the latter through the harsh winter months of January and February, and he still attempted to gain recognition at court, presenting, of all things, a tortoise to the Queen via his patron (and the probable matchmaker between him and Anna), Lady Drury. Finally, on 4 July 1586 Arthur married Anna, having, on 1 July, taken a servant, Dorothy Harcourt 'to serve my wife' and then, on 3 July, sealing 'the writings', the marriage settlement. Before joining his new wife, and her parents, Arthur paid one last visit to court, no doubt still with an eye on gaining favour with Queen Elizabeth, but also perhaps to speak to Bess. He received a gift of five pounds from his mother (which would have enabled him to buy at least three more cod musks, although the moment for such things may have passed), who then sent him off to Colchester, the home town of his new bride and her parents. Arthur, on his arrival, wrote to Bess and sent oysters to his mother, probably packed in a barrel with seaweed: these delicacies were cheap and plentiful on the coast but a rare treat further inland. Arthur had gone to another kind of life, for the time being at least.

Over the course of her brother's courtship and marriage, Bess's own life was one of constant movement, with little if any privacy or solitude. The court moved every few months from one royal palace to another. At times the Queen would go on an official progress, setting up her court in the great houses of the land, at the owners' expense. Hundreds of people would travel with the Queen: courtiers, administrators, counsellors, ambassadors, Ladies and Gentlemen of the Privy Chamber, Maids of Honour, the Captain of the Guard, Grooms of the Privy Chamber, the court physicians. Noblemen dreaded a visit from their monarch, since it would set them back perhaps seven hundred pounds per night (as it did the strangely named Sir Julius Caesar when the Queen visited him in September 1598 at his house at Mitcham before, thankfully, she moved on to her own palace of Nonsuch).

In October 1586 Bess was with the court at Windsor. Arthur was nearby, en route to his new family from a tour of his West Country properties. It was to be a terrible winter for the Queen and for those immediately around her. After over twenty years of plotting, intrigue, compromise and conflict, the end was nearing for Mary Queen of Scots. For months, secret letters had passed from the Scottish Queen to her allies, hidden in a beer barrel: these letters outlined what would become known as the Babington Plot. Every letter was intercepted, copied and then passed to Francis Walsingham. By the middle of July 1586, Walsingham finally had a letter written by Mary herself, direct evidence of treason. There was a clamour for Mary's execution, but Queen Elizabeth still hesitated, unsure about the political wisdom and Christian morality of killing a fellow royal. Through the winter months, the Queen moved restlessly from court to court, and her courtiers watched carefully. The Queen would not make a clear decision, but did not prevent her counsellors from doing so: they gave the orders, and on 8 February 1587 Mary was executed, meeting 'her death with a resolution that Elizabeth had lacked in allowing it'.[15] Months earlier, and up in Leicester, Anne Throckmorton had seen Mary, the figure who had dominated the political life of her husband, pass through the city, on her last journey to the south. She saw a woman 'of stature tall, of body corpulent, round shouldered, her face fat and broad, double chinned and hazel eyed, her borrowed hair auburned'. Now the plump, be-wigged Mary Queen of Scots was dead. Queen Elizabeth apparently received no comfort from the news, but instead was racked with guilt and distress. Worse still, having solved one problem, having removed one threat to the Crown, others quickly appeared. The succession to the Virgin Queen remained unresolved.

One of the beneficiaries of Mary's elimination was Sir Walter Ralegh. The Babington traitors' money and land were forfeit to the Queen. The happy beneficiary of her subsequent generosity was the man she called her 'pug', Sir Walter. It is a rich area of controversy, both then and now, as to the precise nature of the relationship between Ralegh and his Queen, but, measured in material terms, the year 1587 was a particularly good one for Sir Walter. In contrast, Bess may have been settled in her position as Gentlewoman of the Privy Chamber, but she was very short of cash. Anne Throckmorton sought to do something about the situation, and early in 1587 she went to court in an attempt to recover Bess's legacy from her father, loaned out to the Earl of Huntingdon fifteen years earlier and never repaid. Anne's attempt failed. Bess became increasingly dependent on Arthur to help her financially, which he did, sending her the comparatively large sum of thirty shillings, by his man Charles, on 14 December 1586. Bess spent the money on a pearl girdle. Arthur was in return dependent on his little sister for the development of his connections at court. In these years he became close to the man who would be his lifelong friend, Edward Wotton and, more intriguing, became closely involved with the powerful and dangerous Walsingham in the last years of the decade.

Arthur's correspondence during this period is a curious mixture of banal news and much darker hints of dangerous matters. He was in communication with William Ashby, the Queen's ambassador to Scotland, who sent Arthur details of the young prince, James VI. King James was 'chaste' and 'continent', loved to hunt, wrote Ashby, and was adjudged to be in love with a Danish princess, presumably Anna of Denmark, the woman he would eventually marry. None of this was particularly compelling or valuable (and indeed it glosses over crucial aspects of James's sexual and political life), but Ashby's letters also reveal that the two men were exchanging highly classified information: indeed, Ashby warns Arthur that they should wait to talk in person 'for there is no secrecy in pen and paper'. By mid-November, and then throughout the winter, Arthur was dealing directly with Secretary Walsingham about Mr Ashby. Arthur's burgeoning friendship with Edward Wotton appears to be crucial to this new engagement with high politics. In the months leading up to Mary Queen of Scots' execution, and to the birth of his first child, Arthur was talking 'deeply' with 'E:W who sounded fathoms in me'. Wotton would pull Arthur ever closer to the radical Protestant grouping at court, those who advocated the aggressive foreign policy that Arthur's father had worked for. Arthur's friendship with Edward Wotton, who was nine years older than him, was clearly important to him emotionally, but Wotton was also a social and political ally. He was a highly intelligent and extremely well educated man, who had also spent many years outside England, in particular in Arthur's beloved Italy. Throughout the 1570s he had been employed on diplomatic business, and was described in 1579 as a 'creature of Walsingham's'. In the 1580s he had been used by Elizabeth in diplomatic missions to Scotland. A sign of his political and social loyalties, and his prestigious position, came at the funeral of the great hero of the aggressive Protestant cause, Sir Philip Sidney, killed in battle on behalf of the Dutch Protestants. Edward Wotton was one of Sidney's pallbearers. Arthur and Edward became political confederates. Arthur wrote to Ashby 'from Pickering House, Mr Wotton's this 20 of July 1589', hinting at dark secrets and plans, and ending elusively with the proverb 'better a half loaf in the hand than much bread in a common oven'. Arthur advises Ashby to get more bread before he comes home. In a postscript (here in its original spelling), Arthur writes that 'Mr Wotton commendes hym selffe (or d'yallsusute a vos)', the (appalling) French either an indication of Arthur's incompetence, or a joke at their common friend Wotton's expense, since he was known for his superb command of languages.

But it is Francis Walsingham's influence that lurks behind this mysterious exchange in the last months of the 1580s. For over four years, Arthur had been asking Walsingham to use him in some way, his motive, among others, to show his loyalty in the face of the treason of some of his 'name and blood'. As early as March 1585 he wrote that he was 'thoroughly tired with an idle course' and went on: 'I desire in this action to be set on work, and the rather because I would cleanse the stains that some of my name and blood spotted my poor house with, by my own good and dutiful demeanour. I am not so ambitious as to catch at great matters, but shall be contented with what her Majesty and you shall think me worthy of.' The birth of a baby daughter in 1587 provided another opportunity to become closer with Walsingham. The baby girl, delivered 'at half one hour past three of the clock in the morning' after a long and difficult labour, was christened Anna in April. Her godparents included the Lords Stafford, Willoughby and, vitally, Walsingham. Little Anna did not survive, but Arthur's links with Walsingham did, although the historical record remains mysteriously silent as to what Walsingham asked Arthur to do to prove his loyalty in the late 1580s.

In the same year that Walsingham acted as godfather to Arthur's baby girl, Bess's mother came again to London. This was the last time that mother and daughter would be together. In a world in which boy children were invariably more highly prized than girls, Bess, Anne's 'one and only daughter', had clearly been precious to her mother. An important bond between this mother and daughter appears to have been their assertive spirit and confident action in a world dominated, officially at least, by men. By the autumn of 1587, Anne's health was failing, and on 24 November she 'departed this life at 3 in the morning'. Her funeral took place in the darkest days of winter, and Bess saw her mother buried in a grave alongside her father, Nicholas, in St Catherine Cree Church in the City of London.

Arthur was now Bess's closest family member, but his diary shows the stress of his combined roles as husband to Anna, head of the

Throckmorton family and aspiring diplomat and politician. He is constantly paying out money, mainly to his wife; he refers anxiously to brothers Thomas and Robert, worries about little 'Nick' (Bess's youngest brother) and has to send 'cloths' to his older brother William, still dependent on him. In contrast, Bess in 1588 is fully independent.

Anne Throckmorton was gone, but she had been a vital influence on her daughter's life. All Bess had in material terms from her mother were some jewels, some chains, some clothes and some household linen. But she had inherited a sense of her own worth and the confidence to be a political and economic player. What she might do with these qualities was suggested by the dangerously symbolic items bequeathed to her by her stepfather, who had died two Novembers earlier, in 1585. Following the pattern of his earlier property deed, Adrian left his stepdaughter, Bess, material possessions rather than property or money. Bess received the hangings and a bedstead from his first wife's bedchamber and was promised the furniture when she married. These goods were far from worthless: a posted and canopied bed (and one can hardly believe that the Duchess of Suffolk had anything less) could be worth well over ten pounds. The bequest of the Duchess of Suffolk's bed was, however, a vivid symbol of Bess's connection with a whole network of figures involved in some degree with the struggle to succeed Elizabeth.

Was it at this point, in the aftermath of her mother's death, that Bess first became involved with Sir Walter Ralegh?[16] If wealth attracted her, then Ralegh was certainly a rich man. In addition to the lands confiscated from the Babington plotters, he had also received 42,000 acres of prime Irish real estate. In August 1588 his monopoly over the distribution of wine licences was renewed for another thirty-one years. Ralegh's money, however, did not make him any more settled in himself, or less anxious about possible threats to his position. Always busy, he continued to move restlessly from one part of the country to another, and abroad, in September alone proceeding from Cornwall to court in London and then to Ireland. If he became Bess's lover at this time, it would have been a question of seizing opportunities to meet in the midst of these unquiet travels. Bess's own movements were the object of scrutiny. Any woman in the service of the Queen had to demonstrate unquestioning loyalty and discretion, but someone with Bess's connections had to be even more careful. Indeed, another way of looking at Bess's apparent success at court would be to view service in the Privy Chamber 'as a form of protective custody', because the Queen liked 'to keep any woman with a claim to the throne' under surveillance at court.[17] The threat from Catherine and Mary Grey may have vanished, their politically disastrous marriages, their subsequent humiliation and banishment at the hands of Queen Elizabeth, their deaths in poverty and isolation mere memories, but perhaps Queen Elizabeth was keen to keep a close eye on this 'sister' to the dangerous Grey girls.

Bess and Sir Walter's relationship, whenever it began, and whatever its origins, thus merely added to the ferment of sexualized power politics that characterized the court of Queen Elizabeth. Their fellow courtiers may well have suspected that something was going on. They may equally have decided, as they had done in selected other cases, that the whole business ought 'to be repressed and to be buried in silence that it may not be known to her Majesty'. But keeping Bess's secret marriage, let alone her pregnancy, 'repressed and buried in silence' would prove harder and harder with each passing month.

2

'True Within Ourselves': Bess and Sir Walter

————>◦◦◦<————

Bess's task was to act as if nothing was happening to her own body as she maintained her position as trusted Gentlewoman of the Privy Chamber. Sir Walter's task was to continue in the Queen's favour, and to maintain his standing as the richest and most successful courtier and adventurer in the land. His letters at this time are filled with details of boats, of the New World, of financial deals: there is not a word about his personal life. *Her* letters, predictably, don't survive. Clearly, however, Bess had some tough decisions to make, not least how much to tell Arthur. Indeed, how much did he already know? During the autumn of 1591, Bess decided to keep the news of her pregnancy from him. He was, after all, a family man now, guardian of the honour of the Throckmorton name. So when Bess visited Arthur and Anna in September, at the Throckmorton house at Mile End, she concealed her sickness and her exhaustion. Perhaps her brother and 'sister' were conveniently preoccupied with their own baby daughter, nine-month-old Mary, sister to the short-lived Anna, and did not look too carefully at their sister's condition.

As October wore on, and Bess's body, now four months pregnant, adjusted to its new state, the patterns of behaviour and allegiance

established over the summer appeared to be continuing uninter-
rupted. Arthur moved ever closer to the Earl of Essex, and when the
Earl returned from a military expedition to France on 10 October
Arthur finally gained private access to the great man, as he records
triumphantly in his diary: 'I was with my Lord of Essex.' This was a
huge step for Bess's brother, a sequel to his successful attempt in
recent years to convince Walsingham that he was fit to be 'set on
work', and Arthur decided that a superb new ruff was called for. He
paid out fifty shillings for this luxury item. To compare costs, Arthur
would pay twenty-four shillings (or the price of half a ruff) to his
wife's wet nurse for a full three months of work, and nursing was one
of the most lucrative jobs that a woman could do. On 17 November
1591 everything still appeared to be going to plan. The day was one
of general celebration, the anniversary of Queen Elizabeth's accession
to the throne, but it was also a day of personal glory for Arthur, no
doubt in his ruff, because 'the Queen spoke to me and made me to
kiss her hand'. Bess, close in attendance on her Queen, looked on.
The young Throckmortons were doing very, very well.

The Queen suspected nothing. Someone, however, did. Lurking on
the fringes of this intense and sexually charged group of frustrated
courtiers, was Robert Cecil. Just five feet tall, stooped due to a
debilitating back problem, and known to the Queen as her 'little elf',
Cecil had been quietly and unobtrusively making his own moves
towards the centre of power. It helped, no doubt, that his father was
Lord Burghley, the Queen's longest-serving, most respected political
servant. Recent events had been good to Burghley's son. In May
young Robert had been knighted at Theobald's, his father's magnificent estate, during a lavish royal entertainment. In August he had
stepped yet closer to filling his father's shoes when he was appointed
by the Queen to the Privy Council, the youngest-ever man to fill this
role. At twenty-eight he was only two years older than Bess, and he
was willing and able to play the long game, to watch and wait for his
next opportunity for advancement.

The first hints of trouble came only two days after the Accession
Day festivities. Arthur records in his diary (in discreet French) that it
was 'le jour que je saye le maryage de ma soeur', the day he found out
about the marriage of his sister. He does not, however, write that Bess

is carrying a child: it is quite possible, therefore, that this fact still remained a closely guarded secret. Alternatively, he may have discovered the pregnancy and, as head of the family, had thus demanded information about his sister's marital status: perhaps someone, with good or bad intentions, had felt it necessary to inform Bess's brother of his little sister's condition. It is equally possible, however, that Bess told her brother, as part of a controlled campaign to gain wider acceptance for the marriage. Arthur had been benefiting hugely from his sister's influence in the preceding weeks and months, moving from service to Walsingham, to direct access to the Earl of Essex, to having the Queen herself permit him to kiss her hand. Now was a good time to let him in on the secret, when he had most to lose.

Whatever precipitated the revelation, the diary entry confirms that it was not Arthur who pushed Ralegh into the marriage, if he had indeed needed any pushing. Generations of Ralegh biographers have represented the great man as forced into marrying Bess by the oldest trick in a devious woman's book: the myth does not seem to survive the evidence. In November 1591 Arthur was not going to expose his sister, but once he knew about the marriage Bess became once again dependent on the men in her life to sort out the public issues. Her role was to keep quiet and have the baby. Arthur's role as brother was, at first, to protect his sister and his family from the potential wrath of the Queen. He wrote swiftly to Lord Burghley. There is, sensibly, no mention of Bess (Arthur would hope that Burghley knew nothing), but there is a careful plea for continued support and patronage, however circumstances may change. Arthur points out that the world has witnessed Burghley's favour towards him, and therefore it would be a dishonour to him to discontinue it. Arthur clearly also felt that he had at least to talk to Sir Walter, if only to protect the Throckmorton family's interests from any potentially predatory moves. Therefore, on 30 November 1591 he writes: 'Je parleye avec Sir Walter Rawley.'

By December, however, Bess had grounds to feel confident that her marriage had been hushed up by those in the know, and that the most basic and necessary proprieties had been observed. She and Sir Walter were succeeding in their plans. Ralegh's letters over the winter are studiedly banal. He wrote to his half-brother, John Gilbert, on 30

December to say that 'here is no news worth the writing, but all things stand in the same state as of old'. Meanwhile, he was organizing his next great military expedition against the Spanish in Central America. Originally pitched as an attack on the Isthmus of Panama, the voyage turned into an attempt to catch the Spanish treasure fleet at sea. The serious planning began in early 1592, and the ships were supposed to leave in February. Ralegh was in his element, making preparations, ordering '3 score tons of cider' (and that is a lot of cider) to be prepared and brought to Dartmouth in readiness. For the Earl of Essex, too, life continued in a familiar pattern: he was the star of the show at the Christmas court festivities, some of the more stern political commentators suggesting that he was getting carried away with 'light devices or shows of braveries'. The Queen seemed, as ever, to like his style.

It was harder for Bess to pretend that it was business as usual. By February, and as Ralegh prepared for his treasure hunt, she knew it was only a matter of weeks until the birth of her baby. How she concealed the later stages of the pregnancy is a mystery, but apparently she succeeded in doing so. As the birth approached, however, arrangements needed to be made. Bess turned to Arthur, and it was her brother, in familiar territory, who, on Friday 11 February 1592, paid twenty-eight shillings for a nurse 'for 14 weeks from Monday next'. He also 'took a medicine' that day, perhaps a sign of stress at having to deal with his wayward sister. In fact, Bess did not come to her brother's house until over two weeks after the nurse had been engaged. She was cutting it fine, but if she was to keep her non-attendance at court to under a fortnight, she would not need to obtain a licence to authorize her absence. More than two weeks away, and she would not only have to explain herself but her servants would no longer be provided with livery and food at the Crown's expense. This was all part of the attempt to make sure that courtiers did not leave their staff at court living off the state, as well as an attempt to make sure that the Queen's aristocratic servants should actually do the jobs to which they had been appointed. Bess thus left it as late as she could, but at the end of February she packed up and left the court, probably taking her servants with her. At Mile End, Arthur wrote that his sister had come 'to lie here': both meanings were relevant. Bess would both prepare for the birth of her child and continue to deceive the world, all from his house.

Hiding out at Mile End, Bess was not far, physically, from Sir Walter, who was often down at Chatham Docks supervising preparations for the Panama expedition. To see each other was, however, simply too dangerous. Ralegh was successfully maintaining his preeminent position at court, but he had invested an immense amount of money and time in setting up this particular voyage, and its success relied at least in part on his charismatic leadership. He was extremely anxious about the series of delays, the 'many urgent occasions', that were preventing him from leaving the country. He began writing about the expedition as a matter of life and death: 'if we live we hope to repay all again, if not we shall reckon in the kingdom of heaven.' At heart, however, he wanted to be as far away as possible if and when the news of his marriage and child broke to the Queen. Bess did not have the option of escape. She could only fall back on her brother's protection and hospitality at this time, knowing that at any day Sir Walter would be sailing. Bess may have guessed, however, that there were potential advantages to her husband's absence, since his temperament in this kind of crisis had not been truly tested.

But it would be, and by Robert Cecil. As the birth approached, Sir Walter explicitly denied any relationship with Bess in a series of lies to Cecil, who had been pushing Ralegh for some answers. Sir Walter claimed that there had been no marriage, that there would be no marriage, and that he was attached to no one, other than the Queen

> I mean not to come away, as they say I will, for fear of a marriage and I know not what. If any such thing were I would have imparted it unto your self before any man living. And therefore I pray believe it not, and I beseech you to suppress what you can any such malicious report. For I protest before God, there is none on the face of the earth that I would be fastened unto.

What he did not know was that Cecil had, belatedly, found out about the secret marriage with Bess, probably during the week in which Bess had left the court at the end of February. Therefore, when Ralegh wrote this letter on 10 March, Cecil knew that he was being lied to.

Ralegh thus destroyed any precarious bond of trust that had existed between these two profoundly dissimilar men. The letter, born of expediency, was in fact politically crass. Bess and Ralegh clearly *had* imparted their situation to other people, long before Cecil found out. Moreover, while the request to Cecil to suppress the 'malicious reports' was merely naive, for Ralegh to take God's name to a barefaced lie was downright blasphemous.

Above all, the letter was a complete betrayal of Bess, lying in at her brother's house. It left her facing her first experience of childbirth alone and unacknowledged by her own husband. She went into labour on the morning of 29 March: that afternoon, she thankfully and fairly swiftly 'was delivered of a boy between 2 and 3'. What was this first experience of childbirth like for Bess? In many ways it would have been much like the experiences of any one of her contemporaries. She lay in a separate, darkened room and was given 'cordials' (based on alcohol) in order to relieve the pain of the contractions. But in one respect this lying-in was different for Bess. Childbirth often brought generations of women together, and usually involved a wide kinship network of sisters, cousins and aunts. Bess's mother was no longer alive, and she had no blood sisters. More important, the fewer people who knew about the baby boy, the better. Bess's sister-in-law, Anna Throckmorton, was her closest female relative and would have supported her as the birth approached, but she may have been the only female relative involved, although presumably Bess would have been attended by her women servants from court. Sir Walter, still waiting for the wind at Chatham, heard of the birth of his son from Arthur's footman Dick, who rode down with the news that same afternoon.

Sir Walter stayed away (what else could he do?), but he did send his half-brother, Adrian Gilbert, to Bess, with fifty pounds of spending money. This generous sum, Gilbert recalled later, was spent 'at Mile End Green, and about London, when the Lady Ralegh was first delivered with child; and when most of Sir Walter's friends forsook him'. Gilbert remembered that he had been 'requested' by Sir Walter 'to visit' Bess, the visit of a member of her husband's family as important as the gift of money. Ralegh himself, however, did not let the news of the birth of his first son break his stride. Two days after the baby's birth, he was down at Portland in the west of England, immersed in further expedition business.

As the baby's fraught early days passed, there was the christening to attend to. And it is here that Bess's ambition re-emerges, with a glimpse of the stakes she may have been playing for. On 10 April 1592 the little baby was christened with the strange name Damerei. His godfathers were his uncle, Arthur Throckmorton, and, surprisingly to those who did not know the history of the last few months, the Earl of Essex. His single godmother was his aunt, Anna Throckmorton.

No clearer indication of Bess's link with Essex is needed than this, an involvement now encouraged and facilitated by Arthur. Bess's own situation was in some senses legitimized by the experiences of her friend, Penelope Rich, who appeared to be emerging unscathed from her own unconventional domestic arrangements. During March, Penelope had given birth to a baby girl in her brother's mansion, Essex House. The baby's father was Penelope's lover, Charles Blount. Penelope was, however, still married to Lord Rich. The illegitimate daughter was christened the day after Damerei's birth, in St Clement Danes Church, opposite Essex House. Like Penelope, Bess was in many ways reliant at this time on the continued tacit support of the Earl of Essex. Often dismissed as a playboy, or merely the ageing Queen's toy-boy, the Earl's motivations and significance have recently been reassessed. He is now seen as a man for whom 'notions of virtuous behaviour were vitally important . . . they gave his life meaning and allowed him to justify his innate sense of ambition'.[1] It is perhaps within this context that he supported the marriage of his chief political rival to a woman from a solidly and aggressively Protestant family, just as he had allied himself in marriage to the daughter of spymaster and foreign policy hawk Walsingham and the widow of Protestant soldier-hero Sir Philip Sidney. The new political order he envisioned would revolve around these marriages and their offspring. To Essex, the marriage of Ralegh and Bess may have symbolized his vision for England: the honourable soldier and the Protestant gentlewoman would bring forth brave sons to fight for God's own nation.

What, however, did Essex make of the choice of the baby's name? The Raleghs' own aspirations are nowhere more apparent than in the ambitious pretensions implicit in Damerei's name. He was so called because Ralegh had 'proved' with the aid of a genealogist that he was descended from the Plantagenets: that is, that he had royal blood. Back in 1587, Ralegh, ascending fast to his position of power at court, commissioned a history of Ireland from a well-known scholar, John Hooker. Hooker used his dedication to make public new evidence about Ralegh's royal ancestry: you had to go back to the Plantagenets to find it, and you had to accept that one Sir John de Ralegh had married the daughter of de Amerie or Damerei of Clare, a relation of Edward I, but if you accepted these facts then it all made perfect historical sense.

It seems that Essex was not too alarmed by the royal name, because Bess felt confident enough to go on to attempt to use the full force of her link with the Essex family, brother and sister, to push for a new honour for Sir Walter. On 23 April, St George's Day, the Queen would appoint new Knights of the Garter, the most exclusive social group in the realm: the numbers were limited to twenty-five, and since the appointment was for life, new investitures depended on mortality. Only 'the best, most excellent, and renowned persons in all virtues and honour' could receive the honour, symbolized by 'a garter garnished with gold and precious stones, to wear daily on the left leg only; also a kirtle, gown, cloak, chaperon, collar, and other solemn and magnificent apparel, both of stuff and fashion exquisite and heroical to wear at high feasts'. Ralegh would have looked very, very fine. The Earl of Essex did indeed nominate Sir Walter but, unfortunately for Bess, he was the only peer of the realm to do so. Ralegh never did get to be a Knight of the Garter. While Bess pushed for her secret husband's interests at court, he had more pressing concerns at the end of April, as he waited for the tide to take the fleet out of Falmouth. He still clearly wanted to be out of the way if and when trouble came.

Bess's strategy was somewhat different. While waiting to hear what the Queen made of Essex's nomination of Ralegh as Knight of the Garter, she made her own move, backed by a letter from Arthur, loyal as ever to his sister. On 27 April, a mere four weeks after Damerei's birth, Bess returned to court. The baby was sent with his nurse to Enfield, out of sight, but perhaps not out of mind. Just as Bess re-established herself audaciously as a Gentlewoman of the Privy Chamber, the weather and sea conditions were at last propitious for Ralegh, and he could make his escape from Falmouth to sea. Both Sir Walter and Bess were back at last where they wanted to be. An image of Bess from this time survives, but only in the form of a black and white print of the now lost original painting. She is wearing the conventional fashions of the 1590s, her puffed sleeves ballooning out, her lace ruff immaculately starched, her jewels ostentatiously displayed, but there are a few details in the picture that might confuse the onlooker. Bess may be wearing the open ruff traditionally associated with an unmarried woman, but the picture draws the viewer's attention to the thumb of her left hand, on which sits a large ring, possibly a wedding ring (since it was a matter of personal choice as to which finger wore one's wedding ring). Is there even a hint of her recent pregnancy? Her stomach is certainly more rounded than in other women's portraits of the time. These details may or may not be significant, but what is certain is that the woman portrayed, with her wide, flat cheekbones, her long nose, and her slightly protruding bottom lip, may not be a conventional beauty, but nevertheless exerts a strange power over the viewer. Only a day after setting sail, however, one Sir Martin Frobisher caught up with Ralegh and demanded that he return to court, on the orders of the Queen herself. Ralegh, perhaps foolishly, ignored these orders, insisting that he needed to stay with the fleet until they were fully at sea. But he was quick to understand that this was not just another example of the Queen's desire to have her dear pug near her. Rather, it was the first real threat to his special relationship with Elizabeth. The stalling over, on 16 May he was back at Plymouth, and a few days later back in London.

And still the expected storm from the Queen did not come. Perhaps Elizabeth really had been worried about Sir Walter's safety at sea. Relieved, Sir Walter and Bess, clearly both increasingly confident, took steps to regularize their relationship. For Ralegh, this meant beginning to assert his financial and legal rights as a husband. He sent his man, Browne, to Arthur's house in order to draw up an *ex post facto* marriage settlement. This was signed on 19 May 1592 and witnessed by Browne and by Ralegh's cousin, Sir George Carew. For Bess, this meant bringing her baby, and his wet nurse, back to the City of London from internal exile in Enfield. She, Damerei and the nurse all went, on 21 May, to long-suffering Arthur's house at Mile End. Typically, her brother paid the nurse.

The confidence implicit in these actions was ill-founded. A mere three days later, a representative of the Lord Chamberlain came to the house at Mile End. He had a warrant for the arrest and interrogation of Arthur and Anna. They were questioned with the aim of establishing the extent of their involvement with the deception surrounding the two-month-old baby lodged in their house. This may have been the point at which Bess realized just how much her brother and his wife were risking for her, the point at which she realized that it was time for her husband to stand up and be counted, the point at which she had had enough of all the lies. Whatever the case, there is a certain defiance in Bess's next move. On 28 May baby Damerei was at last formally taken by his mother to his father's house. Bess travelled up the river to Durham House, Ralegh's superb London palace on the Strand, lying midway between the City of London and Westminster. For a brief twenty-four hours, the Raleghs were a conventional family in their own home.

Then, after the deceptive lull, the storm finally broke. First, the Queen's men came to question Sir Walter, who was placed under house arrest at Durham House. For two days he was interrogated: during that time he was allowed one private visit from Arthur, during which the two men perhaps attempted to co-ordinate their stories. Bess watched and waited. Maybe her husband and brother could find the right answers for their questioners. They could not. The Queen moved against Bess. Unlike Sir Walter, Bess was not allowed to stay in her own house, but instead was taken by Sir Thomas Heneage, the Vice-Chamberlain, to a 'courtyard' somewhere in London. Heneage was one of Elizabeth's most trusted spymasters, heir to the feared Walsingham, and no doubt his own team of secret agents had been collecting information over the previous days, weeks and months. Arthur meanwhile attempted to get out of town: when he was summoned for a second round of questioning, he replied that he was needed at his country estate at Paulerspury in Northamptonshire. He was nevertheless hauled back to London and made two formal statements on 10 and 12 June. Suspiciously (and frustratingly for the historian), none of these documents survives, but whatever Arthur said appeared to clear his name. He could return to the relative safety of the country and its pursuits: a few weeks later he was hunting with his best friend, Edward Wotton, himself in need of consolation, for his wife had recently died, leaving two young children, Thomas and Philippa.

Bess's position is extremely hard to assess, not least because of the strange lack of records for this time. It is impossible to establish whether, for example, she was allowed to take her baby and his nurse with her when she left Durham House. Whatever was going on was being hushed up, and perhaps because of this there was hope, even at this stage, that the crisis was being managed or at least suppressed, and that the Queen, the most important player, was going to live and let live, if only for the sake of minimizing scandal. At least this particular Throckmorton was a Protestant: throughout these months, the Catholic side of the Throckmorton family remained a thorn in the side of the Anglican state. Whether it was Lady Throckmorton harbouring a priest, stranded in London in his Spanish clothes because he became so seasick he could not sail on to Scotland, or Mary Arden, born a Throckmorton, up in Warwickshire, refusing to attend church, or the 'suspicious nature of those who frequented' Coughton House, the wider Throckmorton family continued to challenge the authority of the Queen and her Church state. Why worry about Bess's sexual transgressions?

Indeed, while she decided what to do about Bess, the Queen appeared to be mellowing towards Sir Walter. On 27 June 1592 she confirmed the transfer of the estate of Sherborne in Dorset to him. He had coveted the place for years: the courtier John Harington recounted that on passing by the house for the first time, riding from London to Plymouth, Ralegh was so excited that he fell off his horse. Even today, it is easy to understand what attracted him: the rich farmland, the superb hunting grounds and the ideal location for a man whose political and adventuring life took him from London to the far west of England and back again on a regular basis. Granted Sherborne by his Queen, he was still, however, not a free man. Deprived of the lifeblood of personal contact with his monarch, he struggled to keep himself together: 'the torment of my mind cannot be greater', he wrote in desperation.

He was angry as well. With typically bitter irony, he complained that Her Majesty thought it was, as he put it, 'profitable to punish' his 'great treasons', suggesting that on the one hand that it would *not* be profitable to punish him (and that it *would* have been profitable to have been allowed to attack the Spanish treasure fleet) and on the other that his solitary 'unfortunate accident' was being grossly inflated into 'great treason'. In each case, however, Ralegh's attempt at irony fails. His secret marriage, his secret baby, were, if not 'great treasons', then certainly a betrayal of his Queen, both politically and personally. And as for 'profit', Elizabeth succeeded in getting far more money out of Ralegh's downfall than she ever got from his success.

What is absent from his letters is any explicit acknowledgement of what he has done. What is more, there is never, ever an acknowledgement of the woman whom he has married and with whom he has created a child, and who is sitting in another part of London waiting, as he was, for judgement to come. This was not only true of Ralegh himself, however. There may have been a whispering campaign going on, but no one appeared willing to spell out exactly what had happened. There is a mysterious silence in the official records as to why Bess, her husband, brother and sister-in-law were being interrogated as they were. It was even unclear whether it was indeed one 'unfortunate accident' or the 'several occasions' mentioned in one fascinated courtier's letter. The atmosphere at court is vividly captured in the Earl of Essex's poetry. He is no great writer, but he knows at first hand that

> heavens, what hell! The bands of love are broken,
> Nor must a thought of such a thing be spoken.

If the precise nature of the charges remains hidden, so do the Queen's motivations. The strange stop-start progress of events suggests that the conventional interpretation (that the Queen, for whom 'vanity was the one constant force' and being fired with sexual jealousy, banished Sir Walter from court 'when he seduced her maid') is inadequate.[2] As Susan Doran points out in her superb study of the Queen's courtships, there is no need to explain Elizabeth's behaviour in terms of deep-seated psychological damage and neurosis, let alone to suggest that she was motivated by vanity and jealousy. Doran writes that

> her anger at the secret weddings of her ladies and courtiers often had a political cause. In general terms she wanted her privy chamber to be apolitical and consequently required her ladies to be free from loyalties to a husband and his kin. By marrying, her ladies were risking their political neutrality; furthermore, when they married secretly (often of necessity), they were demonstrating to their mistress their untrustworthiness and divided loyalties.[3]

Marriages conducted without the Queen's 'privity' – that is, her permission and knowledge – made her 'grievously offended'. Moreover, Queen Elizabeth's responses to the disloyalty of her female courtiers varied from case to case. Mary Shelton had her ears boxed, while Bridget Manners's husband was sent to prison. So why in this case was no one willing to talk about the issue? And more specifically, why was the Queen particularly hostile to Bess?

In the short term, probably because Sir Walter could not keep quiet. Although it was clear that Her Majesty was not receiving his complaints well, Ralegh could not resist one more attempt to get through, his sense of urgency compounded by the knowledge that the Queen was making final preparations for her summer progress. Anyone who was anyone would be leaving London, and time was running out. So Ralegh wrote to Robert Cecil, hoping that he would pass the message on. His letter is an extraordinary outpouring of intense emotion, ostensibly directed at a no doubt bemused and possibly amused Cecil but clearly directed towards the Queen. Ralegh certainly piles on the praise of Elizabeth: 'I that was wont to behold her riding like Alexander, hunting like Diana, walking like Venus – the gentle wind blowing her fair hair about her pure cheeks like a nymph, sometimes sitting in that shade like a nymph [at this point, he crosses out "nymph" and inserts "goddess", having realized he has done the nymph thing already], sometimes singing like an angel, sometimes playing like Orpheus.' Sir Walter hints at the cause of the goddess

Elizabeth's wrath, but always euphemistically and always stressing the singularity of it all: '*once* amiss . . . *one* frail misfortune . . . *one* drop of gall . . .'. This is at best disingenuous, if it could be construed to mean the sexual act that created Damerei, but, judged more harshly, it was a blatantly self-serving lie. Ralegh as victim presents himself as trapped in London (as he indeed was, under house arrest), his beloved Queen going 'away so far off', while he remains incarcerated in 'a dark prison'. Significantly, when he revised the letter, he added the words 'all alone' at this point, thus not merely drawing attention to his prospective loneliness but also emphasizing that Elizabeth had indeed succeeded in separating him from Bess. By the end of the somewhat hysterical letter, Ralegh has completely lost sight of Cecil as audience, and his words are addressed solely to his Queen.

The letter failed completely in its purpose, and probably merely served to exacerbate the situation. Things began to get serious. House arrest, until now seen as punishment enough to both Sir Walter and Bess, was insufficient. The Tower was being talked of: the 'dark prison' of Ralegh's fantasy was going to become, it was said, a harsh reality. Gossip went round London like wildfire. On the Sunday night, Sir Edward Stafford wrote to Anthony Bacon with gleeful cattiness: 'If you have any thing to do with Sir Walter Ralegh, or any love to make to Mistress Throckmorton, at the Tower tomorrow you may speak with them, if the countermand come not to-night, as some think it will not be, and particularly he that hath charge to send them thither.' These revealing comments suggest, first, that the marriage between Ralegh and Bess was not common knowledge (Bess is still 'Mistress Throckmorton'), although clearly her baby was, evident in the snide aside about her willingness to make love. Secondly, there was clearly a power struggle at work behind the scenes. An order sending Bess to the Tower had been drawn up, but someone else was attempting to get that order countermanded. 'He that hath charge to send them thither' believed that the countermand would not be achieved: who this is remains unclear, but it is most likely Robert Cecil, who may well have been secretly delighted with the turn of events.

No countermand came. Queen Elizabeth, now at her palace at Nonsuch at the start of her summer progress, and thus only a few miles away from the house in which Bess had been born, signed the warrant for the arrest and imprisonment of her wayward Gentle-woman. Up to this point the Queen may have believed that the relationship between Ralegh and Bess was simply a matter of rampant hormones, and could perhaps be ignored once a proper show of outrage had been manifested. But when she found out that there had been a marriage, that the baby was legitimate, that the boy's parents claimed that he was descended from the Plantagenets, and had the Earl of Essex for his godfather, and a mother with a family back-ground of treachery and pretenders to the Crown, she acted. Just over a year after Damerei had been conceived, and four months into the life of her son, Bess finally paid the price for her ambitions. On 7 August 1592, as the summer heat worked on the dirt in the city, she was imprisoned in the Tower of London.

Bess's attitude towards her situation and her strategy for achieving release were markedly different from that of her husband, partly out of necessity, partly because of their different characters. Ralegh the wordsmith turned to poetry, clearly not having learned from the failure of his earlier passionate letter sent to Robert Cecil. Well over 500 lines of (admittedly superb) verse later, he must have felt he had captured the intensity of his feelings for his Queen, and having written out his poetic offering in his best italic hand, he sent it to Cecil in the hope that he would pass the poems on to Elizabeth. Cecil unsurprisingly did not. In fact, the poems only resurfaced in the nineteenth century, a remarkable insight into the workings of Ralegh's psyche. In *The Ocean's Love to Cynthia* (Ralegh is the ocean, Elizabeth is Cynthia, goddess of the moon), he writes, dolefully, of his 'body in the walls captived', but claims it is his mind that suffers, tormented by memories of what has been: 'despair bolts up my doors, and I alone/Speak to dead walls.' Ralegh insists that he has done so much for Elizabeth: he has been 'to seek new worlds, for gold, for praise, for glory', and, yet again stressing his isolation, his only reward is to stand 'alone, forsaken, friendless on the shore'. Yet, again and again, his anger, both against Elizabeth and against women in general, seeps through the seeming praise. His Queen is also and only a 'woman', full of the viciousness of 'her kind', a tyrant exacting a cruel and unjust punishment upon him: 'Judgement hath been given', 'the limbs divided, sundered, and a-bleeding'. Ralegh's depiction of himself as a hanged, drawn and quartered traitor sits uncomfortably in a poem ostensibly praising goddess Elizabeth for her eternal beauty.

With Ralegh writing poetry, by turns self-pitying and aggressive, and with her brother Arthur off with his best friend Edward Wotton, Bess started to tap into the network of women friends she had acquired in her years at court. She began with Elizabeth Heneage, who just happened to be the daughter of Sir Thomas Heneage, the man who had first taken Bess from her home at Durham House, back in May. Heneage himself had clear ideas about how gentle-women should behave. He praised his family's chief female represent-ative at court, Bridget Manners, as an 'exceeding good modest and honourable' girl, 'careful and diligent' in her attendance on the Queen, and thus he presumably did not think much of young Bess Throckmorton's behaviour. Perhaps his daughter could put in a word for Bess, could start the long, slow move towards political and social rehabilitation and release.

The political core of the letter shows Bess attempting to formulate a strategy. Sir Moyle Finch, Vice-Chamberlain Thomas Heneage's son-in-law, has advised her to write to his father-in-law, and Bess promises that she will 'perform it tomorrow in such sort as he may show it the queen'. She has already written to the Lord Chamberlain, but recognizes that it was wasted ink: there is no hope of help in that quarter, 'but so I must be ruled'. Robert Cecil has also proved unhelpful, and Bess cannot resist a cryptic attack on him: he has been 'somewhat deceived in his judgement in that, and it may be he findeth his error'. But Bess acknowledges that she must be 'ruled' by men such as the Lord Chamberlain, and also by her husband. For, while she is 'daily put in hope of' delivery from the Tower of London (a daily hope that would be dashed again and again), she is also aware that she may do 'harm' to Sir Walter 'to speak of my delivery'. How far should she plead her case?

As with Ralegh's letter to Cecil, Bess's letter appears to be addressed to one person (in Bess's case, Elizabeth Heneage's hus-band, Sir Moyle Finch) but in reality it contains explicit messages and indeed instructions for her woman friend. The studied cheerfulness and practical considerations almost conceal the perilous situation that Bess finds herself in, but there are clear indications that she is both sick and frightened. The 'plague is greatly seized' and coming closer and closer to the Tower. Bess's opening lines refer to 'the end', to her 'sick estate', and that her illness continues 'even so still'. Bess is extremely grateful for Elizabeth Heneage-Finch's continued kindness (no mean thing under the circumstances) and for the medicine she has sent to the Tower, which she promises to try. She is thankful for Elizabeth's letter, but hints strongly, and with controlled irony, that she would appreciate a visit from her friend in addition: 'when we meet we will talk of it: the Tower stands just in the way to Kent from Copthall.' Bess allows herself hopes of 'delivery' from the Tower, but nevertheless acknowledges that her future, even if she is released, is uncertain. 'Who knoweth what will become of me when I am out?', she asks.

And yet, despite her obvious fears and sickness, Bess, unlike her husband, remains publicly unrepentant, demonstrating the pride and strength of character she learned from her mother. She celebrates her marriage, never showing anything other than a completely loyal and devoted front. She writes to her friend that 'I assure you truly, I never desired, nor never would desire my liberty without the good liking nor advising of Sir W R', and she goes on defiantly, 'we are true within ourselves, I can assure you'. Proud to the last, she signs the letter ER, a public proclamation of her married status, and, disconcertingly, the Queen's own initials.

Meanwhile, still at Nonsuch, and safely out of reach of the encroaching plague in London, the other ER received news of the capture of the richest prize ever to be taken by English ships, the Spanish treasure galleon, the *Madre de Dios*. The galleon, a huge vessel with an enormously valuable cargo, would have been Ralegh's prize if he had been permitted to sail on the Panama expedition. Now it was his political lifeline. The boat contained half a million pounds' worth of treasure, and all the spices and gold, the ebony and ivory, ever dreamed of by an ambitious adventurer. But the distribution of the booty was being grossly mishandled, and by the time the looters had finished their business, the cargo was worth less than 150,000 pounds. Robert Cecil was horrified by the chaos: 'Fouler ways, desperate ways, no more obstinate people did I ever meet with.' But Sir John Hawkins, on the spot and desperate for support, knew who was needed: 'Sir Walter Ralegh is the especial man.'

Ralegh knew this and saw his opportunity. As soon as the *Madre de Dios* came into Dartmouth, he began offering the Queen and her council a financial deal in return for his release from the Tower. On 11 September 1592 Ralegh wrote to Lord Burghley promising hard cash: 'Four score thousand pound is more than ever any man presented Her Majesty as yet. If God have sent it for my ransom I hope Her Majesty of her abundant goodness will accept it.' Alongside the offer of an astonishing eighty grand, Ralegh again deploys the familiar rhetoric of love for his Queen, writing from his 'unsavoury dungeon'. He has a 'faithful mind and a true desire to serve her' (which perhaps glosses over the actions of his unfaithful body), and once again his letter ends with an implied plea direct to the Queen herself.

Whether it was the eighty thousand pounds or the declarations of a 'faithful mind' and 'true desire', the strategy appeared to work. A few days later, in mid-September, the Queen signed the order for Ralegh's conditional release. In a painful irony, Elizabeth was at Sherborne when she did so, the very estate that should by rights have had Bess as its mistress now the resting place of the Queen on her continuing summer progress. The following day Ralegh was out of prison. Within hours he was riding westwards, dashing off letters of thanks to Lord Burghley from London and then another from Hartley Row, on the road west between Basingstoke and Bagshot.

Bess had no such possibility of escape. Some of those who had supported and encouraged her even a few months earlier were quick to fade into the background in her time of trouble, not least the Earl of Essex. All she had was a husband who would not even acknowledge her (there is continued and complete silence about Bess in Ralegh's letters), and who clearly believed that she had ruined his political career. Unable to offer eighty thousand pounds to her Queen, and unwilling to deny her relationship with Ralegh, Bess remained alone in the Tower.

She did have some supporters. Despite or, indeed, because of the fact that neither man liked or trusted Sir Walter, both Robert Cecil and Arthur Throckmorton did what they could for her. The former's ongoing hostility towards Sir Walter is evident in a letter describing his arrival in Dartmouth. The tone is snide and patronizing, although Ralegh's restless energy is reluctantly acknowledged. Cecil notes that Ralegh's 'heart is broken, as he is extremely pensive, unless he is busied, in which he can toil terribly'. Still, however, no one, let alone the careful Cecil, is being open about what has actually happened. Cecil finds Ralegh 'marvellously greedy to do any thing to recover the conceit of his brutish offence', but he nowhere makes clear what that 'brutish offence' is. Whatever Cecil thought about Ralegh, he did, however, write to Sir Thomas Heneage asking the 'good Mr Vice Chamberlain' to 'be good to my poor sorrowful Bess, your cousin'. Arthur also rallied to his sister's cause: it was he who, typically, worked to alleviate some of the practical problems of imprisonment for Bess, attempting, for example, to get a friendly warder for her.

Bess may have been daily put in hope of her delivery, but freedom did not come soon enough. As September continued, the heat in London did not abate. It was the end of one of the hottest summers within living memory, and London was a city of drought. Incredibly, the Thames itself dried up. Conditions in the Tower of London deteriorated as the weeks went by, but worse was to come with October as the plague took a stranglehold on the city. Those who had returned to attend to business or the start of the new law term quickly packed up again and left; even the legal sessions moved well north of London to Hertford. The theatres closed, and playwrights turned to poetry, not plays, to earn their keep: this was the summer when William Shakespeare turned poet. The Queen finally returned from her summer progress but kept clear of the City of London and Westminster, preferring to stop at Hampton Court on 10 October and stay there.

The heat and the plague acted on the weak, on those who could not leave. It was most likely in October that baby Damerei died only six months into his short life: infant mortality was so familiar that there is no record of his death. There is silence in the official records about this small tragedy, and about the fate of his mother. It was, however, no coincidence that Bess and her baby were left in prison in a plague-ridden London. The Queen may well have hoped that her treacherous Gentlewoman would follow the baby Damerei, carrier of such an ambitious name, into the anonymity of a public plague pit.

3

'Him That I Am': Building a Life at Sherborne

At last, on 22 December 1592, Bess was delivered from the Tower. Perhaps predictably, Sir Walter appears to have had nothing to do with it. Instead, on 26 December 1592 it was Bess's brother Arthur who met Lord Chamberlain Hunsdon and Vice-Chamberlain Sir Thomas Heneage, an indication of the people who had exerted most influence in the matter.

Bess did not stay in London but went quickly down to the estate at Sherborne in Dorset. Ralegh, it seems, stayed at Durham House. She had lost so much: baby Damerei, her career at court, her reputation and her ambitions. Now she was in exile, forced to make a new life with a husband who believed that she had destroyed his future and was neither ready to forgive her nor to acknowledge her publicly.

Bess's journey down to rural isolation in the dead of winter was through an England disfigured by failed harvests and by plague. She saw deprivation and dislocation on a scale previously unknown to her generation, as thousands left their homes attempting to flee starvation and disease. Her journey's end was a cold, crumbling medieval castle. Beyond the walls of the castle ran the river Yeo, flooded at mid-winter. Beyond the river, across some water meadows, lay a small hunting lodge, built in the time of Henry II.

A measure of her spirit is that Bess would create, from these beginnings, a new style of living, one that was to be admired and imitated by her contemporaries. The old hunting lodge would become the site of Sherborne Lodge, a beautifully designed country house, constructed to the latest French specifications. Bess's new home would be one of the earliest (perhaps *the* earliest) English houses to use plaster on the exterior walls, while further lightness and elegance were created by the unusually large number of windows and the beautifully worked plaster ceilings, complete with the Ralegh coat of arms hovering above the main bed in the house. The Lodge was functional as well as refined: fresh water was pumped directly into the house from springs on a nearby hill, while the kitchen and bakehouse, in the basement, were spacious, with generous fireplaces. There was a fan-vaulted wine cellar and a barrel-roofed beer cellar: the household would be well provided for.

The very design of the Lodge embodied a rejection of the court and its values. The defining features of the traditional courtier's house, the communal Long Gallery and the Great Hall, were abandoned. The servants' quarters were separated from the rooms of the family, further removing Sherborne from the spatially and socially enmeshed old ways of living.

And yet, despite this confident assertion of a new order, there were hints of anxiety, even fear, in the architecture, hints of an unknown but ever-present threat to the Raleghs' security. One plan of Sherborne is marked with sightlines, as would have been provided in planning an artillery fort, and there are massive door hinges at intervals on the well-worn turret stairs, enabling a retreat to safety within the house itself if under attack. There is a strange tension between, on the one hand, a move towards light-filled sophistication, epitomized by the high windows and the gleaming white plasterwork ceilings, and the emphasis on security and secrecy. Perhaps neither Bess nor Sir Walter ever felt entirely secure, and probably with good reason.

Sherborne Lodge was to create a fashion for studiedly unpretentious country residences, places, as John Aubrey put it, 'to retire from Court in summer-time, and to contemplate'. This was a pretty fiction for the Raleghs, since those hints of paranoia in the structure of the building demonstrated that their Lodge was more than a rural retreat. Sherborne was by necessity their main house, possibly even their refuge.

At Sherborne, Bess's daily life was transformed. No longer at the court, no longer at the heart of the political nation, no longer a personal servant of the Queen, she was, however, now mistress of her own house, acknowledged as Lady Ralegh, with all the responsibilities that entailed. Her day would have been busy, not least because of the need to run the household in the old castle while supervising the building of the new Lodge. The workmen lived on site with her and needed meals: finding the food in a countryside devastated by famine and disease was a daily struggle. Tented workshops dotted the fields, where the teams of freemasons could dress and carve their stone protected from the weather. Jobs were not always done satisfactorily and needed constant supervision. A contemporary bemoaned one builder's 'botcher's beginning', which meant that the columns that supported the entire building had to be moved one foot further out. Getting and keeping good workmen was always a problem, particularly if there were rival projects occurring nearby, and managing their contracts (ranging from a week or two to a maximum of a year) a logistical nightmare.

And there were indeed rival projects, not least that of Robert Cecil, building his own country manor house at Cranborne, not far away from Bess. There was to be no escape from the rivalries of court life, even in rural Dorset. Cecil sent down his own architect to copy the plan of Sherborne, and was in direct competition with Bess for both the necessary men and materials for building. Cecil, to his obvious delight, managed to retain the services of William Arnold, a Somersetshire mason and apparently 'the absolutest & honestest workman in England'.

Yet Sherborne Lodge grew quickly, perhaps an indication of Bess's commitment to the project, her desire to create a new life for herself after the crises of recent years. Around the Lodge, Bess developed the gardens, designing terraces and walks and planting exotic specimens brought back from the New World. Contemporary commentators were both attracted by and concerned about the rage for home improvements in the great houses of England, epitomized at

Sherborne, a process they described as the 'amendment of lodging'. One wrote, 'our fathers, yea and we ourselves also, have lain full oft upon straw pallets, on rough mats covered only with a sheet' with 'a good round log under their heads instead of a bolster'. Pillows were an idle luxury 'thought meet only for women in childbed'. As for servants, 'if they had any sheet above them, it was well, for seldom had they any under their bodies to keep them from the pricking straws that ran oft through the canvas of the pallet and razed their hardened hides'. Bess, however, was having none of this austerity: the household at Sherborne had the linen sheets and feather pillows she had known in her life at court.

While daily life was transformed for Bess, some things remained the same with the new year. Sir Walter still felt aggrieved, and still believed that a direct approach to the Queen herself would solve all his problems. So in January 1593, only a few weeks after Bess's release from the Tower, he wrote to Elizabeth, repeating again the argument that he had been cheated out of the *Madre de Dios* money. He demonstrates complete amnesia about his wife back at Sherborne. Ralegh followed up the letter by returning to London, and by mid-February he was back at Durham House, and about to launch his most audacious, and ill-judged, offensive in the battle to regain favour with the Queen. On 23 February a Member of Parliament called Peter Wentworth was interrogated about his intention to speak the next day in Parliament about the vexed issue of the succession. The interrogation was swift and the outcome was decisive: Wentworth was sent immediately to the Tower. That very afternoon, Ralegh wrote to the Queen, alerting her to the urgency and the spontaneity of his response ('this being after one hour's warning, but one hour's work') and offering his services as a political fixer at this time of crisis. Still, the amnesia concerning Bess continues, Ralegh writing, plaintively, 'I am left all alone in the world and am sorry that ever I was at all'. And still he remains unspecific about the nature of the crime he has committed: 'what I have done is out of zeal and love and not by any encouragement, for I am only forgotten in all rights and in all affairs, and mine enemies have their wills and desires over me.' There are hints that he is beginning to see that he had stumbled in on something bigger and more dangerous than he had originally thought: *his* motives were 'zeal and love', but his enemies now had their 'wills and desires' over him.

Typically, however, this letter was a massive misjudgement. Writing to Queen Elizabeth with an offer to 'manage' the succession for her, when the 's' word was not even supposed to be mentioned, was a high-risk strategy at the best of times. But to bring up the subject when Ralegh's own actions only a few months earlier could have been, and probably were, interpreted as a direct attempt to make a claim for his own potential as a successor was madness.

Throughout this debacle, Bess remained at Sherborne. Used to equality of access to the pleasures of London in previous years, she may well have resented her confinement there, as did her contemporary Lady Anne Clifford who complained 'all this time my Lord was in London where he had all and infinite great resort coming to him. He went much abroad to Cocking, to Bowling Alleys, to Plays and Horse Races.' Anne had to stay 'in the country having many times a sorrowful and heavy heart . . .' until her lord called her to him. Bess, like Anne, had to wait to be invited to join Ralegh, but this he presumably did, at last, in March.

Having made the journey to London, Bess kept well clear of the court and headed straight for Durham House, Ralegh's great house on the Strand to which she had brought Damerei for one short day the previous spring. Now she returned, without her baby. There she would have found her mother's sister's family, the Darcys, already installed: Durham House was big enough to hold two extended families, and it is perhaps a measure of Bess's influence in some areas over her husband that it was her maternal relatives who shared Ralegh's London residence, not his.

Ralegh may have called Bess to him because he was keen to have another child. Many husbands kept diaries of their wives' menstrual cycles and insisted on having sex at what they believed to be the most appropriate time, the irony being that common knowledge had it that a woman was most fertile when she was menstruating. Sir Walter may have been in denial publicly about his marriage to Bess, but in private he made sure he husbanded his wife. By the summer of 1593, the signs were unmistakable. Bess was pregnant again.

Bess lived in a culture in which pregnancy and birth were still a communal experience, with little if any of the emphasis on privacy of our own time. Arthur, Bess's brother, recorded in explicit physical detail his wife's pregnancies, complete with his own, typically Elizabethan interpretation of symptoms. So, with Anna three or four months pregnant, and on the auspicious occasion of the Queen's Accession Day holiday, 17 November, Arthur writes that his 'wife felt live movement in her belly'. This seems rather early for Anna to be feeling the baby moving, but perhaps this was the point at which the pregnancy was confirmed by the continued absence of her 'flowers', her monthly bleeding. Medical textbooks informed anxious parents that 'the infant . . . will stir in ninety days', a third of the way through pregnancy as measured at that time. This was the moment of quickening, a time, 'some moralists urged, when the woman should "quicken" to repentance, as religious and physiological concerns became fused'.[1] At five months, Anna worryingly 'had belly ache', but four days later Arthur notes happily that 'my wife had masses of milk in her breasts'. Again, in physiological terms he is completely misguided, but he obviously felt that a milestone had been passed. At last, on 25 April 'my wife began to give birth about one o'clock in the morning and a daughter was born between 8 and 9 in the morning'. Arthur's comments are very much of his era: he notes the astrological details of the time of birth, the saint's day and that he has given Goody Collingwood two shillings and sixpence for washing. The next few days were anxious ones. Interestingly, Arthur's diary suggests that Anna was breast-feeding her baby at this early stage, since he notes, in specific detail, the onset of full milk after the first few days of colostrum. Mother Sparrow, the midwife who had presided over the successful delivery, was paid the handsome sum of three pounds.

Bess was familiar with all of this, a visitor and helper at the sociable childbed gatherings of her female friends and family, the experiences of other women such as her 'sister' Anna, both a source of support and of terror. Anna went through three pregnancies, suffering a late miscarriage, a stillbirth, and then a baby's death after only a few days, before her fourth pregnancy, when she gave birth to a healthy girl, Mary. Bess, of course, already knew what it was to go through labour herself, and she knew, most painfully, what it was to lose her baby. To the burden of these painful memories was added the knowledge that the forthcoming months would be dangerous to herself. These very real anxieties were perhaps compounded by the attitudes of her time to the workings of divine providence. Although there are no records to show how Bess, in her own conscience, viewed her behaviour over the previous years, if she did believe that she had sinned, did she fear that her unborn baby would show the signs of God's anger? If a child was born misshapen, the deformity was seen as a direct punishment for the sins of the parents. Perhaps she already interpreted the death of Damerei as God's just punishment for the sins of the mother.

This time, however, the baby growing inside her was the legitimate product of a legitimate marriage. Bess was fulfilling her primary function as a wife, to bear children. She was expected to remain active and sociable, since pregnancy did not mean that a woman retired from her normal activities: in 1565, the year of Bess's birth, one noblewoman, seven months pregnant, was sent down to Kent from London (a journey of several days by rough roads) to greet a visiting princess who was herself even closer to giving birth. As her due date approached, women became a particular focus for social visits. One male writer recounts how he visited in the space of three days his niece 'newly brought abed', another niece 'that looks very shortly', and the cousin of his friend, who 'is ready to lie down and looks hourly'. Interestingly, when Bess began to look very shortly, she returned to Sherborne. There, in a suitably darkened room (light and air were thought to harm the newborn baby), and attended by women from her household and by a professional midwife, Bess gave birth to a baby boy. In precisely this year, an Elizabethan doctor, John Jones, when questioned as to who should be present at a birth, replied that there should ideally be a few 'godly, expert and learned women', rather than 'a rude multitude given either to folly, banqueting or bravery, as in the towns of the West Country is too much used'.[2] Bess was without doubt in the West Country: we can only guess who attended her during her labour, and whether there was much 'banqueting or bravery' involved. What is more certain is that, once the baby's navel had been cleaned, the 'child, being washed and wrapped in his swaddling clothes, before he suck the breasts or take any meat, must be laid by his mother, lying in her bed, on the left side near the heart first of all; for they think, as they are persuaded, that the mother doth attract and draw to her all the diseases from the child . . .'. As the mother drew diseases from the new baby by her presence at his side, she herself would be offered restorative drinks, broths and caudles to sustain her energies, and plasters, dressings, ointments and salves were applied to quell her bleeding and reduce inflammation.[3] A week or so later, on 1 November 1593, the baby was christened in the little country church of Lillington, near Sherborne. This time there was no ambition in the choice of name. Bess's son took the name of his father, Walter.

There are no clear records for the following few months, which perhaps indicates they were relatively peaceful ones after the succession of crises characterizing the previous years. Walter's more precious christening presents safely stored away, the more useful ones, such as mounted coral for the baby to cut his teeth on, put to one side in the short term, there were more celebrations to come, not least Bess's churching. This was a ceremony of thanksgiving for the safe delivery of the mother, and it took place about four weeks after a baby's birth. Women were churched even if their baby was stillborn or had died in the first weeks of infancy, and the ritual could be a crucial part of coming to terms with the loss: the ceremony signalled the woman's status as a mother, her community's recognition of her experience and her own thanksgiving for survival. Bess had presumably not been churched in the spring of 1592 after the birth of Damerei, since at the relevant time she was attempting to return to court as if no baby had ever existed. Now she was attended to church by her midwives and 'gossips', and went on to a lavish feast, washed down with plenty of celebratory ale. Soon after this festive occasion came Bess's first Christmas at Sherborne, the house decorated with mistletoe, holly and yew and lit with hundreds of candles. The rooms were filled with the smells of aromatic compounds of dried herbs, flowers and spices, since this was the season to make up 'sweet powders' and renew old ones with dried rose petals stored from the summer before. The twelve days of holidays were filled with feasting and entertainments. Wat, as little Walter was known, was with his mother at Sherborne, and Bess was surrounded by her new household of relatives, friends and servants. Sir Walter's wealth could not buy him or his wife a place at court (yet), but it could protect them and their household from the continuing famine: at Sherborne, no one went hungry.

Bess's Christmas of 1593 had many things in common with our own modern Christmas celebrations:

> Good bread and good drink, a good fire in the hall,
> Brawn, pudding and souse, good mustard withal.
> Beef, mutton and pork, shred pies of the best,
> Pig, veal, goose and capon, and turkeys well dressed.
> Cheese, apples and nuts, jolly carols to hear,
> As then in the country is counted good cheer.

This poem leaves out the Elizabethan Christmas cake, a rich march-pane concoction, distantly related to our modern marzipan but closer to a heavy macaroon biscuit mixture. These cakes weighed three to four pounds or more and were dazzling to look at, each cook vying to produce the most elaborate decorations: gold and silver icing, intricate designs of coats of arms or mythical beasts, flowers and hearts. But it was the 'shred pie' that was most characteristic of an Elizabethan Christmas, and that has endured longest in English households: 'Every Family against Christmas makes a famous Pie, which they call Christmas Pie.' Inside the freestanding shell of pastry, a 'great Nostrum' of ingredients were mixed, most (apart from the meat) still familiar in modern mince pies: 'Neats-Tongues, Chicken, Eggs, Sugar, Raisins, Lemon and Orange Peel, various kinds of Spicery', together with suet and alcohol. As a historian of cookery writes:

> Admittedly, no modern meal bears any exact resemblance to the sort of spread laid on by Tudor and Stuart cooks for a company still accustomed to eat with the fingers. But it is not perhaps going too far to detect traces of the medieval origins of English cookery in all the standard ingredients (except for the roast potato) of a conventional Christmas dinner consisting of turkey, bread sauce and cranberry jelly, plain buttered vegetables and gravy enriched with red wine, followed by boiled plum pudding and sherry or brandy butter, not forgetting the

little dishes of sweets, nuts, candied peel and crystallized fruits that are the nearest most people at home ever come nowadays to a final banqueting course.[4]

Christmas was above all a time of hospitality. The household at Sherborne would have fluctuated in size each day, as guests came and went. Again and again the tables would be piled with food and drink and strewn with colourful dried flowers and sweet-smelling herbs. Guests would leave with little gifts – ribbons or small baskets of sweetmeats – after feasting with their hosts. The hospitality extended to those who lived around Sherborne, since Christmas was still a time when the wealthy landowners held open house. A Christmas table 'represented the triumph of summer over winter, art over nature, plenty over want': for Bess, the Christmas of 1593 was a particularly powerful celebration of renewed life, after the dangers and bereavements of the previous years.

Comfortable this life may have been, but apparently it was not what Bess saw as her future, for in February 1594, and with Wat only three months old, she began making the first semi-independent moves to regain her position at the heart of the political world. These moves suggest that the traditional image of the devoted wife providing a haven of domesticity away from the public world is somewhat removed from Bess's actual experience.[5]

Two initiatives indicate both her continued tenacity and renascent ambition. The first was her resurrection of the apparently long-dead issue of the Huntingdon money. Twenty-three years earlier, when Bess was only six, the five hundred pounds she had inherited from her father had been loaned to the Earl of Huntingdon by her mother. The money had never been repaid. Most women would have given it up for lost, or accepted that it was a small price to pay to gain the support of a leading nobleman. But to Bess this money was symbolic, perhaps of her father's hopes for her, perhaps of her own independent income. It may even have been a matter of pride: to recover the one material thing she was bringing to her marriage to Sir Walter. The first step in her campaign to recover the money was to confirm the validity of the debt, and this she achieved early in 1594.

A few days later Bess began her second offensive, writing directly to

Robert Cecil, ostensibly about her husband's plans. Ralegh's most eminent Victorian biographer assumes that Sir Walter was the initiator of this letter, and that Bess merely copied out his words. It is true that she uses 'we' at times in writing to Cecil (which is more than her husband did at this time), but Bess also directly addresses the Queen's Privy Counsellor in terms of her own intimacy and friendship with him. She thanks him for a New Year's gift, writing: 'I received your tables of no less rare device than the sentence within was comfortable.' These 'tables' may have been ornamental tablets inscribed with a 'sentence' of 'rare device' (a piece of cleverly devised wisdom), or possibly even a backgammon set (the game was then called 'tables') containing a note from Cecil. Whatever these 'tables' were, Bess finds the message one of comfort. A somewhat elusive passage follows, perhaps referring back to Cecil's words: 'Yet I fear that my Mistress, if all hearts were open, and all desires known, might without difficulty read her own destiny in a plain alphabet.' Bess echoes the familiar language of the Book of Common Prayer ('Almighty God, unto whom all hearts be open, all desires known, and from whom no secrets are hid: cleanse the thoughts of our hearts') and in doing so suggests a dangerous contrast between the deceptive world of the Queen and the transparent kingdom of the all-powerful God that controls Elizabeth's 'destiny'.

At this suggestive point, she appears to describe the dynamic of her marriage: 'We are both great believers, and therein we flatter ourselves and nourish our own minds with what we would.' Is there a hint here that she is increasingly aware that Ralegh is only ever the 'great believer', that he flatters himself with what he 'would' were true, rather than acknowledging the real situation, as perhaps Bess suggests she does? She herself is still bruised by the events of recent years, perhaps even alluding to the death of her first child. She has 'bought sorrow at a high price': now all she wants is some stability, to be 'steady' for a time, since 'alterations will but multiply misery of which we have already felt sufficient'.

She moves from this poignant reflection on the past into advising Cecil on how to deal with Ralegh in the future: 'Now sir, for the rest, I hope you will rather draw Sir Walter towards the East than help him forward toward the sunset, if any respect to me, or love to him, be not forgotten.' Bess imagines Cecil as a magnet, drawing Sir Walter wherever he pleases, which is, of course, flattering to the Counsellor's power ('I know only your persuasions are of effect with him', she writes), but also perhaps a despairing hint that she was unable to influence him herself. The sunset, or West, Bess refers to might literally be the West Country of England (that is, Sherborne) but is probably even further west, the Americas. Bess may well be alluding to the fact that Ralegh was already thinking about a bold expedition across the seas in search of the gold of El Dorado. Bess wants her husband, the 'great believer', to look to the East, the court in London, not to the illusion of gold in the New World.

Rather than Ralegh putting Bess up to write to Cecil, therefore, it is far more likely that the opposite was true. Bess set up the lines of communication with Sir Robert, writing letters such as the above: only then does Sir Walter begin writing to him, invariably in a far more detached and businesslike way. This letter also demonstrates that Bess was quite happy to acknowledge her married status. The days of secrecy were long past. Yet, through these months and indeed years, there is no mention of Bess in any of Ralegh's letters. She is completely invisible, even when he writes to those to whom he is close.

It is this lack of acknowledgement that may have goaded Bess into exploring quasi-independent sources of money and patronage, such as the Huntingdon debt and the goodwill and influence of Robert Cecil. Bess may have been wealthy, able to create a beautiful home, but there is a sense that she was searching for a more public identity and role.

Arthur, the person closest to Bess for the longest time, was having problems of his own adjusting to the marriage of his sister. There was a distinct lack of friendship between Arthur and Sir Walter, perhaps unsurprising under the circumstances. Arthur never once calls Sir Walter his brother, while Bess from the start calls his wife Anna her 'sister'. Arthur may not have liked Bess's choice of a husband, but he remained loyal to his sister, coming to Sherborne to visit her and his eight-month-old nephew, Wat, at mid-summer. Little Wat was thriving, and, unlike the offspring of many elite families, he had not been sent away to a wet nurse, but instead the wet nurse came to live in the house at Sherborne. Arthur generously paid the nurse ten weeks of wages while he was there, a material sign of his sense of responsibility for his sister. There is no mention of Ralegh in Arthur's account of his visit, and even if Sir Walter had been keen to show himself a devoted husband, circumstances were such that he might not have been able to do so that summer. Earlier in the year, he had once again been in serious trouble, this time a formal inquiry by the Court of High Commission into his religious beliefs. The evidence brought before the court dated back to the previous summer. Shortly after the mysterious death of Christopher Marlowe, with Bess well into her pregnancy, the Raleghs went out to dine with some friends and family near Sherborne. Over the meal, the discussion was of religious matters. Sir Walter kept pushing the argument further and further, challenging every definition ('neither could I learn hitherto what God is . . .') and appealing to what he called 'our mathematics' for certainty, rather than to the Bible. There was no stopping him, and there were those present who remembered the conversation, and months later used it to attempt to destroy him. The Court of High Commission's task was to establish whether Ralegh had indeed 'called the godhead into question', and throughout March 1594 those present at the dinner party the previous summer were questioned intensively. It was a close-run thing, but Sir Walter convinced the court that he was no atheist. He spent the next few months travelling restlessly around the West Country, attending to the political and military business conferred on him, more and more the provincial outcast.

With Ralegh absent, in body or spirit, so much of the time, Bess was busier than she had ever been. She had a young child to raise, and two households to run, in London and the country. From the moment she broke her fast, sitting down with the rest of the household to eat early in the morning, she would have had business to attend to. She would eat again in the late morning, and this would be her dinner, the main meal of the day, with a light supper taken at about 5.30 in the evening. In London much, but by no means all, of the household's food could be bought from the markets, but at Sherborne it was a different matter. There, Bess was involved with all aspects of house-wifery and husbandry: supervising in the kitchens, tending the gardens, organizing the granary; she may have even gone fishing. In the kitchens, food would have been prepared for the whole household, but first it had to be grown or caught. From the land around Sherborne came fowl, geese and rabbits, while the dairy produced butter and cheeses from the milk of the cows on the estate. Fruit was picked in the orchards, while game birds and venison were shot in the woods. Bess throughout her life was known for her talents as a brewer and distiller, and no doubt she kept both households well supplied with drink. Cakes and sweetmeats were baked, waters distilled, fruits preserved. There was wool to be weighed and spun, honey to be collected and stored, and the linen to be washed. Plain sewing and embroidery took many hours, while Bess may have, like many women, acted as a doctor to her household, preparing and dispensing medicines and helping to nurse the sick. Then there were letters to read and letters to write, whether in one's own hand or dictated to a secretary: Lady Anne Clifford would sign '33 letters with my own hand' in one day. With Ralegh away much of the time, estate management devolved to Bess. It was Bess who would have kept the accounts, paid the servants, and may even have represented her husband in some of his local duties. For recreation, there were bowls and cards, reading and visiting friends. All of this does not take into account one of the most vital and time-consuming components of many women's lives: religious observance. A typical afternoon in the life of one of Bess's contemporaries includes hours of public and private prayer: 'I took order for supper, dressed my patients, and returned to private meditation and prayer: after I went to supper then to public prayers, and lastly to bed.' Others, of a rather less religious nature, found time to enjoy themselves: 'after supper I played at Glecko [a card game] with the steward, as I often do after dinner & supper', but this card-playing diarist also notes a session of Bible reading with the resident household minister on the same day.

Not only was Bess extremely busy, but she would not have been lonely. Her household functioned as an extended family and contained a wide variety of people. Perceptions of class were very different from our own and far less rigid in some ways. Many so-called servants

90

were of a similar social status, broadly speaking, with their employers: they might be a young gentleman learning about estate management, or an older female relative without independent means who would help with the household tasks. When Arthur visited Bess in the summer of 1594, the household he described contained two such individuals: Christopher Harris, a longtime friend and servant of the Raleghs, and Mistress Hull, probably Ralegh's widowed sister Margaret. There were also 'servants to my sister, Ball, Hillis, Myers, Fullford, Smith the cook, Thomas Laighton, William the Butler, Jockey, Peter, and Smith the Cook's brother'. The roles of Smith and William, cook and butler respectively, are obvious, but it remains unclear not only precisely what functions the other ten people fulfilled in the household but where the boundaries between independent family member or friend (Harris), dependent family member or friend (Hull), and paid servant (Smith the cook) lie. Even these distinctions do not explain the presence of 'Smith the Cook's brother', perhaps brought into the household out of charity to Smith. Arthur does not bother to list all the members of the household by name, but there were probably between twelve and fifteen adults in the household at Sherborne.

In this busy and diverse household, Bess was very rarely alone. Not only that, but she was responsible for keeping everyone happy. Perhaps she, like Lady Anne Clifford, had a particular servant friend who kept her informed about any potential conflicts: 'after Supper I walked in the garden and gathered Cherries and talked with Josiah who told me he thought all men in the House loved me exceedingly, except Matthew and 2 or 3 of his consorts.' There was one place, however, where a woman might have some privacy and could escape trouble-some household members such as Matthew and his consorts, and that was her closet.

This was a small room, usually situated at the end of a series of rooms. Since the corridor was not yet a common feature in houses, with, instead, rooms leading from one to the other, the closet was one of the few household spaces that could be locked without blocking a route through the house. It was a space which provided solitude and concealment, a place for chests, caskets, hampers and books. In the permeable Elizabethan house, with its absence of privacy, the closet may well have been a sanctuary for women. Sherborne Lodge had some interesting design features, not least small rooms in the turrets. One of these is considered by architectural historians to have been Ralegh's study: it is equally plausible that Bess had her closet, her room of her own, in another of the corner towers.

All was going well for Bess during the summer of 1594, although to modern eyes the frequent absence of Sir Walter might indicate that the marriage was not thriving. Then again, to look for or to expect romantic, or even companionate, love in late-sixteenth-century marriages is misguided. Romantic love, although of course it was experienced, was far from the ideal and was seen to have little to do with marriage. Intense emotion made fools of men, and was invariably mocked at every opportunity. When Ralegh himself writes about marriage, whether in letters or his longer prose works, he expresses a rather stern, detached, even cynical attitude. On the death of Elizabeth, the wife of Robert Cecil, during her third pregnancy, Sir Walter wrote an astonishingly hard-headed letter of condolence to the widower, the only consolation offered him being that Elizabeth has at least 'left behind her the fruit of her love . . .'. The woman herself is not worth his tears, seems to be Ralegh's overall message. The marriage has achieved its purpose, an heir.

Handbooks of the time relentlessly asserted the need for wifely submission and obedience, catechizing their readers to drum home the message: 'Question: What is the particular duty of the Wife? Answer: Wives must be in subjection to their husbands.' A popular 'Preparative to Marriage' published in the year of Bess's own marriage explained the reason for this: 'the first subjection of woman began at sin, for when GOD cursed her for seducing her husband, when the serpent had seduced her, he said, "He shall have authority over thee".' In turn, the result of disobedience in women was obvious to all: 'If she be not subject to her husband, things will go backward, the house will come to ruin.'

Bess, marrying late for a woman of her class, had had more time than many of her contemporaries to absorb her society's ideas about the duties of the wife and the responsibilities of the husband. She read of the ideal woman: 'You could seldom or never have come into her house and have found her without a Bible or some other good book in her hands. And when she was not reading, she would spend the time in conferring, talking and reasoning with her husband, of the word of God and of religion, asking him, what is the sense of this place, and what is the sense of that.' Silence (except for discussion of the word of God), placidity and, of course, obedience were the most valued qualities in a wife. Her world ideally revolved around that of her husband: 'When her husband was abroad in London or elsewhere, there was not the dearest friend she had in the world that could get her abroad to dinner or supper, or to any disports, plays, interludes or pass-times whatsoever.' Another conduct book asserted that 'At public plays she never will be known, and to be tavern guest she ever hates', and another points out helpfully that 'we call the wife huswife, that is housewife, not streetwife, one that gaddeth up and down'.

So the manuals had it. The day-to-day reality for married women was often very different. Indeed, a traveller to England from Germany comments that Englishwomen had a greater degree of social freedom than in any country he had visited. He describes London:

> There are a great many inns, taverns and beer gardens scattered about the city, where much amusement may be had with eating, drinking, fiddling and the rest, as for instance in our hostelry, which was visited by players almost daily. And what is particularly curious is that the women as well as the men, in fact more often than they, will frequent the taverns or ale-houses for enjoyment. They count it a great honour to be taken there and given wine with sugar to drink; and if one woman only is invited, then she will bring three or four other women along and they gaily toast each other.

While it is difficult to assess, in general, the balance between social theory and social practice in early modern marriages, it is particularly difficult to draw conclusions about the nature of the Raleghs' marriage in its early years. There is nothing to indicate that Bess was badly treated, and there is plenty of evidence to suggest that she was not short of money. On the other hand, there is not much evidence of closeness, in its emotional and its spatial senses. Ironically, however, if husband and wife were not often together, then that may well have been a positive advantage to Bess. If Sir Walter had been living with her more often, she would perhaps have had to conform more closely to the stereotypical view of the wife.

Such was the beginning of Bess's life at Sherborne. Then, on 20 September 1594, twenty-one months after her retreat to Dorset, and nearly three years after her marriage, a remarkable event occurred. Sir Walter Ralegh mentioned his wife in a letter. He was writing from London, from Durham House, to Robert Cecil, and his staccato delivery suggests his panic: 'I had a post this morning from Sherborne. The plague is in the town very hot. My Bess is one way sent, her son another way, and I am in great trouble therewith.' Sir Walter at Durham House may have been in 'great trouble therewith' but his Bess must have been desperate. Little Wat was not yet even one year old, hardly older than Damerei had been when plague had struck the Tower of London back in the summer of 1592. Bess knew that it was the sensible thing to separate the mother and child, in the hope that at least one might survive, and yet how terrible to have to part with her baby under those circumstances. Perhaps she was advised by her more godly friends to stay and wait upon providence: to flee would be to attempt to escape God's judgement. If she was so advised, then she did not listen, but acted to save both herself and her baby. Bess and Wat survived this time, but around them starvation and death continued to mark their country. Those who could fled famine- and disease-stricken areas, some heading for plague-free towns, where the councils attempted to provide grain, flour and bread at subsidized prices. The situation was, however, spiralling out of control: 'plague was catastrophic not only to the families who were left bereaved and perhaps indigent, but to the whole community. Work stopped, trade was paralysed, the people impoverished.'6

For Ralegh, however, this brush with plague appears to have finally put an end to his public amnesia about his wife. Once he has mentioned Bess, he does not stop and she features in his very next letter to Cecil. With a man as complex and as capable of deception, both of himself and of others, as Ralegh, it is still hard, however, to assess the nature of his feelings for his wife. It is possible that Ralegh's public acknowledgement of Bess was directly linked to his almost obsessive interest in little Wat's future and his desire to confirm the boy's legitimacy. Although the Raleghs were still wealthy, Sir Walter nevertheless spent the early years of his marriage completely absorbed in providing a secure inheritance for his surviving son. Provision for his wife was simply not a priority. When he reviewed his finances in 1594, and when he wrote his will in 1597, Sir Walter allowed Bess a mere two hundred pounds a year after his death, which certainly would not have kept her in the manner to which she was accustomed. Everything else was to go to Wat. While not particularly surprising, this is certainly not generous.

Ralegh, however, appeared to take steps actively to *exclude* Bess from his financial dealings. He wrote in one letter that 'all the interest [by which he means the equity] is in my son', since the lease on the Sherborne estate has been assigned to Wat 'without power of revocation'. If and when Ralegh dies, Bess gets no property and no influence over the property, just her two hundred pounds a year. Even so, Sir Walter expresses anxiety about this deal, and desires his correspondent to keep quiet about the details: 'And besides by that means my wife will know that she can have no interest in my living, and so exclaim.' This statement is ambiguous: does Ralegh mean 'interest' in the sense of equity, in which case he is anxious that Bess will realize that she has absolutely no stake in his property and land (his 'living') and will thus complain of her unfair treatment? Or does it mean that Ralegh is worried that Bess would see the two hundred pounds as something valuable, and that she would therefore have no interest in him living, more interest in a regular income after his death? Either way, his worry is that Bess will 'exclaim'. This evocative word carries its modern sense of crying out vehemently, but had two other possible meanings in Ralegh's time, both characteristic of Bess's behaviour. One was to 'accuse loudly'; the other to 'expose an injustice': as one of Christopher Marlowe's characters says at a particularly bloody moment, 'I curse thee, and exclaim thee, miscreant'.

Therefore, while it is clearly a travesty to represent Bess (as one of Ralegh's twentieth-century biographers does) as 'a devoted honourable wife' complete with 'blue eyes and blond hair', it is also possible to challenge the great Ralegh scholar Agnes Latham's verdict that 'the marriage was, without doubt, a happy one, Ralegh being obviously genuinely relaxed in his wife's company'. The letter above suggests that Ralegh was not very 'relaxed' about Bess, and feared her reactions. More important, was Bess 'relaxed' in the company of Ralegh, the husband who would not even acknowledge her existence for the first three years of their marriage, and who actively sought to constrain her financially in the event of his death? For a woman who appeared to value honesty and straight talking so highly, what did she make of Ralegh's lies and evasions? It has been suggested that deception on the scale Ralegh used it suggests that a man is either devastatingly clear-sighted or completely self-hypnotized, or indeed both.[7] He was, a heady combination of these qualities, a man characterized by duality: intellectually brilliant but also unable to control his passionate emotions, capable of extraordinary exertion (even Cecil acknowledged that he could 'toil terribly') but also of extreme passivity and depression. Bess had allied herself to one of the most visionary, mercurial men of her generation. It would be difficult to be relaxed in the company of a man who lived so intensely, but it may well have been exciting.

And when he was up, he was up. Having seen off accusations of atheism and the threat of plague, by the end of 1594 Sir Walter was increasingly in London, 'very gallant', the freewheeling adventurer again. Bess remained at Sherborne with Wat. In early December the Queen at last granted Ralegh permission to 'offend' the King of Spain, and by Christmas he had the necessary boats and men organized for a voyage in search of the gold of El Dorado, deep in the heart of Spanish South America. Bess's pleas to Robert Cecil to use his power to 'stay' her husband had fallen on deaf ears. Christmas and New Year came and went, and Ralegh waited, at Sherborne with Bess, for the right wind to take him out into the Atlantic. As the voyage came closer, his mood swung back towards depression. He wrote to Robert Cecil, shortly before setting off, that 'the body is wasted with toil, the purse with charge and all things worse. [. . .] There is no news from hence worth the writing.' Ralegh had used this line before, in the weeks leading up to the birth of Damerei.

As Ralegh waited, miserably, for a good wind to take him across the ocean to El Dorado, Bess insisted, on 3 February, that a bond should be drawn up between her and one William Sanderson, the man who had been responsible for raising much of the money for her husband's voyage. Bess demanded some protection against the possibility of a lawsuit by Sanderson, who would wish to recover his investment from her if Ralegh did not return. If she herself was not going to gain from Ralegh's death at sea, then at least she did not want to be saddled with his debts.

On 'Thursday the 6th of February in the year 1595' (as Ralegh's famous and compelling published account of his voyage begins), Bess's husband set out for Trinidad, the Orinoco river, and the illusory gold of El Dorado. Three days later Bess was staying with Arthur, at the Throckmorton family house in London, at Mile End. Her brother writes rather cryptically in his diary: 'La mia sorella Eliz: Rayely inenima a cazza mia.' The key word here is 'inenima' and one can only guess what Arthur meant.[8] Possibly he thinks that Bess animates, or enlivens his household, or he might mean that Bess was in a filthy mood.

Was Bess envious of Ralegh's chance to explore a New World, a place he would later describe as an earthly paradise? She had spent much of her life watching her father, and her brother, and her husband travel to foreign places. Sir Nicholas loved France, Arthur was passionate about Italy, Ralegh drawn to 'the large, rich and beautiful empire of Guiana'. As for Bess, there are no records to suggest she ever travelled out of England. Yet whatever Arthur is getting at in his creative Italian, an impression of his sister's vitality, for good or for bad, comes across. This vitality may not have been allowed to express itself in great voyages beyond the seas, but there were things that Bess could do now that Ralegh was away. Ever the realist, she had done her best to prevent Sir Walter from going, had then attempted to protect herself if he were not to come back, and now she seized her opportunity while he was away to pursue her own ambitions.

On 20 March, with Ralegh three thousand miles away attacking Spanish-controlled Trinidad, Bess renewed her letters to Robert Cecil. Writing from Sherborne Lodge, she expresses her gratitude to Cecil for his kind letter, and also politely thanks him for looking out for her, remembering her, while her husband was away. 'Sir Walter's remembrance of me to you at his last departure shall add and increase, if it were possible, more love and due respect to him.' The letter goes on to express her anxieties about her husband's safety and her feelings for him: 'I am in hope, ere it be long, to hear of him, though not of long time to see him.' When she does, she promises to 'fly to' Cecil in all her 'cumbers': her heavy clothes, perhaps, or with her pleasurable burden of little Wat, or maybe Bess is referring metaphorically to the encumbrances or problems she faces while her husband is away. Cecil, and his wife Elizabeth, had clearly invited Bess to spend time with them while Sir Walter was at sea, but Bess claims that she would not be good company for them: 'a hermit's cell' is 'most fit for me and my mind at this time; being for a time thus dissevered from him that I am'.

This is a fascinating clue to her feelings for her absent husband. The words express both her love for Sir Walter and her sense of the significance of their shared experiences, their union in marriage. They also convey a conscious or unconscious recognition of her status as wife, subsumed within the identity of her husband: 'him that I am'. (Ralegh's most pre-eminent Victorian biographer reassures his readers that 'him *whose* I am' was what Bess meant to write.)

Bess moves on swiftly from this moment of emotional lucidity to talk business, drawing attention to her exploitation of her husband's absence:

> I must entreat your favourable word to my Lord Keeper that he will suffer me to follow the course of law to my Lord Huntingdon. I desire no favour therein, but only sufferance. This bearer can tell you the matter. I rather choose this time to follow it in Sir Walter's absence, that my self may bear the unkindness, and not he: the money being long time past due to me.

This is the first distinct indication that Bess is determined to take the vexed matter of her inheritance to court, and although it is couched in the language of submission, both to the powerful Cecil and her absent husband, the message is clear. She wants her money back, and she will do whatever is necessary to get it. 'The bearer' who takes her letter to Cecil would have been fully briefed as to the case in question: Bess seems sure that Cecil will listen. Her growing confidence is evident in other letters from this spring and summer, in particular those that recommend, or mediate between, male relatives. Although she often apologizes for troubling Cecil with her 'desiring letters', she nevertheless writes forcefully, for example, in defence of 'this my kinsman' (Alexander Brett) who is involved in a dispute with a more powerful adversary. Brett, who would become an important figure in Bess's life in later years, is here praised by her as a man of 'honesty and plain truth'. 'Only his choler [temper] is something to be condemned, which men that stand so much upon their true honesty, as I know this man doth, will be moved if they receive wrongs.' Bess, quick to righteous anger herself, does not condemn the quality in others.

While it is hard to untangle who is trying to do what to whom over the Huntingdon money, the Earl clearly sensed danger from the increasingly confident Bess, and felt it necessary to make moves to cover himself. While Bess had to ask Cecil to put in a 'favourable word' to the Lord Keeper, Sir John Puckering, Huntingdon could go straight to the man himself. On 25 April he received a report from Puckering, which claimed that Sir Walter Ralegh was pushing for repayment of the debt. Bess's letter to Cecil reveals, of course, that she was behind the initiative, since Ralegh was already at sea. Puckering also warns Huntingdon that a member of the Privy Council is giving the initiative his full support and is going to 'move' Her Majesty, on behalf of Sir Walter, for justice in the Court of Chancery 'for his Wives Portion' (that is, her dowry). The Privy Counsellor is presumably Cecil, who must have written back to Bess agreeing to support her claim against Huntingdon.

Bess was clearly having some success in proceedings, but at this point her brother Arthur attempted to get involved, claiming that he was the person who should be managing the entire business, since he was the executor of his parents' estate. As head of the family, and having weathered the storm of the previous year, he was consolidating his own position, receiving in 1593 two-thirds of 'the London house' from his older brother William. Quite why Arthur not only inherited the main family estate in Northamptonshire (Paulerspury) and now took dominant control over the London property ahead of his older brother William remains unclear, but scraps of evidence such as Arthur's regular payments to and on behalf of William do suggest that the boy born during Sir Nicholas Throckmorton's trial for treason back in 1554 was unable to take on the responsibilities his birthright conferred upon him.

In 1595 Arthur's intervention was a complication for Bess, and her brother's motives are not entirely clear. Puckering writes that Arthur 'till he were better satisfied how his sister stood well dealt withal . . . made stay, and would not consent that any Process should be sued out upon that Recovery in his name . . .'. Robert Cecil then challenged Arthur, saying 'that if Mr Throckmorton stood to be further satisfied, concerning his sister's marriage, it would not be abydden [tolerated], but would be taken in great offence: and for any satisfaction, touching any assurance for his sister, it was needless for her, who desired no help of Him'. Bess, it is argued, is quite content, 'so far satisfied, as that she had sent her Messenger to me (as indeed Mr Gorge came to me in her name) to desire that Order might be taken that Sir W. Rawley might be paid the Money.' This is news to Arthur: 'I sent for Mr Throckmorton, making him acquainted herewith.'

Two vital aspects of Bess's experience as a woman (and the historian's task in re-creating her life) become acutely visible in this document. First, Puckering's letter renders Bess almost entirely invisible, at best a fleeting presence as a 'sister' or 'wife': her agency is never once acknowledged. Secondly, the proceedings illustrate Bess's potentially vulnerable position caught between the various men who sought to control her life: husband, brother, Privy Counsellor. Despite the fact that Bess was directly responsible for the initiative in the spring of 1595 (not least because Sir Walter was over a thousand miles away in the Atlantic Ocean) and that she succeeded in her tactic of a direct approach to a Privy Counsellor, and that he in turn 'moved' the Queen, who gave her support to Bess's claim against Huntingdon, the letter quoted at length above gives all the agency to first Sir Walter and then Arthur, husband and brother respectively. As indeed was appropriate on one level: she can claim the money only insofar as it is owing to her husband, the aim being that 'Sir W. Rawley might be paid the Money'.

This document gives an intriguing hint of Arthur's anxiety on behalf of his sister. He appears still to be questioning the legal and financial basis of her marriage to Sir Walter, still demanding 'satisfaction'. Three years on, Arthur is still not convinced that the marriage had been properly conducted. His doubts are, however, dismissed as offensive, and were not going to be tolerated. Moreover, for all Arthur's worries, Bess appears to be throwing in her lot with her husband, 'him that I am'.

For however much this initiative suggests confidence and self-assertion, the best that could come of it for Bess would be the recovery of the money and then its immediate absorption into Sir Walter's estate. As a woman, Bess was subject to the doctrine of coverture (or *femme covert*), which meant that husband and wife were one person at law. Put bluntly, everything that was the wife's before the marriage became the husband's after the marriage, to do with as he willed: 'if before marriage the woman were possessed of Horses, Meat, Sheep, Corn, Wool, Money, Plate or Jewels, all manner of movable substances is presently by conjunction the husband's, to sell, keep or bequeath if he die . . . he may discharge himself of the whole, or of part, as himself shall think meet and convenient . . .'. Coverture eclipsed the legal identity of the married woman, leaving her unable to sign a contract or sue or obtain credit in her own name. And yet, despite these constraints, and with her individual identity erased from the documents, Bess still made the effort to recover the money. What is more, having dealt with the intervention from Arthur, she set a deadline for its payment. Huntingdon claimed that he had not had enough time to raise the money, but 'them that followed for Sir Walter' (that is, Bess, through her spokesman Brett) 'answered that Your Lordship's self had desired not further Time for payment than the last Christmas'. Bess wants the money by mid summer, and Puckering finds 'no willingness in them, to yield any further Time': pay up, he advises Huntingdon, 'lest otherwise, her Majesty may be moved'.

While Bess attempted to get her five hundred pounds back, if only to pay off her husband's debts, Sir Walter was doing what Sir Walter did best: leading magnificent but doomed expeditions. The voyage had begun well, and Ralegh and his men had successfully taken the island of Trinidad, at the mouth of the Orinoco, from the Spaniards. Sir Walter then led a canoe expedition up the Orinoco river, in search of the fabled gold to be found in the interior. His great money-making venture would, however, fail. Unsurprisingly, he never found El Dorado's city, nor, more unluckily, did he find the workable gold mines on the shores of the Orinoco. Bess would indeed see her husband 'safely landed' in England in September, over seven months after he had sailed to seek his fortune, but he came back empty-handed. In a further sign of her growing significance, it was Bess who breaks the news to Robert Cecil. It was time for a change of strategy.

4

'A Most Dangerous Woman': The Return to Power

The one burning political issue consuming the country that Bess's husband returned to in the autumn of 1595 was precisely the one burning political issue that no one was allowed to talk about: the question of the succession. It was certainly not mentioned at the Accession Day celebrations in November, when sermons and speeches across the City of London and the land affirmed the eternal power of the Queen. At Whitehall Palace, thousands of spectators packed into the tiltyard to witness the Earl of Essex vowing that 'this knight would never forsake his mistress' love whose virtue made all his thoughts divine . . .'. The Queen liked the show, and Essex was 'much commended in these late triumphs'. No mention of the passing of time was allowed to cloud the image-making. And when the Bishop of St David's gave a sermon at court a few months later and took as his theme the death of the Queen, Elizabeth was horrified by his presumption. Sent swiftly to prison, the Bishop was reminded forcibly that his Queen was, of course, eternally young, possibly even miraculously self-renewing. Yet the Bishop had only spoken the truth. The Queen was moving closer and closer to her inevitable death, and the chief political players in the state jockeyed, silently, for pre-eminence under the yet unknown regime that would follow her. The stakes were high, and betrayals large and small became the currency of personal and political life.

What did Bess have to play with? She had no inheritance of her own. On her marriage, she had united herself with a man who was dependent for his income on his actions, whether as a lover of the Queen or as an adventurer, rather than the more reliable wealth of an established noble family. Both her older brother Arthur and her younger brother Nicholas were able to turn to their fathers-in-law for financial support: neither Bess nor indeed Sir Walter had that option. They were thus similar in their isolation from the traditional sources of familial income, similar in their dependence on what their personal initiative could win for them.

Sir Walter was not in good shape, however, on his return from Guiana. He appears to have experienced some sort of crisis of faith, and in October it was 'much commended and spoken of' that he went 'daily to hear sermons, because he hath seen the wonders of the Lord in the deep'. Ralegh also met the intellectual John Dee, who dined at Durham House. After these weeks in London, hearing sermons and talking about ideas, he returned to Sherborne and was, if anything, even more miserable. In November he wrote to Cecil that 'from this desolate place I have little matter, from my self less hope . . .'. Ralegh occupied his time in writing an account of his voyage to Guiana which, like his earlier *Cynthia* poems, was sent to Cecil. The work was designed to justify the expedition and to raise funds for a new attempt on the gold of Guiana, and it failed in this respect: Ralegh was simply not believed. Yet *The Discovery of the Large, Rich and Beautiful Empire of Guiana* is a marvellous work, in all senses of the word, a classic of the travel-writing genre, a tale of discovery, dangerous adventure and eventual noble defeat.

While Ralegh wrote his way out of his depression, Bess worked to effect a détente between the four disparate men who most influenced her life: Sir Walter, Arthur, Robert Cecil and Robert Devereux, Earl of Essex. As with her letters of mediation to Robert Cecil in previous years, when she regrets that a quarrel between two men she knew well had 'grown farther than I wish with all my heart it had, they both being my very good friends', Bess had to use all her powers of persuasion to bring any form of *rapprochement*. She was helped by the formation of a new offensive alliance with France, against the old enemy Spain, which was agreed in May 1596. With ever-increasing anxiety in England about the threat from Spain, Ralegh emerged as a key military adviser and actor for his Queen, a role that had made his reputation back in the early 1580s. Now, in the summer of 1596, a strike was planned against the Spanish mainland itself, on Cadiz. The initiative represented the kind of bold gesture for which Ralegh and indeed Essex had been campaigning for years. The alliance with France suited Bess ideologically (she was her father's daughter in this respect) and offered Ralegh a vital outlet for his restless energy. But it also gave opportunities for peacemaking closer to home, in the first instance a chance for Sir Walter to establish better relations with Bess's brother.

In early May Bess and Sir Walter came to stay with Arthur at Mile End, bringing their toddler Wat with them. The Throckmorton house was the perfect base for Ralegh, as he worked from eight in the morning, and then 'till it was night . . . up and down on the river continually busied'. The bad weather that spring made preparations for the voyage difficult, and Ralegh complained of rowing up and down the River Thames, from Gravesend to London, pressing men to serve on his ships. He ended up exhausted, wearily writing that he was stranded in a 'country village, a mile from Gravesend, hunting after runaway mariners, and dragging in the mire from ale house to ale house'. For all the complaining, this was what Ralegh did best: he could indeed 'toil terribly'. As for Arthur, his brother-in-law's expedition would offer him an opportunity to relive his soldiering youth: at nearly forty, Arthur was going to join in the attack on Cadiz.

The growing bond between the two men, evident in their happy co-existence at Mile End, was cemented on the voyage itself. One night Arthur (described rather implausibly as a 'hot-headed youth', but more plausibly as 'at table in drink') actually got into a fight with a fellow officer, all in defence of his brother-in-law. Although it is not clear what the subject of the quarrel was (it is described as 'this scandal-stone'), it seems likely that Bess's sexual proclivities were a topic of drunken conversation. Arthur's defence of the honour of his sister and brother-in-law resulted in his being cashiered, but was indicative of the new friendship existing between himself and Sir Walter.

Back in England, however, rumours were coming in of a disaster to the fleet at Cadiz. It was 'a general speech throughout London' that Ralegh had been drowned. Bess was desperate for information but could not get any reliable news. At last, she heard that her husband was alive, and not only that, he had been the hero of the hour 'for that which he did in the sea-service could not be bettered'. Better still, Arthur had received a knighthood.

Bess's happiness would have been short-lived, however. Her husband may have been the hero, but this had, if anything, exacerbated the tensions between him and the other courtiers involved in the military action. It emerged that the entire expedition had been a rather pitiful example of men behaving badly. Unable to put their personal rivalries to one side, Queen Elizabeth's finest soldiers squabbled among themselves as to who should lead the attack on Cadiz. The fallout from the expedition was not pretty, as each leading figure sought to put their own version of events to their Queen and indeed to the public. Ralegh complained that, although he had received 'good words, and exceeding kind and regardful usance', he nevertheless had 'possession of naught but poverty and pain'. The latter may have been true, since he had received a serious wound in the leg, but the claim of poverty neglected to mention the spoils he had brought back. Durham House and Sherborne were filled with his booty: plate, pearl, gold ornaments, Turkey carpets, tapestries, wines, hides and a chest of precious books.

It was no surprise that by September the fragile alliance between Ralegh, Essex and Cecil had broken down. As one historian expresses it, 'the Cadiz expedition crystallized the tensions which had built up over the preceding years and introduced open factionalism into high politics in 1596'.[1] Most significantly, Cecil and Essex were now violently opposed. Allegiances were once again to be tested.

But which man to choose? Both were close to Bess in age, both had been or were close to her politically: instead of choosing one over the other, why not work again towards an alliance between them? Neither man was as strong as he thought he was, and the winter of 1596–7 exposed their vulnerabilities further. The Earl of Essex, never very emotionally stable, was clearly feeling the strain, and became ill to the extent of withdrawing from court. In January Robert Cecil's wife, Elizabeth Brooke, died in childbirth. The Raleghs rallied in their different ways. Sir Walter wrote a stoic, passionless letter to Cecil, perhaps seeking to appear as a newly controlled and mature man, in sharp contrast to the kind of overemotional, almost hysterical language that had characterized some of his earlier letters to Cecil. Bess's response was more practical: an offer of help in raising Will, the Cecils' young son. Cecil was duly grateful: a correspondent noted that 'Mr Secretary has lent part of his house in Chelsea' to the Raleghs. By March 1597 Bess had persuaded her husband that he should act as mediator between the two men, and this he did. Sir Walter was 'very often in private' with them individually, and others, such as Sir Robert Sidney, watched and hoped 'how much good may grow by it'. Then, on 18 April 1597, Ralegh had dinner at Essex House: Cecil made up the party. As one correspondent put it, with echoes of another famous political meal in Islington in the 1990s, 'after dinner they were very private all 3 for two hours, where the treaty of a peace was confirmed'. This 'treaty of peace' ironically centred on a new military initiative, the so-called Islands Expedition, an attack on Spanish territories and ships in the mid-Atlantic. All three men would ensure that this went ahead, and also ensure that Cecil gained the Chancellorship of the Duchy of Lancaster and that the Earl of Essex would receive the Mastership of the Ordinance. Ralegh, most wonderfully, would be restored to his position as Captain of the Guard with the full backing of Cecil and Essex.

As the summer went on, the new alliance between the three men appeared to hold. But others looked on and noted that neither Essex nor Ralegh (referred to in code, Ralegh is 24, Essex is 1,000) was doing as well as he would like with the most important player, the Queen. The Earl was 'wearied with not knowing how to please', while Ralegh 'once spake with the queen but not private', and 'comes seldom to court, and then but to the presence'. For all the gains of the previous months, Ralegh was still struggling to gain access to the Queen's Privy Chamber, instead, having to compete with all the other political aspirants in the Presence Chamber. But at least he was no longer depressed. With England on alert for an imminent attack from

Spain, Ralegh's letters of the summer of 1597 are fired up with desperation and excitement: 'Hast post hast, hast for life' or 'Hast post hast Hast for life with [all] speed possible', he scribbles, dashing letters from coastal defences or from 'Sherborne at 12 at the night'.

Once the Islands voyage was under way, Bess could again only wait, increasingly impatiently, for news. When it came, it was not good. 'Sir,' she wrote to Robert Cecil, 'I know not what to think.' Bess is confused and frustrated because the 'gentlemen that are come from the Fleet' bring only news that Sir Walter (she spells his name Watter) has 'gone before me Lord General' and that 'his ship the *Guiana* is cast away'. The gentlemen who bring news to Bess from the fleet have arrived in a 'little pinnace, *The Darling*'. Bess knows that this was the 'only ship' that Ralegh 'had left him' and it has 'come away unknown to him, appointed so by me Lord General'. A frightening picture is emerging: Ralegh has lost all his ships, save one, which has been ordered back to England by the Lord General of the expedition, the Earl of Essex. Ralegh, with no ship of his own, has been called up in front of his commander. No wonder that Bess ends her letter with an urgent plea to Cecil, 'For God sake, let me hear from you the truth; for I am much troubled', although she is conscious that her directness is perhaps unwise: 'pardon my haste and scribbling', she adds.

This is not the place for a detailed narrative of the troubled expedition to the Azores (Robert Lacey gives a fine account in his biography of Ralegh). It is enough to acknowledge that again and again Ralegh came into conflict with the Earl of Essex, whose actions and decisions as commander-in-chief of the expedition were at best inconsistent, at worst positively dangerous to the men under his command. After a series of unexplained and inexplicable delays on the part of Essex, a frustrated Ralegh led an unauthorized but highly successful attack on the town of Fayal. As Robert Lacey has it: 'Someone had to creep forward to reconnoitre the best route for attack, and there was but one man for the job – Ralegh. As in Cadiz harbour, Guiana and Ireland, Walter was showing that, whatever his strategic and political failings, he could be a very brave man.' Essex was not happy and sought to court-martial Ralegh for his disobedience, a crime punishable by death. He failed, but, as Lacey concludes: 'Sir Walter was never to take to the sea again as a naval commander, nor was there much point in his ever pretending that he could be a close or a true friend to Robert, Earl of Essex.'[2]

In the aftermath of the Islands expedition, 'me Lord General' Essex was increasingly perceived as a threat, hostile to Sir Walter and thus to Bess. Over the following months it was thus the widowed Robert Cecil, already her best and most reliable source of information, who received the full impact of Bess's generosity and hospitality. She made dinner for him and she sent him porcelain, accompanied him to 'plays and banquets' and generally made much of the widower. Cecil certainly did miss the housekeeping abilities of his dead wife, and some years later would ask the Queen to send 'my Lady Scudamore . . . with a needle and thread' to manage one of his London homes. Bess's charm offensive appeared to pay off, as Robert Cecil belatedly began to take Ralegh's diplomatic abilities seriously. In early March 1598, he and Sir Walter travelled to France on an extraordinary embassy to prevent a new alliance between France and Spain. It is almost as if Bess was creating her husband in her father's image, as the international statesman, conducting negotations in and with France.

Yet her letter to Cecil asking for the 'truth' about Ralegh on the Islands voyage began with the telling words 'I know not what to think', and unwittingly these words expose her own marginal position, dependent for information and indeed power on the men around her. All her efforts to effect *rapprochement* between husband and brother, between Ralegh and his political rivals, did little to improve her own situation. There is, however, evidence that over these same years Bess continued to take small, but increasingly independent, steps towards the achievement of her own ambitions, both large and small. She always worked, however, within and around what was possible in her role as wife to Sir Walter. Four letters serve as indicators of her gradual development. These letters may well represent the tip of the iceberg, since this was a culture based on letter-writing, but the survival rate for women's correspondence is so poor that it is only from these fragments that a fuller picture can be glimpsed

Apart from actually seeing someone, gaining access to their 'presence', letters were the most important means of communication. All correspondents worried about the security of their letters (Anne

Bacon, for example, warned her son sternly: 'Let not Lawson, that fox, be acquainted with my letters. I disdain both it and him. He commonly opened underminingly all letters sent to you from counsel or friends') but women in particular worried about their skill with the pen. It was common practice to send a verbal, often confidential, message with the carrier of a written message so that there could be no danger of information falling into the wrong hands: Bess often writes that 'the bearer' will tell the recipient more. But in both cases, women were dependent on men: in the first instance, women often felt that men's rhetorical skills were needed to make their cases, and in the second, in practical terms, women relied on male family or servants to deliver their confidential messages.

Bess used letters, as a woman, to write to women on behalf of women. For example, she wrote to Lady Walsingham (the Earl of Essex's wife) to complain about the behaviour of one John Meeres 'for he took into his house a sister of his wives who had some 200 mark portion which the knave had cussined [cheated] her of and turned her off a begging'. This everyday tale of one man's exploitation of his wife's sister clearly moved Bess to act on the woman's behalf. (Sir Walter, in contrast, is condescending towards the women involved: Meeres's wife is 'a broken piece that I think few or none would have had'.) Another time, Bridget Kingsmill wrote to Bess to ask for her help in her struggle to manage her own inheritance. Bridget enclosed a draft of a letter she had written to Robert Cecil: 'I trust if Sir Walter will take the pains to polish them, he shall also prevail in the subscribing.'[3] The need for a woman to get a man to 'polish' her words and then to do the actual petitioning is rarely more apparent. Shortly after, Ralegh did indeed write on her behalf, not to Cecil but to Lord George Carew. The case was finally resolved in Bridget's favour, in that it was made possible for her land to be inherited by her daughter. Bess herself was still preoccupied with her own inheritance struggle, when in 1596 she made a new attempt to recover the Huntingdon money. The Earl had died the previous December, childless: now seemed a good time to pursue the debt from his executors. Typically, the official record has Sir Walter Ralegh behind this move, but the chronology of events suggests otherwise, because precisely at this time Ralegh was engrossed in preparations for the Cadiz voyage.

In addition to this kind of intercession on behalf of women, Bess was also involved in the worlds traditionally seen as male-dominated, such as expedition arrangements and the management of land and money. In July 1596 it was Bess who wrote to Robert Cecil with news of the follow-up voyage to Guiana, led by Lawrence Keymis, and she knows her stuff. She writes:

> Sir,
> I understand that *The Darling* wherein Keymis went to Guiana is come in to Yarmouth safely, some eight days past. As yet, I have not heard one word from him or any of my men there, which I wonder at, but that I think they are running about with the pinnace for London. As soon as I hear where they are, if it please you to send down a man to them, as I will send then one to them, that you may know what they have brought; which cannot be any thing, as I think, much worth, for that the Spaniards are already possessed in Guiana. I mean along the shore, so as they durst not land. And also Topiawari the King, that was her Majesty's subject, is dead and his son returned. Thus Sir you hear your poor absent friend's fortune, who, if he had been as well credited in his reports and knowledges as it seemeth the Spaniards were, they had not now been possessors of that place [or *bin poscisars of that plas*, as she actually writes]. Thus, humbly taking my leave in haste. Mile End, this Wednesday. Your poor friend. E Ralegh.

Bess has her men ready down at Yarmouth, in the Isle of Wight, waiting for news, but she already has a good idea of what will emerge. She knows very well that 'the Spaniards are already possessed in Guiana' (something Sir Walter repeatedly glossed over in his attempts to raise funding) and she has a good understanding of the internal politics of the region.

With Ralegh at sea so much of the time, it is no surprise that he delegated a lot of his business to others, but it is noticeable that, as the decade wore on, he defers increasingly to Bess. From her various bases, including the Throckmorton house at Mile End, Bess seeks out and conveys news, acting astutely for her husband, Cecil's 'absent friend'. So, on 25 August 1599 Ralegh wrote a long and tedious letter to Robert Cecil, from the English Channel. The gist of the letter is the complaint that a certain John FitzJames has managed to get land and money that is rightfully Ralegh's, and Sir Walter does not stint on the details. What is interesting is the final sentence: he will let the matter rest only if 'my wife be satisfied [compensated] by FitzJames to her liking.' This acknowledgement of Bess's authority, his recognition that the deal must be arranged to 'her liking', is testimony to Bess's growing importance in Ralegh's business and financial dealings.

All these small moves were achieved within the legal and social context of being a wife and mother. One of Bess's friends fulfilled both these functions in the conventional way. Lady Barbara Sidney had numerous children and presided over the Sidney family home, Penshurst. She gained the unstinting praise of the poet Ben Jonson, who lauded Barbara for her traditional feminine virtues, her 'high housewifery' and the fact that she was a 'noble, fruitful, chaste' wife. Barbara, it was said, 'used' Bess 'most kindly', and it was noted that 'the two ladies wished there were love and concord amongst all'. The women bonded over their ambitions for their husbands, their hopes that they 'might be preferred'. In contrast to Barbara, however, Bess, after a number of years of marriage, still had only the one child. Tradition had it that a woman was deemed fit for sexual intercourse again about one month after the birth of a baby (which coincided for many women with the churching ceremony). Therefore, ever since December 1593, Bess had been expected to welcome Ralegh into her bed. What was more, the medical textbooks would have told her that regular orgasms and 'moderate venery' were essential for the good health of both men and women. This was a culture in which women's sexual pleasure was deemed as important as the man's (so long as the aim of sexual activity was procreation), since a woman 'having great and fervent desire to any man' produces a seed which 'doth issue from this foresaid place down along to the woman's privy passage, moistening all that part as it were with a dew'. In a Christian physiology, Aristotle's argument that this 'dew' had no other purpose than 'to excite, move and stir the woman to pleasure' was rejected: the moisture must have a 'just, great and necessary cause', and, since sexual pleasure could not possibly be an end in itself, then it must be designed 'for the generation and increasement of posterity': that is, making babies.

And yet, rather conveniently, considering the major health risks involved (most women bore between eight and fifteen children, and saw perhaps half of them die, while the risk of their own death in childbirth increased dramatically after the fifth child), Bess herself did not have another child after Wat. Quite how she managed this remains a mystery, since any deliberate attempts to inhibit conception were regarded as a sin, and would hardly be the subject of letters. There is always the possibility that Ralegh had become infected with syphilis, perhaps on his Guiana expedition, and thus his potency was reduced: many of the symptoms of the illnesses he suffered from in the later 1590s could have been caused by the disease. A shadowy presence in her life was an earlier product of her husband's excessive 'venery', his illegitimate daughter. Born probably in the late 1580s, this young girl's life remains obscure. Sir Walter certainly took increasing financial responsibility for her during the 1590s (although she is never mentioned by name), during which time it seems she was being raised with her mother in Ireland. Yet there is some evidence that the girl came to live with her father, possibly in London, almost definitely in Jersey in the early 1600s. While in Jersey, it seems she was married to Daniel Dumaresq, Seigneur de Saumarez, Ralegh's ward and page and a family that Ralegh was closely involved with during his time as governor of the island.

Bess's status as mother to only one child gave her a certain freedom, but if she questioned at any time what it meant to be a wife (and there are no indications that she did in any theoretical sense), her husband's will of 1597 would have left her in no doubt as to her position. Ralegh's vast estate is bequeathed to little Wat, who had turned four in the spring. Sir Walter makes no charitable bequests, but there are gifts for his male friends: the mathematician Thomas Harriot gets all his black suits, and Arthur Gorges gets his best rapier and dagger. Anything that is not actually mentioned in the will still goes to Wat, who has already been bequeathed his father's plate, bedding, household stuff, furniture and jewels. There is one significant exception: 'my wife's pearls' can return 'unto the said Elizabeth, my now wife'. These pearls were Bess's vital, material link with her mother, Anne, and even Ralegh recognized their emotional and financial value to his wife. If Wat died, however, 'before he be married or of full age, and have no heir of his body', then Bess would receive 'all the residue of' Ralegh's 'said plate, bedding, household stuff, furniture of house and jewels'. In a cruel irony, Bess would be wealthy only if she could outlive both her husband and her young son.

There is one area, however, where Bess may have influenced the will. If Ralegh were to die before Wat reached his majority, the estate would be managed by overseers. The men he chose were Arthur Throckmorton, Alexander Brett, George Carew and Thomas Harriot. Two of these men at least had close family connections with Bess: Arthur was, of course, her brother, and Brett was a cousin and good friend. If Ralegh died, Bess would be working with people she knew and trusted to manage the estate of their wealthy little boy.

There is, finally, an intriguing paragraph embedded in the will that speaks volumes about Ralegh's sense of the energies (for good and for bad) of his wife. His 'will is that so long as I, the said Sir Walter Ralegh, or my son, Walter Ralegh, have any issue of either of our bodies, the said Elizabeth my wife shall not make any grants by copy of court roll, by her self or any of her officers, of any of the premises last bequeathed, nor shall dispark my park of Sherborne, or plough up any part of the same park, or commit any wilful waste, spoil or destruction in the said Castle or in other the premises or new erected buildings in the said park, gardens, orchards, walks, fish ponds, conduit pipes of lead, timber, trees, new planted trees or hedges in the same park, nor shall take any woods or under woods out of the several grounds enclosed called by the name of Honycombe woods, Thorney Leaze, Whitefield Woods or Candell Woods.' This long sentence is carefully designed to make sure that Bess ('by her self or any of her officers') is prevented from making changes to the Sherborne estate so long as Ralegh, his son or his son's sons are alive. But the very fact that he is worried that Bess might attempt to issue grants, 'dispark' his park, plough lands, knock down buildings, pull down woods or reverse enclosures suggests that the possibility of her doing just that was a very real one.

The long sentence also reveals what a spectacular estate Sherborne was becoming, with its park, garden, orchards and walks, woods and fish ponds. Whatever the legal and practical constraints placed on her as a woman, to be mistress of Sherborne would have had its pleasures. Through these years, Bess moved from country house to London to country house, increasingly able to enjoy the good things on offer to a woman moving in the highest aristocratic circles. So, one late summer evening there was a delightful party at the Sackville family's superb country house at Knole. Sir Walter and Bess, Arthur and Anna were all 'very much made of and feasted'. Even now, the decorative gatehouses, the beautiful carved wooden screen in the Hall and the elaborate chimneypieces survive from Bess's time. Aside from house parties at Knole, Bess also socialized with her namesake, Bess of Hardwick, both in London (Bess of Hardwick lived only a short distance from the Throckmorton house in Mile End) and at her spectacular new house, Hardwick Hall in Derbyshire. The architect, Robert Smythson, had designed a special room at the top of one of the turrets, ornamented with rich decorative plasterwork: the views were, and remain, awe-inspiring. Here, guests would be treated to banquets or move on to a purpose-built banqueting house in the garden at Hardwick. Feasts and banquets did not merely involve food. There were games and dancing, singing and music, and often some sort of dramatic interlude or entertainment provided by players, either members of the household or travelling bands. Music was provided by a 'broken consort', and everyone joined in the singing of madrigals and airs. Old tunes would receive new words, or old words gain a new tune: much of the most memorable poetry of the period was originally designed to be sung, with Sir Walter himself the author of numerous popular and eloquent verses.

Bess was married to a man who could and did write song lyrics in moments of idleness or in response to challenges from rival courtier-poets. He made literary exchanges with, among others, Sir Thomas Heneage, the Earl of Essex, John Donne, Christopher Marlowe and indeed the Queen herself. These exchanges were not always playful. One of Ralegh's greatest poems (and one that is hard to imagine set to the music of his own time), 'The Lie', generated a range of acutely hostile responses. 'The Lie' commands the poet's soul to go forth and tell the truth to the world, to tell the world of its lies. To do this invites death, but the task must be taken on: 'go since I needs must die.' Ralegh does not pull his punches:

> Say to the court it glows
> And shines like rotten wood.
> Say to the church it shows
> What's good yet doth no good.
>
> Tell men of high condition
> That tend affairs of state
> Their purpose is ambition
> Their practice is but hate.

The cynicism continues relentlessly ('tell love it is but lust, tell flesh it is but dust'), but ends in passionate bravado:

> Although to give the lie
> Deserves no less than stabbing –
> Stab at thee he that will
> No stab the soul can kill.

This is the spirit of defiance that linked Bess to Ralegh but also attracted angry responses from their contemporaries: the poem, punned one courtier, contains 'so raw a lie [sic], No stomach can digest' it. Further poetic responses were quick to come, allegedly from the pen of the Earl of Essex: 'If Rawhead this deny, Tell him his tongue doth lie' and, more ominously, 'Such is the song for such is the author, Worthy to be rewarded with the halter'.

While poetic exchanges went on in the great houses of England, superb works of drama were available to Bess when in London. A short wherry-ride across the river from her, whether she was staying at her own Durham House or with Arthur at Mile End, lay the theatres of the South Bank. By the end of the century she had up to four theatres to choose from. Among them was the Globe, the new theatre occupied by the Chamberlain's Men. There, on its opening night in 1599, Bess might have seen *Henry V*, a new play by the company's chief dramatist, one William Shakespeare. On playing days as many as 4,000 people travelled across the river in search of entertainment, choosing from 'two, sometimes three plays running in different places', as an awed visitor to London noted, and 'competing with each other' for the 'most spectators'. Although women were excluded from the theatre world as actors or writers, they could still be involved as shareholders and investors, and above all as audience. Going to the theatre was not, however, without its dangers. Bess travelled to Southwark knowing that she would meet 'a great number of dissolute, loose and insolent people' as she passed through 'noisome and disorderly houses, poor cottages, habitations of beggars and people without trade, stables, inns, alehouses, taverns, garden houses converted to dwellings, ordinaries, dicing houses, bowling allies and brothel houses'.

Once at the theatre, the atmosphere was no more salubrious. Playhouses were accepted sites for prostitution: 'Pay thy twopence to a player', wrote Thomas Dekker, and 'in his gallery may thou sit by a harlot.' Whether engaged in activity with a harlot or not, audiences were expected neither to sit still nor keep quiet, and if bored would quite happily play dice or cards to while away the time. Food and drink were 'carried round the audience, so that for what one cares to pay one may also have refreshment'. If Bess tired of the theatre, there were other amusements nearby on the South Bank, such as rings for bull-baiting and bear-baiting.

As for Ralegh, he at first appeared to be reaping the benefits of the post-Cadiz realignments. It was even rumoured in the summer of 1598 that he would be admitted to the Privy Council. But over the following months he remained unrewarded and unrecognized, and by 1600 the gossips were now saying that he was dissatisfied with his political fate. He had retired to the country, they said on 19 April, and indeed two days later he was back at Sherborne. The military crises of 1597 had taken their toll on him, as appears in a portrait of 1598 now in the National Gallery of Ireland. Bess's husband, in his mid-forties, looks suddenly haggard. Whether it was nervous and physical exhaustion brought on by the continued military expeditions, the leg injury suffered at Cadiz or even the impact of syphilis, the disease he may have contracted in the Americas, there is no doubt that Ralegh had aged considerably.

Perhaps Ralegh's sense of his own limitations led to a new awareness of his dependence on Bess. In a letter of 29 April 1600, to a new friend and political ally, Lord Cobham, he uses the pronoun 'we' for the first time, writing from Bath that 'we attend [wait for] you'. Moreover, Sir Walter explicitly brings Bess's voice into the letter: 'My wife will despair ever to see you in these parts if your lordship come not now. We can but long for you and wish you as sharing our lives wheresoever you be.' It is, at last, 'our life'.

Bess, in contrast to her depressed husband, appeared to be enjoying an enviable social life and magnificent houses in London and the country. She had her son, her nieces, her brother. She was becoming more and more visible and active in her husband's public life. Her postscripts begin to be added to his letters, her knowledge is deferred to in a legal suit, her abilities as go-between are recognized and exploited. Bess is re-emerging from the years of exile as a formidable individual. What of the woman who had attempted to destroy her back in the summer of 1592? A detailed record of a meeting with Queen Elizabeth, written by a foreign ambassador, suggests a complex picture of both anxiety and confidence, frailty and power, of great freedoms but at the same time a frighteningly constricted life, lived always in the public gaze. The ambassador writes that

> she looked at me kindly, and began to excuse herself that she had not sooner given me audience, saying that the day before she had been very ill with a gathering on the right side of her face, which I should never have thought seeing her eyes and face: but she did not remember ever to have been so ill before. She excused herself because I found her attired in her nightgown, and began to rebuke those of her Council who were present, saying, 'What will these gentlemen say' – speaking of those who accompanied me – 'to see me so attired? I am much disturbed that they should see me in this state.'

The entire interview involves a dance of etiquette: the taking off and putting on of headwear, the standing or sitting down of Queen and ambassador, conducted in front of the assembled gentlemen, and all played out with the Queen in her nightgown.

It was, however, no ordinary nightgown. Its lining was 'adorned with little pendants of rubies and pearls, very many, but quite small', and the dress itself was of 'silver cloth, white and crimson, or silver "gauze", as they call it. This dress had slashed sleeves lined with red taffeta, and was girt about with other little sleeves that hung down to the ground, which she was for ever twisting and untwisting.' That bodily movement alone suggests the nervous energy that drove the Queen. Throughout the interview 'she would often rise from her chair, and appear to be very impatient with what I was saying. She would complain that the fire was hurting her eyes, though there was a great screen before it and she six or seven feet away; yet did she give orders to have it extinguished, making them bring water to pour upon it.'

Some of the nervous tension came no doubt from the increasing disjunction between her image of eternally young goddess and her far more complex (and older) personality. On the one hand, the Queen wore a 'great reddish-coloured wig, with a great number of spangles of gold and silver' and kept the 'front of her dress open' so that 'one could see the whole of her bosom, and passing low, and often she would open the front of this robe with her hands as if she was too hot'. Yet the façade of youth could not conceal that her face 'is and appears to be very aged. It is long and thin, and her teeth are very yellow and unequal, compared with what they were formerly, so they say, and on the left side less than on the right. Many of them are missing so that one cannot understand her easily when she speaks quickly.' The ambassador further notes, with the confidence of the patriarchal voyeur, that her bosom was 'somewhat wrinkled as well as one can see for the collar that she wears round her neck, but lower down her flesh is exceeding white and delicate, so far as one could see'.

In the face of this kind of scrutiny, and perhaps in response to what has been described as the 'searching realism' of the royal portraits of the early 1590s, the Queen's features were transformed by art to that of a much younger woman. As Roy Strong argues, all the evidence from the mid-1590s suggests that the Queen ordered the destruction of portraits deemed offensive, and that she never sat again to have her portrait taken from life. Nicholas Hilliard, the creator of exquisite miniatures, such as the one of a young Ralegh in his magnificent ruff, but by now 'an exponent of an already outmoded aesthetic, was called upon to evolve a formalized mask of the Queen that totally ignored reality'.[4]

This ageing yet ever youthful Queen was presiding over an increasingly fractured kingdom. By the end of 1597, the Elizabethan political world was torn by what have been described as 'fierce and increasingly unmanageable political rivalries'. These rivalries had occurred before, of course. Things had been bad in the 1560s and again in 1579–80 with the negotiations for the Anjou marriage. But Elizabeth had been well able to control or at least play off the various competitors for her political attention, and once open war with Spain had begun in 1585 there was less energy left over for personal rivalries. But the Cadiz action, in which Essex had attempted to bolster his position, merely opened old wounds, encouraging talk of conspiracy and dissensions. Put simply, 'if factionalism at court was nascent in 1595, it became overt in 1596, and deeply rooted by 1597'.[5]

There was an irrevocable falling out between Cecil and Essex. The former, since 1596 acting as Secretary of State and continuing to go from strength to strength, had recently successfully beaten his younger rival to the lucrative post of Master of the Court of Wards, and then persuaded Essex to accept the no-hoper job of sorting out Ireland. Essex, like so many Englishmen, returned chastened after only six months, having failed to pacify the country. He returned in a state of distraction, at last unable to contain the political and military ambitions that had tormented him for over a decade. In a dangerous gesture, he broke, unexpectedly, into the Queen's bedchamber with a group of armed men and denounced Ralegh and Cecil to the startled and no doubt frightened Elizabeth. Ralegh in turn branded Essex a 'tyrant' and recommended that Elizabeth cast him off. In a letter to Robert Cecil, he argued that, if the Queen neglected to show Essex favour, he would 'decline to a common person'. The beneficiary of this decline into obscurity, argues Ralegh, would be none other than Will Cecil: lurking in the shadows of the letter, however, is Ralegh's ambition for his own son, Will's young friend Wat. The Earl was indeed cast off by his Queen and confined to Essex House with his followers, close to the Raleghs' own Durham House on the Strand. Ralegh watched carefully and, sensing that trouble was brewing, tried at least to protect one of his friends and kinsmen, Sir Ferdinando

Gorges, from his involvement with the Earl. Ralegh invited Gorges to Durham House: Essex for his part warned Gorges against going to the enemy's house and insisted on the two men meeting in the middle of the Thames, near the two mansions on the Strand. As the boats drew together, Ralegh 'being all alone', advised Gorges to leave Essex House and London. At this moment, shots came from Essex House. Ralegh was the target. He fled to the court, where there was already furious activity. Senior Crown officials, learning of Essex's plans, had earlier gone to Essex House. There they had been locked in his study while the Earl set off with two hundred followers for Sheriff Smythe's house near the Royal Exchange. He thought he had the support of the London Trained Bands, but, although crowds formed to watch the armed procession, the people of London did not rise in support of his attempted coup. Nor did Sheriff Smythe: instead, he closed off the City of London to the Earl, who, after a brief battle with the very Trained Bands that he had believed would support him, could only attempt to escape back to his house on the Strand. The only available route was by the Thames, and by the time he got back the house was surrounded.

In March 1601 the Earl was executed. The crime for which he was condemned was treason, since he had led an armed rebellion against his Queen. But others saw his fall as emblematic of a deeper-seated disease in the country, saw that there was something rotten in the state of England. Arbella Stuart, who knew this world as well as anyone, believed that Essex had been doomed from the very moment he had burst in on his Queen without warning, puncturing the façade of the eternal goddess even as he kissed 'that breast in his offensively wet riding clothes'. Both Bess's husband and brother saw a deeper significance in the Earl's downfall. Sir Walter believed, in a variation of Arbella Stuart's interpretation, that Essex's 'Insurrection' did not cost him his head but rather that he had 'told Queen Elizabeth that her conditions were as crooked as her carcass'. That speech alone, focusing at it did on the Queen's physical body rather than her majestic image (and one wonders where Ralegh heard the speech), cost the Earl his life. Arthur Throckmorton, typically, simply records what he hears and hopes for the best: the Earl 'confessed he meant to surprise the Queen in her court', and that 'he would have altered the state of government, called a parliament. And I know not what.' Arthur concludes that 'it seems the state was sick. I hope this letting blood will do it good.'

The state was indeed sick, but 'this letting blood' certainly did Bess no harm in the short term. Instead, she consolidated her position, enjoying still more the power and influence of being mistress of Durham House. This was a splendid palace built in the time of Henry III. Five hundred feet square, 'it standeth on the Thames very pleasantly', wrote one traveller, while the outbuildings fronted on to the Strand, with its busy shops.* There were two large courtyards, and 'the hall whereof is stately and high, supported with lofty marble pillars'. Fresh water came from a conduit in the courtyard, piped from a spring in nearby Covent Garden. Bess probably managed the extensive orchards and vegetable gardens, as did her female contemporaries. Maria Thynne writes (in the sure knowledge that she is writing in hope rather than expectation) that her garden is 'too ruinous', but that she intends 'to plough it up and sew all variety of fruit trees at a fit season', while the devout Margaret Hoby followed a morning of prayer by spending 'almost all the after noon in the Garden sowing seed'. Gardeners of the time succeeded in producing a range of vegetables throughout the year, which were then prepared into elaborately designed salad dishes, their presentation on the banqueting tables of Durham House echoing the intricate, formalized patterning of their planting. One recipe of the time calls for 'lettuce, spinach, watercress and other greens, alternating with pickled samphire and broom buds, capers, olives, raisins, currants and nuts'. This eclectic selection of ingredients were then to be arranged in a series of concentric rings or shallow circular steps rising to a model of a castle (carved from a turnip and gilded with egg yolk) in the centre of the mound. The final touch was a little green tree stuck with spring flowers.[6] It was a world in which even a salad was an aesthetic delight.

Durham House was lavishly furnished, 'dressed' in different ways in different seasons and for different occasions. Wall paintings and wall hangings set off the rare and beautiful things acquired by Ralegh

* Almost exactly where the Savoy Hotel stands today.

on his journeys. Quite how legitimately these items came to be in Durham House was another question. One October, for example, Ralegh wrote to his nephew John Gilbert, who was down in the West Country at Plymouth. Gilbert's privateering ship, the *Refusal*, had recently taken a Brazilian vessel laden with porcelain and silks. Gilbert was suspected of having removed part of the cargo and of allowing it to be 'stolen'. Sir Walter was not backward in coming forward in his requests for some of the booty: Bess wants porcelain, Sir Walter wants 'pied silks for curtains'. Indeed, Ralegh makes a half-joke about his request (Gilbert should get hold of these things 'if you mean to bribe me'), acknowledging the reality of political and social life in these times.

This letter, written by Ralegh to a trusted family member, and lacking his often overplayed rhetorical flourishes, offers a glimpse of the man that Bess was loyal to: when confident, he is direct and knowing, charming and persuasive. The problem was, of course, that he was invariably on the defensive or anxious. A couple of weeks later he was still trying to get nice things from Gilbert, reminding him about the porcelain and adding a request for a certain fine saddle and some luxurious wall hangings. And, in a surprise move, he asks for some 'silk stockings' for himself. Once again, Ralegh's taste for clothes shines through.

With a husband in silk stockings, and a table laid with the finest porcelain, Bess was ready to play host to some of London's most interesting and cosmopolitan gatherings. Of course, the foreigners, or 'strangers' as the Elizabethans would have called them, in her household were more often servants than guests, although the servant/friend/family member boundaries were extremely porous. Where did Cayoworaco, Leonard Ragapo and Harry, native Americans brought by Ralegh to England, stand on this spectrum, for example? Certainly not slaves, nor were they equals, and they may well have hovered somewhere between the two, ever gazed upon as curiosities. Most is known about Cayoworaco. He was a young son of the tribal chief with whom Ralegh had made an alliance during his exploration of the Orinoco. As Sir Walter remembers it, the old tribal chief 'freely gave me his only son to take with me into England, and hoped, that though he himself had but a short time to live, yet that by our means

123

his son should be established after his death'. As ever, Ralegh's mindset is of fathers and sons, and of establishing sons at the father's death. Cayoworaco would indeed, as his father hoped, return across the Atlantic to rule his kingdom of Arromaia briefly, as Bess acknowledges in the letter to Cecil quoted earlier. It is hard to imagine this son of a king being treated like a common servant.

Far more likely to be consigned to servitude were the black Africans in Bess's household. Another sea captain down at Plymouth, one John Hill, was attempting to organize the return of some 'negers' who were 'taken' by a certain Captain Clements of Weymouth.

These 'negers' are described in the same terms as the porcelain or rare books or jewels that seem to fall off the back of ships throughout these years and find their way into the Ralegh household: Hill begs 'favour for procuring one of the negers remaining with my Lady Ralegh, that I may speedily return'. Bess was not alone in participating in the exchange of, and indeed benefiting from the services of, the human victims of war with Spain. A proclamation of 1596 warned 'that there are of late divers blackamoors brought unto this realm, of which kind of people there are already here too many', and predictably insisted that any black people brought recently to England should be rounded up and expelled. In these 'hard times of dearth', the 'negers' have 'crept into this realm'. Once in England they 'are fostered and relieved here to the great annoyance of her own liege people who want the relief that these people consume'. What is worse, most of them are 'infidels'. How many black Africans were in England 'already'? Did Bess 'foster and relieve' those 'taken' by Captain Clements? Or did she exploit them as slaves? Did she share Sir Walter Ralegh's at times complex sense of cultural relativity in religious and cultural matters, or did she see it as her duty to convert these 'strangers' to her own Protestant Christianity? The historical records, for black people's experience as for many of Bess's beliefs, are simply not available to begin to answer these questions.

Sherborne, like Durham House, was growing every month in splendour. In the late 1590s Sir Walter finally obtained the freehold of the property. More than Durham House, which was theirs only by grant of the Queen, Sherborne was the Raleghs' own estate. Bess and Sir Walter became more and more appreciative of what Sherborne had to offer: 'every day this place [Sherborne] amends' and London 'grows worse and worse'. There were good social and political reasons to remain at Sherborne in that, as a result of the continued unrelenting rain and failed harvests of the mid-1590s, famine became widespread throughout England, the same 'dearth' that had been used to justify the expulsion of black immigrants. The Queen issued proclamations that compelled 'all good householders' to remain in their own counties 'for the relief of her people' and 'there in charitable sort to keep hospitality'. Bess, as mistress of Sherborne, would have been one of the conduits of charity throughout these terrible years of deprivation for the vast majority of Englishmen and women.

Sherborne was also valuable as a base from which she and little Wat could welcome and see off the ever-moving Sir Walter. Wat may have just started toddling when his father left for Guiana in February of 1595, and was not yet two when his father returned. In Wat's third year of life, Sir Walter was away fighting in the Cadiz expedition, and in his fourth year his father was sailing to the Azores. Wat saw a bit more of his father after his fourth birthday, but then, when he reached seven, the pattern of farewells resumed when Ralegh gained the governorship of Jersey. If Wat did not see much of his father on a day-by-day basis, Sir Walter's notional role, as head of the family, and Wat's symbolic status as sole male heir were clear to all.

> Upon the male heir devolved all the hopes and anxieties of the rest of the nuclear family, and his circumstances and personality . . . did much to determine the fortunes of the whole. Immense care was often lavished upon his education and advancement [. . .] the marriage of the heir was critical.[7]

With regard to education, little Wat was taught at home, although stern theorists warned against boy children spending too much time with women, certainly once they passed the age of seven, the age at which they went into adult clothes, into doublet and hose. An influential early-Tudor writer, Sir Thomas Eliot, advised that when a boy reached this dangerous age he should be 'taken from the company of women' and consigned to 'a tutor, which should be an ancient and worshipful man'. At home, the young boy would learn about manners, morals and proper behaviour from parental example and precept:

in his 'own home, as in a free school', the young boy would 'shape and form himself'. It was Bess who would have taught Wat to read and write, would have taught him the basics of religion, would perhaps even have taught him basic French. As for the critical issue of the marriage of the Ralegh heir, there were moves made to arrange a lucrative alliance between Wat and Elizabeth, the daughter and heir of William Bassett. Elizabeth Bassett was worth three thousand pounds a year.

Ralegh's own vision of himself as father is expressed in a remarkable painting, where he stands alongside his son and heir, who, at age eight, attempts to adopt a suitably martial expression. Bess is, of course, entirely excluded from this almost iconic image of patriarchal identification and ambition, and thus the portrait tells only one part of the story of Wat's childhood. Without the relevant evidence, however, it is difficult to assess, even in general terms, and more so in specific instances, just how close mothers and young children were, and how that closeness expressed itself. In Wat's early years, it may well have been significant that Bess was wealthy enough to have his wet nurse in the house with her, or travelling with her. This meant that she was not separated from her baby in his earliest months and indeed years: breast-feeding was the main source of nourishment for babies to a far greater age than is now the fashion in Western countries. Wat was tutored at home, mainly at Sherborne, and there-fore also stayed close to his mother once he had started his education. Together, Bess and Wat travelled to greet and to say farewell to Sir Walter. One time, Ralegh sailed for Jersey, where, as Bess reports, 'he was safely landed and royally entertained with joy'. Sir Walter 'was two days and two nights on the sea, with contrary winds': this, Bess knew, was not a happy experience for her husband, who, surprisingly for a man who went to sea so often, was a bad sailor. In particular, he found it hard to sleep while at sea, complaining one August while in the English Channel of 'the unwieldiness of these huge ships, in which I shall never sleep at night if I be here till Christmas'. The bad weather on the way to Jersey was a surprise because, as Bess goes on, Sir Walter 'went from Weymouth in so fair a wind and weather, as little Wat and my self brought him aboard the ship'.

Bess took on maternal responsibilities towards other young chil-

126

dren, most obviously her nieces, Arthur's daughters, and possibly Ralegh's illegitimate daughter, now reaching her teens. Outside her own family, she became something of a surrogate mother to Robert Cecil's son, Will, who was three years older than Wat. The two boys became friends and spent happy times together, often at Sherborne. On the same trip to Weymouth when Wat went to sea, perhaps for the first time, Bess wrote intimately to Will's father, Robert, that his son (whom she describes as 'my cousin Will') is 'here, very will, and looketh will and fat with his bathing'. In an age that loved puns, Bess was no exception, while her idiosyncratic spelling merely adds to the joke. Bess's impact must have been great on the motherless boy, although his devotion to Sir Walter is what has been noticed by historians. As Robert Cecil's biographer noted, 'to his father, William would pen a short letter in Latin, referring only to his studies, whereas, when he wrote in English to Ralegh, he wrote freely that in his absence he felt he had lost his "Captain" '. Sir Walter 'had won affection where Cecil had respect'.[8]

Another visitor to Sherborne was Will Cecil's maternal uncle, Henry Brooke, Lord Cobham. Both Bess and Sir Walter developed a passionate affection for their new friend, not least because Cobham had crucial access to the Queen and could present gifts on behalf of the Raleghs. Cobham was lively and exciting company, ready for anything, but also famously poor, despite his noble blood. Throughout these early years of friendship with the Raleghs, he was looking for a wealthy wife, and in the widowed Lady Kildare he found one. They married at Christmas 1600, and everyone including his own brother-in-law, Robert Cecil, gossiped that 'mere necessity makes the Lord Cobham a married man'. The marriage did not change Cobham's lifestyle, and early in the new year following, Ralegh and he were instructed to escort Virginio Orsini, Duke of Bracciano, nephew of the Grand Duke of Tuscany, to Hampton Court. This kind of high-profile diplomatic mission, Cobham's status as brother-in-law to Cecil, and his own strategic military position as Lord Warden of the Cinque Ports, all combined to make Henry Brooke's friendship a symbol of the Raleghs' impressive social and political future.

Bess, however, would have a troubled relationship with Cobham's new wife. Born Frances Howard, her father was Charles Howard, the

Lord Admiral. Lady Kildare had as strong a personality as Bess, and she certainly had a temper: 'she threatens to break the neck of that weasel (which was her own term) that had disgraced her', commented an onlooker about one particular courtly conflict. Few people understood her marriage, 'her strange affection' for Cobham, 'whom never woman loved or will love, besides herself'. Contrary to this letter-writer's belief, Bess was a woman who did seem to be attracted to Cobham and her friendship with him went from strength to strength, based on her typically personal and feisty approach: 'Bess remembers her self to your lordship with a challenge that she never heard from you.' When he was expected down at Sherborne, Ralegh wrote: 'I hope your lordship will be here tomorrow or a [on] Saturday or else my wife says her oysters will be all spoilt and her partridge stale.' Ralegh then writes from both himself and Bess: 'I pray your lordship to send us word whether you have taken up the house at Bath or no, that we may send thither.' By this stage in 1601, it is clear that the Raleghs are operating as a political team, signalled in those plural pronouns, and that Bess is exploiting the language of hospitality, of oysters and partridges, to try to shore up their political alliances. This letter, like so many, ends with a personal and teasingly threatening message from Bess: 'Bess remembers her self to your lordship and wayes your breach of promise shall make you fare accordingly.'

Bess's close relationship with Robert Cecil, now Secretary of State, also continued and appeared to intensify. One autumn she sent him a pair of gloves, with a playful, but pointed request that 'it is indented [stipulated] that if they serve not your own hands you must of your grace return them again'. A week after this letter, one from Ralegh adds a message directly from Bess to Cecil: 'Bess says that she must envy any fingers whosoever that shall wear her gloves but your own.' Robert and Bess wrote directly to each other as well. He wrote to her with news of a fire at Durham House, and she replied to reassure him that the fire had not in fact been too serious, and that what she calls 'all our poor substance of plate and other things' had not been damaged. Bess insists that her only regret is the loss 'of your company which I think by this means we cannot enjoy this winter'. Presumably she means that she will not be able to entertain Cecil at Durham House in London. A postscript, however, asks Cecil to act on her behalf to punish the woman Bess sees as responsible for the fire: it was all the fault of 'me cousin Darcy's servant – a woman that dwelleth just under our lodging, and annoyeth us infinitely'.

A cryptic sentence in this letter concerning the fire hints at both her continued anxiety and ambition:

It will be now a fit time for you to get some interest in that rotten house for your self and for your friend: other wise, I know none so unwise that will bestow so many hundred pounds as Sir Walter hath done, without further interest or assurance of it. I beseech remember it now, so shall not the Queen be troubled to build the Bishop's old stables.

This can be interpreted in a variety of ways. Perhaps Bess is genuinely suggesting that Cecil put some money into Durham House, that 'rotten house', although why he should do so remains unclear. Underlying the words is an anxiety about Sir Walter's 'unwise' actions: he is investing hundreds of pounds in a property that is only his by the grant of the Queen. The anxiety here suggests that, however enjoyable and impressive socializing with the nobility might have been, only 'nearness' to the Queen could ensure the 'interest and assurance' that Bess craved.

Bess was getting closer in these months, however. When, in September of 1601, a French delegation, led by the Duc de Biron, came to England, the Raleghs were given the job of looking after the Duke and his followers, the Elizabethan equivalent of corporate entertainment. The Queen decided to entertain the French outside London and travelled down to Hampshire, 'a country pleasant of soil, and full of delight for Princes of this land who often make their Progress therein; so it was well inhabited by ancient Gentlemen, civilly educated, and who live in great amity together'. One of them, the Marquis of Wiltshire, was the lucky, but soon to be impoverished, choice of host, his house at Basing becoming the Queen's residence to his 'great charge'. Four days after the Queen's arrival, the French arrived: the Duke came with twenty noblemen of France, and four hundred other men, and were 'entertained with all favour and gracious usage'. Wall hangings and plate from the Tower of London and Hampton Court were brought to Hampshire, as were seven score beds and pieces of furniture, 'which the willing and obedient people of the County of Southampton, upon two days' warning, had brought thither, to lend the Queen'. The feasting and entertainment were on a magnificent scale, the Queen enjoying 'many devices, of singing, dancing, and playing-wenches, and such like'. Sadly, while other great houses that Bess would have visited, such as Sion, Penshurst and the Vine, have survived, Basing was burned to the ground in 1645. Nothing remains now but a garden wall. Ralegh, ever the follower of fashion, was keen to look the part, and noted anxiously that 'the French wear all black and no kind of bravery at all, so as I have only made me a black taffeta suit to be in and leave all my other suits'. In a postscript the acute urgency of the fashion crisis is fully revealed. Ralegh must get to London: 'I am even now going all night to London to provide me a plain taffeta suit and a plain black saddle and will be here again Tuesday night.' Bess was married to a man who would ride hundreds of miles in order to make sure that his black suit of clothes co-ordinated with his black saddle.

When the Queen left Basing, she created ten new knights, a greater number than she had ever created at one time before, including Carew, Sir Walter's older brother. In a rare glimpse of Bess's day-to-day life, a document survives which shows that she was ill at Basing. Ralegh's half-brother, Adrian Gilbert, spent ten pounds of his own money in 'two journeys to Basing when he carried with him Christianus, a physician, to minister physic to the Lady Ralegh, by Sir WR's appointment'. There is only one other oblique mention of physical illness in all the documents connected with Bess, when she thanks her friend Elizabeth Heneage-Finch for medicine while imprisoned in the Tower in the summer of 1592. In contrast, her brother's diary shows a man who was frequently ill. Indeed, every single detail of every single illness is recorded by Arthur in explicit detail, as are the cures, some of which are even more unpleasant than the diseases themselves. Similarly, Sir Walter's health became increasingly poor through the later part of the 1590s, and he did not conceal the details of his afflictions in his letters to his friends. Both men, like their contemporaries, understood their symptoms in terms of a theory of humours. Men, it was believed, were hot and dry, while women were cold and moist. It followed, as night follows day, that men were active, women passive: men were energetic, brave and strong, while women were gentle, tender, kind and timorous. The humoural theory also posited that women were less healthy than men: due to their 'passive condition', they were 'subject unto more diseases'. Medical theories of the time cannot have helped Arthur and Sir Walter, afflicted with agues and ruptures with grim regularity, to understand Bess's apparently rude health. It is, however, quite possible that Bess was ill as often as her brother and husband, but that her health was simply not seen as an important topic for discussion, either by herself or by those close to her. If a woman was, as Aristotle argued, an error in creation, an imperfect version of the male, if she was, as Genesis had it, created second, the tempter of Adam, condemned by God to bring forth children in sorrow, then why pay attention to the perfectly natural expressions of woman's defectiveness: illness and pain?

Crucially, however, Bess continued to escape the physical grind of relentless pregnancy and childbirth familiar to many of her aristocratic contemporaries. During these years, her relationship with Ralegh appeared to strengthen and mature. Bess was indeed 'one in all with Sir Walter', as she wrote in another postscript to one of Sir Walter's letters, this time to Lord Cobham. She was certainly growing in confidence.

But all was not as it appeared. In part because of the elimination of the Earl of Essex, low-born Ralegh's pretensions to power seemed even more threatening to both the traditional noble families, such as the Howards, and to Secretary Cecil. Anxious about the future, the cannier English courtiers began to turn towards the most likely successor to the Virgin Queen, James VI of Scotland, and started to poison the prospective King's mind against their political rivals. These were anxious times for Cecil. If his secret correspondence with the Scottish King had been exposed, he would have lost all the trust of his Queen, and, indeed, he came very, very close to precisely this crisis. He was the man for the long game, however, and he pursued relentlessly his campaign to ensure that he, Cecil, would emerge as the new King's chief minister. The obvious corollary of this was the removal of his rivals, gathering their own forces at Durham House.

As early as 1600 Cecil began a secret correspondence with Lord George Carew, Sir Walter's own cousin. The movements of Ralegh, referred to in code as 2048, were tracked, his ambitions noted. However many pairs of gloves Bess sent, however many happy times Will Cecil spent with Wat Ralegh, tensions between Cecil and Sir Walter rose. There was 'some little feud' between the men, Sir Walter was 'not well pleased', and yet still he wrote to Cecil in the language of generous hospitality: 'We do wish you more cordially here than you can wish your self.' In the margin, he writes: 'Bess returns you her best wishes notwithstanding all quarrels.' Bess, the peacemaker, was still trying to keep everyone happy.

Aware that there were 'quarrels', she was unaware that she herself was being highlighted as the root of the problem, precisely because of her increased influence over the group at Durham House. Cecil was damning in private: 'But Sir,' he writes, 'for the better man the second wholly sways him, and to which passions he is subject who is subject to his Lady, I leave to your judgement and experience.' Henry Brooke is the 'better' man (after all, he was Cecil's brother-in-law) who is swayed by 'the second' (Ralegh): but, more ominously, Ralegh himself is 'subject to his Lady'. Correspondents were horrified by what they saw as a dangerously inverted hierarchy on display at Durham House: social superiors subject to social inferiors, man subject to woman.

Cecil was unable to shake off illness and exhaustion through the autumn and winter, and when Queen Elizabeth 'reviled' Cecil 'notably for I know not what', his misery pushed him into an explicit denunciation of those he increasingly saw as his enemies: he was 'perturbed by the ambitions of Durham House'. Bess, still unaware that Cecil was so hostile, turned to him for help in March of 1602, asking for his support in her ongoing feud with Lord Cobham's wife. The situation is complicated in the way that only petty feuds can be, but centres on Cecil's anxiety that people were saying he had been critical of Lady Kildare (who had, it appeared, 'dealt' badly by Bess with the Queen) to Bess. Bess, predictably, was furious, but she was quick to reassure Robert that she had not received the news of Kildare's slander from him: 'as you know, I never understood it by you; neither did I ever see you, or hear from you, since her ladyship did me that good office.' Bess's sarcasm merely brings out her fury at Kildare, who has now not only slandered Bess to the Queen but put about the rumour that Cecil was a political gossip. This is all her 'mistaking, which she useth too much'. The letter ends with frosty politeness: 'I wish she would be as ambitious to do good, as she is apt to the contrary.'

Bess's anger in this case merely drew more attention to her danger-ous energy. At some point during this spring, a vicious letter singled Bess out in terms that built on the innuendos contained in Cecil's earlier whispering campaign. The letter writer was Lord Henry Howard (and thus Frances Howard's, Lady Kildare's, close relation) and he goes one step further than Cecil, arguing that Queen Elizabeth's mind should be poisoned against Ralegh, Bess and Cobham. Howard, helpfully, gives suggestions of the kinds of slander that could be used:

> She must be told what canons are concluded in the chapter of Durham, where Rawley's wife is presedent [does he mean precedent or president? One or the other condemns Bess]: and withal how weakly Cobham is induced to commend the courses that are secretly inspired by the consent of that fellow-ship.
>
> His wife, as furious as Proserpina with failing of that restitution in Court which flattery had moved her to expect, bends her whole wits and industry to the disturbance of all motions, by counsel and encour-agement, that may disturb the possibility of others' hopes, since her own cannot be secured.

Ralegh is, for Howard, 'the greatest Lucifer', but Bess is Proserpina, the daughter of Zeus and Demeter, abducted by Hades to be his queen, dangerously 'presedent', in the lower world. Howard has Bess and Ralegh as monarchs of hell and yet, ironically and no doubt unconsciously, somewhere acknowledges Bess's power and even her fertility: Proserpina's curious biannual movement between hell and the upper world was a symbol of the naturally fecund cycle of the seasons. An intriguing footnote to this identification of Bess as Proserpina is a portrait said to be of Bess which can be dated to this period. The attribution is extremely dubious: there is little, if any, facial resemblance to other, more reliably ascribed, portraits, but the image is a fascinating curiosity nevertheless. In the portrait 'Bess' appears as Cleopatra, complete with brandished snake and bared

133

breasts. In the corner of the portrait is a scroll with a quotation from a popular play of the time, Samuel Daniel's *Cleopatra*. The quotation contains the inflammatory lines 'and now proud tyrant Caesar, do thy worst'. Were Bess and Sir Walter perceived as the Antony and Cleopatra of the London world? London was, after all, according to the Tudor myth, the new Rome. The analogy succeeds at a push. It was indeed true that, all along, Cleopatra/Bess had challenged the 'proud tyrant' Caesar/Elizabeth, possibly even through her own sexuality. The defiance ('do thy worst') is entirely characteristic of Bess, and it is just possible that there is an acknowledgement that Antony/Ralegh is not quite the 'triple pillar' that he once was, to quote a rival playwright on the subject. It is all, however, very tenuous. In both the Proserpina and Cleopatra analogies, however, Bess's wantonness and wit, her very femaleness, echo through representations of her power.

Apart from these libels, Howard had some more practical suggestions to ensure the downfall of the Durham House inmates. His first plan was to expose their own secret communications with the Duke of Lennox in Scotland; the second was to encourage them to negotiate with Spain. Indeed, Howard believed that Cobham was already involved with Spain, citing his suspicious visit to Boulogne in 1600 as evidence. Howard's third strategy was to deny money to Ralegh and then to watch what he did. He went to Ralegh's jugular here, because, coming from a great family himself, Howard knew very well that his rival had no such dynastic network to fall back on. Exposed as the pretender that he is, the Queen will censure 'so great sauciness in so great infirmity' in her ex-favourite. A final, dramatic strategy is toyed with, but rejected: a full-scale attack on Durham House, similar to the one launched against Essex House a couple of years earlier and for the same reasons: that is, just for the hell of it, 'to prove what sport he could make in that fellowship'.

'Hell did never show up such a couple', wrote Howard, but increasingly he would concentrate his venom on Bess, indicating where he saw the real power in Durham House. Bess, for Howard, was 'a most dangerous woman', and, fascinatingly, he describes her as 'full of her father's inventions'. Sir Nicholas Throckmorton, traitor to Queen Mary, lurks as an absent presence over Bess's reputation. Howard also notes that 'the league is very strong' between Bess and Lady Shrewsbury, better known to us now as Bess of Hardwick: this other Bess had her own agenda in these years, being stepmother to Arbella Stuart, who had one of the strongest claims to the English throne. Above all, however, Bess is threatening because 'much hath been offered on all sides to bring her into the Privy Chamber to her old place'. Bess was closer than she had ever been to a return to 'her old place', and on her own terms.

Her husband, however, was not doing so well. He was still attempting to use the language of love and devotion (over a ground bass of ever more grand financial offers) that had characterized his earlier relationship with his monarch.

> Her Majesty knows that I am ready to spend all I have, and my life, for her in a day, and that I have but the keeping of that I have, for all I have I will sell for her in an hour and spend it in her service. Let the Queen then break their hearts that are none of hers: there is little gain in losing her own. These things should not torment me if I were as others are, but it is true, *ubi dolor, ibi amor, exue amorem, exueris dolorem* [where there is pain, there is love: lay aside love, and you will have banished pain].

These passionate lines are embedded in a letter to Robert Cecil which has as its main theme proceedings in Parliament and some business about taverns. All the lovesick lamenting in the world wasn't going to do any good. The time for this kind of language from Sir Walter had long gone, even if Cecil would have passed on the message to the Queen. Meanwhile, others were adopting the pose that Ralegh had made his own through the 1580s and 1590s – that of lover towards Queen Elizabeth – with great success, suggesting that it was not the language that had gone out of fashion, but the man. None other than Lord George Carew wrote to the Queen on 1 October 1602, a letter full of references to beauty and sacrifice. The Queen's 'beauty adorns the world', her wisdom is the miracle of the age, he, George, is willing to sacrifice himself at her royal feet. Robert Cecil was rather pleased with the performance, and congratulates his friend, writing that 'the Queen liked your letter very well'. Ralegh returned again to Jersey, feeling, quite rightly, that he was 'in the wilderness'. But unlike earlier voluntary or forced exiles, this time he acknowledged that he had Bess: writing again to Cecil, he pleaded, 'Bess will convey me your letters if you send any'.

Cecil did keep writing letters because he was determined that neither Bess nor Sir Walter should suspect the fact that he was utterly betraying them. He even lent Ralegh four thousand pounds in May 1602. By this time, however, he had developed what had begun as an instinct for political survival into a bitter hatred of both Ralegh and his wife. So when in early June even Lady Kildare showed signs of mellowing towards the residents of Durham House, in part because they were seen to 'rail' less loudly in public, Cecil argued that it was all just cunning. With tensions running high, no incident was without sinister implications. On 1 April 1602 there was a burglary at Durham House. According to the offical record, two men 'broke burglariously into the dwelling house of Sir Walter Ralegh, knight . . . and stole two linen pillowbeares . . . fitted with silk and gold worth 10 pounds, a linen "cushing cloth" adorned with silk and gold, worth five pounds'. While it is possible that the burglars were truly after the household linen, it may well have been that they were also after further evidence to bring down the Raleghs. By the end of June, Cecil was writing to Lord Carew, now addressed as 'George', in growing intimacy, swearing to get revenge on the Raleghs: 'know it, we will be merry, and yet believe me 2 old friends use me unkindly, but I have covenanted with my heart not to know it, for in show we are great, and all my revenge shall be to heap coals on their heads.'

Bess, when at Durham House, lived next door to the visible signs of Robert Cecil's encroaching ambition. On the Strand, between the Savoy and Durham House, Cecil was building the imaginatively named Cecil House. Finally he moved in, lonely, according to his biographer, in a 'house poignantly unshared by those of his family he had loved'.[9] This did not stop him desiring to expand his property on this prime piece of London riverside real estate: these months marked the start of Cecil's plotting to take Durham House away from Ralegh.

The façade of support continued, however. With the new year, 1603, he offered to provide half of the costs for 'victualling': that is, fitting out one of Ralegh's ships. His letter confirming the offer barely conceals, however, the major fault-lines in the two men's relationship. Cecil begs that Ralegh should 'as much as may be, conceal our adventure, at the least my name above any other'.

Bess and Sir Walter still did not realize the extent of Cecil's hostility, or they might have acted earlier to protect themselves. Something, however, in the winter of 1602–3 led them to take action. It may well have been the knowledge that the Queen's physical and mental health was deteriorating rapidly. It may have been a genuine crisis of funds: Ralegh had complained of poverty so often that it is hard to assess whether his claim that his estate was 'weak and far in debt', and conscious of his 'neglect' of 'a son and a wife', was true now or not. Or it may have been a belated recognition of the hostility surrounding them. The steps they took included the off-loading of Ralegh's Irish estates, for a paltry thousand pounds, to the Earl of Cork and the placing of Sherborne in trust. Both these actions would haunt Bess for the rest of her life, but at the time the sale of the Irish lands would have seemed a wise increase in liquid assets. The idea of placing the Sherborne property in trust suggests a deeper anxiety. Lying behind the legal moves was the spectre of treason charges. Bess and Sir Walter knew only too well what happened, physically, to those convicted of treason. But they also knew, Bess because the Throckmorton family had suffered it, and Sir Walter because he had benefited from it, what happened to the traitor's property and land. The process was grounded on the principle of escheat whereby property and land (the 'fief') of a tenant reverted to the lord when the tenant died, if there was no successor qualified to inherit under the original grant. Since an attainted person (according the doctrine of the corruption of blood) could have no legal heir, his property suffered automatic escheat: his heirs, however innocent, could not inherit. Instead, the estate 'lapsed' into the control of the Crown. By placing Sherborne in trust for his son, Ralegh, if convicted of treason, could not forfeit to the Crown what he did not possess. If he lived, he could receive income from the estate. If he died, the property would stay in the Ralegh name. Sir Walter did absolutely nothing for Bess. He could have done, since the Statute of Uses of 1536 permitted married men to devise land in trust to their wives, but instead he focused everything on ten-year-old Wat, then on his brother and his brother's sons. There is no clearer indication of Bess's utter exclusion from the business of property inheritance and thus her complete dependence on the goodwill of the male members of the family into which she had married, no better indication of her status as a *femme covert*.

The trust was set up only just in time. Already Queen Elizabeth had been 'by fits troubled with melancholy some three or four months'. By the close of February, the end was drawing near for the Queen. For two weeks she was 'extremely oppressed': she would neither eat nor see a doctor, and would not even go to bed to rest. Finally, her will gave way, and she was persuaded to lie down. She knew that death was near. The most important men in the land stood around her to watch her die, led in prayers by the Archbishop of Canterbury. Then night fell, and the important people left, leaving the Queen alone in her Privy Chamber with 'all but her women that attended her'.

5

*'My Dead Heart':
The Traitor's Wife?*

―――――⇒⊃●⊂⇐―――――

Looking back at her youth, Lady Anne Clifford described an anxious night in London spent waiting to hear of the death of the Queen: 'my aunt Warwick sent my Mother word about 9 a clock at night – she living then at Clerkenwell – that she should remove to Austin Friars her House for fear of some Commotions.' In the north of England, the same fears were felt. Lady Margaret Hoby and her husband went 'towards York, thinking to continue there until all things were established'. At last the word came through the streets of London, and then along the roads to the rest of the country, that the Queen had died at 2.30 in the morning. News also spread that there had been a dangerous power vacuum for only a few hours, since at 'about 10 o'clock King James was proclaimed in Cheapside by all the Council with great joy and triumph'. Mary Queen of Scots' only child, James VI of Scotland, was now King of England, achieving the crown his mother had struggled towards for much of her life. No wonder Anne Clifford 'went to see and hear. This peaceable coming in of the King was unexpected of all parts of the people.' The unforeseen and slick transfer of power after so many years of suppressed, whispered anxiety about the succession was a triumph for Robert Cecil and a relief for those who had feared 'commotions'. Reassured, Anne Clifford wrote that 'within 2 or 3 days' she and her mother returned to their house in Clerkenwell while the Hobys 'both returned . . . to Hackness where we found all quiet, god be praised'. For Bess, however, the old Queen's death signalled the start of a series of terrifying events.

In London a 'great company of Ladies' attended the Queen's corpse as it lay in the Drawing Chamber, but all eyes were turned towards Scotland. Within days of the Queen's death and burial, courtiers began riding north, hoping to be among the first to be noticed and favoured by King James. Sir Walter Ralegh started early, but in an ominous move he was stopped in his tracks by Robert Cecil and forced to return to London. The signs were not good, and just three days later Ralegh sealed the deed that conveyed the whole of the Sherborne estate to trustees, further evidence if this was needed that this action was not merely a matter of tax evasion.

Things went from bad to worse. Prevented from gaining physical access to the King, Ralegh attempted to write to him. On 25 April 1603 an informer reported back to the increasingly omnipotent Robert Cecil that Ralegh's opinions 'hath taken no great root here', although his letters had been presented to King James. From being merely ignored, Ralegh moved to being actively humiliated. By the end of the month he was stripped of the position of Captain of the Guard, and a week later, when the new King revoked all the monopolies and licences issued by Elizabeth, Ralegh lost his most lucrative sources of income. Finally, on 29 May four eminent legal figures ruled that Ralegh (and Edward Darcy, his brother-in-law) had no right to Durham House: the buildings were to be returned forthwith to the Bishop of Durham.

What hit Sir Walter in all this was the sheer pace of events. Of course, the humiliation, financial ruin and eviction did not affect only him. The attack on Sir Walter was an attack on his whole household, as he points out, desperately, in a letter to the Council begging for more time at Durham House. He has

made provisions for 40 person in the spring and I have a family [household] of no less number and the like for almost 20 horse. Now to cast out my hay and oats into the streets at an hour's warning and

140

to remove my family and stuff in 14 days after is such a severe expulsion as hath no been offered to any man before this day.

There is bitterness mixed in with the desperation: Ralegh claims to have spent 'well near' two thousand pounds on the property and is appalled that he has been forbidden to take any of his improvements with him. This was all, however, part of Cecil's plan to destroy the 'dangerous counsels' at Durham House, the first step being to take over the building itself. It is no surprise that the stables and other outbuildings were acquired almost immediately by Cecil.

While Ralegh appealed, ineffectually, to the Lords about the confiscation of Durham House, Bess attempted to circumvent the hostile new King and go direct to his Queen, Anne of Denmark. Bess, who had begun her career serving one queen, hoped to regain the political initiative with another. The signs were hopeful. On 15 April King James, having travelled as far south as Yorkshire, gave orders that 'some of the ladies of all degrees who were about the [old] Queen . . . or some others whom you shall think meetest and most willing and able to abide travel' should travel up to meet Queen Anne. Bess had certainly been 'about' the old Queen, and she certainly was 'willing and able to abide travel'. James's letter was, however, addressed to Robert Cecil, and he was not in the mood to do Bess any favours. Instead, Cecil chose a handful of unexceptional women, and, more troubling for Bess, her old enemy, Frances Howard, Countess of Kildare, the wife of Lord Cobham.

Rival groups of women joined the race north: 'diverse ladies of honour went voluntarily into Scotland, to attend her Majesty in her journey into England.' Lady Anne Clifford gives a graphic account of her participation in the struggle to be the first to meet the new Queen. First there is a problem about horses, which delays Anne and her mother, but once they are mounted there is no stopping them as they attempt to catch up with the main party: 'my Mother & I went on our journey to overtake her, & killed three Horses that day with extremities of heat.' They arrive late at night at a great house 'where we found the doors shut & none in the House, but one Servant who only had the Keys of the Hall, so that we were forced to lie in the Hall all night till towards morning, at which time came a Man and let us

141

into the Higher Rooms where we slept 3 or 4 hours'. In the morning they were off again, still hoping to be amongst the first to greet Queen Anne in her progress south.

However fast they travelled, and however many horses were sacrificed to these women's political ambitions, all the 'diverse ladies of honour' nevertheless had to halt their journey in the far north of England, just south of the Scottish border. News filtered through that Queen Anne had suffered a miscarriage and that she was not well enough to travel out of Scotland. This, however, did not stop the Countess of Kildare, as one contemporary noted, since she 'quit her companions at Berwick and went to Edinburgh', where Anne was due to make her first appearance after the miscarriage. Kildare's initiative seemed to pay dividends, because even before the Queen crossed the border into Berwick on 6 June, the Countess had been appointed governess to the young Princess Elizabeth, King James and Queen Anne's only daughter. Anne then travelled slowly south, towards her new court in Westminster.

Bess, obviously not one of Cecil's chosen few, did her best. She and Wat, not to mention an extended household of forty, were being evicted from Durham House at precisely this time. The deadline to be out was 12 June, and Bess had even more than usual to do, since after his exertions at the end of May, Sir Walter had fallen ill. Nevertheless, having put the retreat from Durham House in motion, Bess rode north. She did not know that Cecil was recording her every move. The man she begged to accompany her to meet the new Queen wrote later to his master, Robert Cecil: 'I was entreated by his wife to ride another idle journey to my charge to meet the Queen, where she received but idle graces.'

Queen Anne was clearly either unwilling or unable to offer Bess any support. 'Idle graces' were not what she had need of as the summer wore on. July came, and the situation worsened on all fronts. Plague struck London, and Robert Cecil started to move in for the kill. Having ousted the Raleghs from Durham House, having stopped their sources of money, his aim now was to destroy them completely, if the plague did not get them first. To do so, he would have to prove them traitors, and to that end Cecil started probing the connections between Lord Cobham, Sir Walter and one Aremberg. The last named was the ambassador who represented the Spanish Netherlands at the English court, and his diplomatic mission was to achieve peace between England and Spain.

Throughout July Cecil watched and waited. One of his informers noted that Cobham, who had been begging for permission to travel since the end of May and had now been granted a licence to do so, had left the country: 'surely something is in hand.' Cecil believed that Cobham's aim in travelling was merely to get hold of the money to fund some as yet undiscovered plot against James. It was no coincidence that Cobham would travel from the Spanish Netherlands and then into Spain itself, returning to England via Jersey, where Ralegh (with 'a pestilent brain of his own') remained, for the time being at least, governor.

On his return to England in mid-July Cobham was at last brought in for questioning. He was interrogated for four days. Meanwhile, his brother George Brooke was also being questioned, and on 18 July 1603 Cecil got what he was looking for – a confession from Cobham's brother. Even though this confession contained only unsatisfactory hearsay about Ralegh, it gave Cecil the chance to haul Sir Walter in for interrogation. By 20 July he was imprisoned in the Tower of London. Ralegh did not handle this test well. When asked about his involvement with Cobham, he made the mistake of claiming different things, one after the other: he first denied any knowledge, then hinted at his suspicions (clearly attempting to extricate himself) and then, most damningly, got in touch with Cobham to reassure him that he had revealed nothing sinister. Meanwhile, Cobham himself was doing no better under pressure. Two days later, apparently provoked by evidence of Ralegh's 'double dealing', Cecil extracted an incriminating confession from him. Although Cobham immediately retracted this, the damage had been done.

What Cecil found was a complex labyrinth of plots, with at their heart two aims. The aim of the secondary or so-called 'Bye Plot' was to force a degree of religious toleration. This plot brought together such unlikely bedfellows as radical, sectarian Protestants and Catholic priests, both groups seeking a measure of freedom to practise their religion. The more ambitious and deadly aim of the 'Main Plot', however, was to stir up rebellion, invite a foreign invasion and then kill the King and his two sons and put a puppet (and conveniently female) monarch on the throne, the young Lady Arbella Stuart. The huge sum of money necessary to implement this bold treason was, it was claimed, being raised by Ralegh and Cobham by means of the latter's old friend, the Count of Aremberg.

There was little hope for Ralegh. Bess was running out of people to turn to for support. Around her, the nation was once again devastated by plague. The disease had re-emerged in March, and by the summer thousands were dying each week in London alone. Thirty thousand would die during the epidemic of 1603, mainly from the poorer classes, as the disease went to its deadly work in the overcrowded parishes just outside the City gates. As one of Shakespeare's rivals, Thomas Dekker, expressed it: 'Death (like a Spanish Leaguer or rather like stalking Tamberlane) hath pitched his tent in the sinfully polluted suburbs.' Unable to understand the indiscriminate disease, contemporaries could only view the plague as a sign of God's displeasure. For Bess, the death and destruction surrounding her wherever she went provided an apocalyptic backdrop to her own personal tragedy, a further sign that her world was disintegrating. She was once again separated from Wat, probably sent with his tutors down to Sherborne, away from the tangible physical threat to his young life and the less tangible political assault on his parents.

In these desperate days Bess wrote to a man whom she must have known was her enemy: Henry Howard, described aptly by one historian as a 'reptile', and certainly not a man who would be normally sympathetic to her interests. Although her letter to him does not survive (as is so often the case), Howard's long, indeed very long, reply does. It is a remarkable onslaught on Bess, which perhaps says more about the writer than it does about her. The letter helps, however, to make clear why Bess was such a threat to men such as Howard and the values they upheld.

He begins by pointing out that he does not usually write his own letters, but that Bess's words, what he calls her 'exceptions' or criticisms of him, have stung him into action. He is clearly shocked by her 'own vein of delivering your mind and the spirit of audacity that prompteth you, esteeming little what be said or thought'. Her letter is mere 'invective', the 'colour and pretence of sorrow' masking 'a

Bess as a young woman (c.1591)

if the greeued Teares of a unfortunat woman, may reseeuf
ani fauor, or the unspeheabell sorros of my ded hart
may reseeuf ani cumfort Then let my sorros cum bel-
for you wich if [thei] Trewly knew, I asur my selfe
you wold pitti me, but most espescially your poour
unfortunet frind wich relyeth holy on your honnarable
and wonted fauor: I knoo in my one soule wich
sumthing knooeth his mind that hee douth and
euer hath doon not idly honered the keng but
naturally loueth him and god knooeth far: from
him to wish him harme, but to haue spent his
life as sound for him as ani cretuer liuing: I most
humly, besech your honnar euen for god sake to be
good un to him, to oms more make him your
cretur, your resited frind, and dell with the
keng for him, for oon that is more worti, of
fauor Then mani eles hauing worthe and
onnesti and wisdom to be a frind; pitti the fname
of your anciant frind and his poour littell cretuer
wich may leue to honnor you That wee all may
lift up our handes and hartes in praydar for
you and yowres, bind this our poour fanelies
to prayses your honnar and wonted good natur
let the hole world prayses your loue to my poour
unfortunat hosban: for cristis sake wich rewardeth

all mercies, pittieng his Iust case: and god for his rufem mari bles you
for euer, and worthe in the keng meiei;
I am not abell I protest beffor god to stand un my
trembling leges therfor sitis I woll hand waitted hon
you: or be delieued hout by yorsi

E Ralegh

Bess' hand-written letter to Robert Cecil, November 1603

Right: *'Bess as Cleopatra'* – *a doubtful attribution*

Below: *Bess in middle age (c.1603)*

Bess in widowhood with her son Carew (c.1619)

Nicholas Throckmorton, Bess's father

Right: *Sir Walter as a young man (copy of a miniature by Nicholas Hilliard, c.1585)*

Below: *Sir Walter in 1588*

Above: *Sir Walter with his son Wat (1602)*

Right: *Bess's miniature of her son
Wat (c.1619)*

Left: *Sir Walter in middle age (c.1597)*

Below Left: *Queen Elizabeth I: the Rainbow Portrait. An idealized image from the last years of the Queen's life.*

Right: *Queen Anne of Denmark*

Below Right: *King James I*

Robert Cecil, Earl of Salisbury

SERO, SED SERIO

Robert Devereux, 2nd Earl of Essex

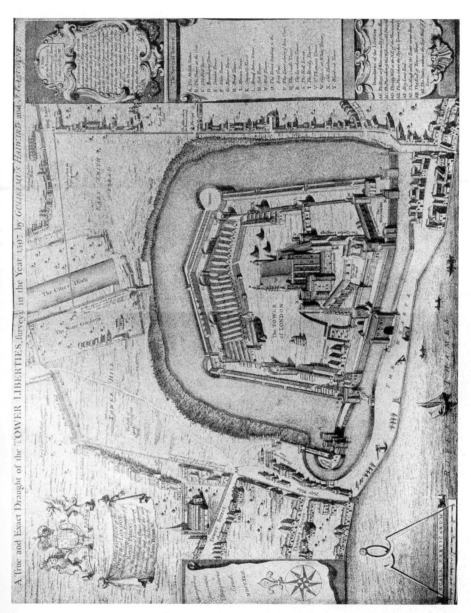

The Tower of London in Bess's time
(from 'A True and Exact Draught of the Tower Liberties, survey'd in the year 1597')

Present day Sherborne Castle – the central part was built by the Raleghs

A typical Jacobean interior – the Hall of Chastleton House, completed in 1612

flagon of pride'. Bess's flagon of pride would not have liked Howard's patronizing request that she should reconsider her words ('those characters which flow out of your pen with heat of passion') once her blood has cooled down.

Again and again, Bess's own words are thrown back at her. Howard can see only the 'infested bitterness' in her words, but when he quotes directly from her own letter it emerges that she is asking him only to 'pity the persecuted because true honour is no tyrant', and to 'not only forgive but do good'. She begged Howard 'not to heap sore upon sore, affliction upon affliction', but he challenges her in reply: 'you must prove him to be clear of all exceptions.' Bess must prove Ralegh's innocence, otherwise to defend him is to charge 'the state it self with injustice'. She is treading on dangerous ground, by suggesting that the state itself may be wrong in its judgement. Rejecting Bess's request that Howard examine his own behaviour ('that conscience which your ladyship inclines me to examine and regard'), he begins to threaten her subtly. Ralegh, he hopes, will by 'trial prove himself as innocent as you': is there a hint that she may yet have to prove her own innocence? Howard remains unconvinced that everything that went on at Durham House has come to light, and suggests that Bess herself may not have an 'unspotted conscience': interestingly, he uses the image of pearls being hidden in cabinets to illustrate the secrets that may yet emerge. Howard is torn between painting Bess as a devious conspirator and as a foolish woman standing by her man. Later, he warns her that, before she 'conclude him to be a martyr', she needs to prove Sir Walter's innocence: 'God grant your husband prove himself the man that you presume.'

Was Ralegh the man she presumed? The most plausible element of the charges against him focus on his inability to keep quiet. Although the documentary evidence is simply not available to establish the true extent of his dealings, it seems that Ralegh, spurred by a particularly humiliating incident with Robert Cecil, gave his verbal support to the plan to create a domestic political crisis, a crisis that would be heightened by the spectre of imminent foreign invasion. In these desperate days, the instability that would be caused by a Spanish attack may have seemed a welcome alternative to the political wilderness that beckoned under the continued rule of James Stuart. But Howard is concerned to establish just how much Bess really knew of Sir Walter's aims and ambitions, how much she herself may have been involved in the plots of the summer of 1603. Did she indeed have an 'unspotted conscience'? Howard was not sure, but to an extent Bess was protected from his taunts because she was a woman. Back in 1601, Penelope Devereux, sister to the Earl of Essex, had been named as one of the conspirators in her brother's failed coup. She was confined to the house of one of the gentlemen of the queen's Privy Chamber, but she was not executed, suggesting that her being female may have shielded her in some way. Ironically, a political culture which systematically excluded women from official positions of power, indeed a political culture that had difficulty imagining women wielding that kind of power, may have also found it difficult to imagine women as serious political threats. But this same political culture meant that Bess's arguments would be dismissed by Howard, because she offended Howard's sense of what it was appropriate for a woman to say. He reminds her of the 'rule that barreth women to discourse of matters' and the even more important rule that 'barreth them to judge of questions or considerations of state'. Bess was, in the end, only a woman. What could she do?

She turned to Arthur. On 23 July 1603 he wrote to Robert Cecil, forwarding a letter he has received from Bess. His covering letter, written from his estate in Northamptonshire, reeks of fear for himself and for his sister. He is extremely wary about showing anything other than simple brotherly support of a sister in her time of need.

> May it please your Lordship having received this letter here enclosed from my sorrowful sister whereby she desiring my coming to her I have thought for my part as well for my duty to the king's majesty as for mine own safety to avoid all suspicion, to send her said letter to your Lord, as also the copy of my answer unto her, humbly desiring withal that you will be pleased to let me understand whether it will stand with his Majesty's liking, and the Council's pleasure, to give me leave to come up unto her, without whose counsel I mean not to come to her, though with their allowance, I would be contented to yield her in this grief all the lawful brotherly comforts I may.

The letter ends with Arthur 'humbly desiring to know' whether 'his

Majesty will like of my coming up to my sister' and a final flourish of yet further humility towards Cecil. While Arthur attempted to gain permission to come to his 'sorrowful sister', and while she attempted (in somewhat aggressive fashion) to enlist noble support for Ralegh's case, it became clear that Ralegh himself was not going to come back fighting from 'affliction upon affliction'. His jailer in the Tower wrote that he had never seen such a 'strange and dejected mind' as that of Sir Walter, and that he was 'exceedingly cumbered with him'. Indeed, Ralegh was not a model prisoner, calling for his keeper 'five or six times in a day', and in a state of 'such passions as I see his fortitude is not competent to support his grief'. Ralegh's 'fortitude' under this test was indeed 'not competent to support his grief' and it certainly did not extend to supporting his wife, now thirty-eight, and his child, aged ten.

While waiting to see if Arthur would be allowed to join her in London, Bess received a letter from her husband in the Tower. Its contents were shocking. Writing to her and to Wat, Sir Walter explained that he simply could not bear that they were both going to be 'left a spoil to my enemies' and that his name was to be dishonoured. He tries to convince Bess ('unfortunate woman') and Wat ('unfortunate child') that he would have 'bettered' their poor estate if he had been granted just a few more years of life. Denied those few years, he now contemplates his own death.

The letter turns into a set of instructions for Bess once Sir Walter is gone, in particular advice concerning her remarriage. 'Thou art a young woman and forbear not to marry again. It is now nothing to me: thou art no more mine nor I thine.' She should, however, show her love for him by not marrying 'to please sense' but merely 'to avoid poverty and so preserve thy child'. A further instruction follows, reminding Bess again of the child Ralegh had fathered in Ireland back in the 1580s. To demonstrate her love for her husband, Bess was to be kind to 'my poor daughter to whom I have given nothing. [. . .] Be charitable to her and teach thy son to love her for his father's sake.'

Alongside the instructions, there is also anger, mainly directed against Cobham, the man who has 'separated us asunder, he hath slain my honour, my fortune, he hath robbed thee of thy husband, thy

147

child of his father and me of you both'. But Robert Cecil is also condemned, although Ralegh begs Bess, at least in public, to appear to forgive Cecil. This is not just Christian virtue but political expediency: 'But do not thou know [admit] it for he must be master [guardian] of thy child and may have compassion of him.' This was a wise assessment: Cecil had been appointed Master of the Wards in May 1601 and therefore would take over the administration of the estate during Wat's minority.

All of this was terrible enough, but Ralegh's key point was hidden in the sentence concerning his illegitimate daughter. Bess is to do all these things 'for his sake who will be cruel to himself to preserve thee'. Ralegh was not going to wait for trial and execution; he was going to kill himself. He regarded suicide as the only way to escape the dishonour he had brought upon himself and his family, as the only decent thing he could do. He justified himself, knowing full well that 'it is forbidden to destroy our selves', by arguing that he did not despair of God's mercy (the implication being, of course, that he did, in contrast, despair of any mercy from the King).

Ralegh turns briefly to business. He assures Bess that his estate is conveyed to 'feoffees', Bess's cousin Alexander Brett, her brother, Sir Arthur Throckmorton, and Ralegh's old friend and adviser, Thomas Harriot. The estate will remain in the family. He then returns to his own pain exclaiming: 'Oh God I cannot resist these thoughts.' He is tormented by the 'intolerable infamy' of the accusations that he has turned Spaniard, and cannot bear to live to be 'made a wonder and a spectacle'. Building up the rhetoric (and after all, Ralegh was and is one of the great writers), he hopes that death will bring 'dark forgetfulness' and he begs death to release him from torment: 'O death destroy my memory which is my tormentor: my thoughts and my life cannot dwell in one body.'

What he does not ask of himself, he asks of his wife. She must go on living, she must learn to forget, she must endure the dishonour and she must marry again, if only to pay the bills. Sir Walter instructs Bess to forget him:

> But do thou forget me, poor wife, that thou may live to bring up thy poor child. Forget me in all things but thine own honour and the love

of mine. I bless my poor child. And let him know his father was no traitor. And whosoever thou choose again after me, let him be but thy politic husband, but let my son be thy beloved for he is part of me and I live in him, and the difference is but in the number and not in the kind. And the Lord for ever keep thee and them and give thee comfort in both worlds.

Bess is thus permitted a 'politic husband' and instructed to redirect all her love towards her son, who will become her 'beloved', of the same 'kind' as Sir Walter. She is then consigned by her husband to the care of God, who will 'keep' her and give her 'comfort'. Quite how God was going to pay off the debts or manage the estate or keep Cecil at bay was another matter, and one that Bess had to attend to: her faith that God would indeed provide was being tested during these weeks and months.

Biographers of Ralegh have been stern about this letter, partly because of the continuing taboos surrounding suicide, partly because of what has been seen as its rather crass, even 'effeminate', emotionalism. It has been described as essentially a fake, designed to draw attention to Ralegh's predicament, as 'nauseating and meaningless'. Presumably it did not seem nauseating or meaningless to Bess. Here was a letter showing that the man she loved was in utter despair and seeking his own death, and there was nothing she could do to help him. Here was a letter showing the man she had married, the man who was responsible for her and for maintaining her, renouncing that role and passing her over to the care of God, who would 'keep' her. Here was a letter urging her to stop feeling, to stop caring, to stop loving Sir Walter, to turn all her emotions towards their son, and to work towards a 'politic' and loveless second marriage.

The letter was not an empty threat. Ralegh acted to end his own life. Like any prisoner, then and now, he was denied any possession with which he could have harmed himself, but on the evening of 28 July a witness reported that 'being at dinner' he 'stabbed himself with his knife that he ate his meat with': the situation was fraught, no one knew 'whether he be dead or alive'. More details filtered out of the Tower: Sir Walter had 'stabbed himself upon the breast and struck the rib and broke the knife'. He would live. His attempt to take his own life had failed, and the judicial system moved relentlessly towards the same end. Ralegh was attaindered: condemned as a traitor to death, with all his civil rights and capacities extinguished. His entire estate, both real and personal, was forfeited to the Crown, and his blood decreed to be 'corrupted', so that Sir Walter could neither inherit nor transmit by descent. This is what he had feared and what the conveyance of Sherborne to trustees was designed to circumvent.

Ralegh still had to be tried, and, in no fit state to act on his own behalf, Bess continued to support her husband in any way she could. There are indications that she worked to get a sympathetic jury. The first jury was dismissed, to be replaced by Sir Edward Darcy (Bess's uncle) and Sir William Killigrew, from the family closest to her parents in their time. She was to be thwarted, however, because these second set of jurors were all changed from one night to the next. Bess called in her French connections, again harking back to her father's network of contacts, convincing one Frenchman of her husband's innocence and hoping that he would press Ralegh's case at court. The summer had ended, and it was well into September when a letter of support came from Paris, addressed to the King himself. It was, however, a dangerously double-edged appeal. The writer, a Catholic, argues that King James should show compassion towards Bess, since 'Sir W. R.'s wife was the daughter of Sir Nicholas Throckmorton, who was a Protestant, but yet in his time did very grateful service in England to you and your mother; which should lead you to have compassion upon her in case he suffers death, and his lands and goods be confiscated to your service'. Since Nicholas Throckmorton, Bess's father, did all he could for Mary Queen of Scots, James's mother, then James, as son, should do everything he can for Bess, as daughter. The letter acknowledges implicitly that there is no hope for Sir Walter. Even Bess could not have believed that her husband could repeat the legal coup achieved by her father – the only man to be acquitted by a jury of a treason charge. The inevitable result of Ralegh's trial would be his execution as a traitor, and then the confiscation of all his lands and property, technically known as an 'escheat'. Everyone knew this, and so the vultures started closing in, attempting to be first in line for the redistributed wealth, just as Ralegh himself had been back in 1584 when the Babington lands were forfeited.

It was Robert Cecil who would be responsible for the redistribution of the lands. By mid-October Cecil was already weary of the process, tired of the number of suitors approaching him in readiness for the escheat. He also notes, equally wearily, that Bess was not giving up without a fight. Cecil complains that 'the wife of Sir Walter hath made such means by some of good reckoning about the king as she shall hope to obtain a gift of all his goods, besides that all his chattels will hardly pay the debts he oweth, bona fide to divers creditors'. Cecil may be gloating that Bess will only get enough to pay off her husband's many debts, but her energy and political canniness shines through, since to have got this far has meant getting through to those 'of good reckoning about the king'.

Bess's concern to salvage some financial security from Ralegh's ruin did not, however, indicate that she had given up her attempt to keep her husband with her. Indeed, her next actions showed her desperation to preserve Sir Walter's life at all costs, even when he himself appeared willing to die. Having made her case, to those in 'good reckoning' with the King, for her right to his goods and chattels in the event of his execution, Bess spent the next two weeks petitioning for Sir Walter to be tried in the Star Chamber. Again, this showed both her knowledge of the legal system and her willingness to pursue extreme courses of action. The court of the Star Chamber was an anomaly in the justice system even then, a court which did not obey English common law, and which was presided over by the Privy Council and two judges appointed by the King. There was thus no jury. The key issue, however, for Bess was that, although to be tried in the Star Chamber was to acknowledge, before one even started, the guilt of the offender, the court could not impose a death sentence.

Petitioning was not enough. Bess knew that a bribe was needed – and fast. Somehow she made her way down to Salisbury, knowing that the King himself was due to come to the city. Somehow she raised the money, and she went for a huge sum: one witness notes that 'my Lady Rawligh [sic] hath offered £5,000 to bring her husband's business to a Star Chamber', but, the writer goes on, he fears 'it will not prove so well for him'. Despite the letter-writer's sense that things would not 'prove well', he adds an urgent postscript, asking his correspondent in

151

London whether he has heard anything about the 'success' of Bess's efforts.

Meanwhile, Cobham and Ralegh were busy sorting out important things, such as male honour. During the month of October, while Bess was making her legal and financial salvage efforts, Cobham succeeded in smuggling letters to his 'friend' Sir Walter, from one part of the Tower of London to another. The letters exonerated Ralegh of any involvement, and presumably made everyone feel just fine. Cobham, at this stage at least, ignored the advice of his wife, the Countess of Kildare, who made her own heartfelt plea to him to place all the blame on Ralegh: 'Help your self if it may be' and 'draw not the yoke of other's burdens'. Reconciled to Cobham, Ralegh was taken down to Winchester for his trial. On the journey, one witness said, he spotted an old man to whom he owed money 'in sight upon Hounslow Heath'. Ralegh insisted the coach be stopped and, in a state of great agitation at the thought of the amount of money he owed, said: 'I beseech the King to be good to this worthy Gentleman: Both of them weeping upon my oath.' The image of Ralegh weeping over his debts is strangely plausible.

He was being taken to trial at Winchester in part because of the continued virulence of plague in the capital. By the end of October it was not thought worth counting the dead in the city, only the living. For some, the scale of the epidemic demonstrated clearly that England had been abandoned by her God: 'Lord grant that these judgements may cause England with speed to turn to the Lord.' But it was not only the plague that made London unsafe for the trial: tensions were running high, and traitor Ralegh, 'the best hated man in England', was so unpopular that it was believed his trial might incite mob violence. Indeed, on 13 November there was a riot in London, apparently directed against Ralegh, and no doubt fuelled by the kind of comments coming from the king's Ministers. Ralegh was a 'viper of hell' said Chief Prosecutor Edward Coke, the leading lawyer in the land and thus supposedly impartial in the case.

Bess had done all she could and now had to stand and wait. These were frightening times, and it is unclear where she made her base. Durham House was no longer hers; indeed, there was nowhere that was her own in London. Sherborne might have seemed a safe haven, far away from the city, but she would be isolated there from events in the capital and in Winchester. Of the houses of her childhood, Beaumanor in Leicestershire was long gone. Perhaps she stayed with Arthur at Mile End in London, or perhaps she returned to her uncle's house at Beddington in Surrey, the house of her early childhood and the house most closely associated with her mother, Anne. Bess's mother had, of course, experienced an uncannily similar crisis fifty years earlier: indeed, the trial of her husband, Nicholas, for treason would in turn have reminded Anne of the night when she, as a child, went to say farewell to her own father in the Tower of London. In a horrible continuation of the pattern, Bess would know now how her mother, both as daughter and wife, had felt. All she could hope for would be that Sir Walter could do as her father had done: talk his way out of a charge of treason.

Ralegh tried hard to repeat his father-in-law's feat. He had to contend with the fact that, by the time of the trial, Cobham's charges had changed, his entire effort now concentrated into the argument that Sir Walter had been the ringleader. Cobham, now apparently listening to his wife, the Countess of Kildare, argued that it was Ralegh who urged him to mediate with Aremberg to get an annual pension of fifteen hundred pounds for foreign intelligence, and he gave a damning account of a time that Ralegh came straight from Greenwich with inside information for sale to Aremberg. Unsurprisingly, the Greenwich story has Cecil at its heart: Ralegh 'had arrived full of discontent upon certain words that that day as he said had passed between the lord Cecil and him'. Ralegh's anger with Cecil that day allegedly encouraged him to suggest that Cobham should get in touch with the King of Spain, who would bring an army to Milford Haven.

Although Cobham attempted now to place the blame on his one-time friend, the evidence against Sir Walter was nevertheless deeply flawed. Throughout the trial, Ralegh did what he would always do best: speak in his own defence with brilliance. An historian of the case acknowledges that Ralegh's performance was superb, with his prosecutor Coke's delivery, in contrast, poor: 'by exchanging insults with the prisoner, by permitting him to exercise his eloquence on the most public of stages, and by opposing any move to allow Cobham to testify against his alleged associate, Coke turned Ralegh – literally overnight – from villain to hero.'[1]

Ralegh may have been a hero, but this was not enough. His enemies wanted a conviction, and it was a conviction they got, on 17 November 1603. Despite the fact that the proceedings were highly irregular, despite the fact that Ralegh exposed them as such, despite the presence of Edward Wotton, Arthur Throckmorton's great friend, as one of the trial judges, despite the fact that it was said that the Crown Prosecutor, Edward Coke, himself was surprised that Ralegh was condemned for treason, when he had been charged only with *misprision* of treason, despite all of this, Sir Walter was condemned to a traitor's death.

Bess and Sir Walter knew only too well what would happen to him now. His public execution would indeed be a 'wonder and a spectacle', and his death would be carefully choreographed to have the strongest impact on the eager audience. He would be allowed to speak on the scaffold, but only to confess and then repent of the crimes he had committed. Then he would undergo the full penalty for treason: to be hanged, cut down from the gallows while still alive, and thus forced to witness his own disembowelling and dismemberment. His traitor's heart would then be displayed to the crowd, the public proof of his hidden treachery.

These were desperate days. Ralegh wrote to the King, begging for mercy, asserting his own innocence: 'I never invented treason, consented to treason, or performed treason.' He wrote also to Cecil of his innocence, still hoping 'your lordship will find that I have been strongly practiced against'. Cecil did not need to be told that Ralegh had been 'practised against', since he had been the one responsible. Cecil, now the most powerful man in the country, had spent the final years of Elizabeth's reign quietly destroying Bess's husband's reputation and the first six months of James's reign bringing him to the scaffold. Whatever his feelings for Bess, Cecil was not the man to prevent the final elimination of a potential political rival for the sake of a past friendship. Unknowing, Bess writes to him of 'the unspeakable horrors of my dead heart'. The letter may be hard for a modern reader to follow in its original spelling, but to read it as she wrote it allows some of the terrible urgency to come through.

To the most honnerabell me Lord Cissell

if the greved Teares of an unfortunat woman may resevef ani fafor, or the unspekcabell sorros of my ded hart may resevef ani cumfort, then let my sorros cum before you wich if you trewly knew, I asur my selfe you wold pitti me, but most espescially your poour unfortunate frind ich relyeth holy on you honnorable and wontid fafor: I knoo in my owne soule wich sumthing knooeth his mind that he douth, and ever hath doon, not unlly honered the keng, but naturally loveth him, and god knooeth far: from him to wish him harme, but to have spent his life as soune for him, as ani cretuer leveng.

I most humly beseich your Honnar – even for god sake – to be good unto him; to onns more make him your cretur, your relifed frind; and dell with the Keng for him – for onn that is more worti of fafor than mani eles; having worthe, and onnesti, and wisdom to be a frind. pitti the name of your ancient frind on his poour littell cretuer wich may leve to honnor you. That wee all may lift up ouer handes and hartes in prayer for you and youres, bind this ouer pooure famlies to prayes your honnar and wonted good natur let the hole world prayes your love to my pour unfortunat hosban. for cristis sake, wich rewardeth [at this point, Bess runs out of space on the sheet, so she moves to writing vertically in the margin] all mercies, pitti his just case; and god for his infeni marci bles you for ever, and worke in the keng merci: I am not abell I protest befor god to stand on my trembling leges otherwies I wold have watted now on you: or be derectid holy by you: chee that will trewly honnar you in all misfortun E Ralegh.

All the practical efforts Bess had made over the last three months had, it seems, sheltered her from the full impact of Ralegh's downfall. Only now can she fully imagine Ralegh dead, as dead as her own heart. She can only beg 'me lord' Cecil in the name of God to make her husband live again. And yet the letter is also defiant. Nowhere does Bess acknowledge Sir Walter's guilt. Instead, she offers a litany of his virtues: worth, honesty and wisdom. She appeals to the old friendship between Sir Walter and Cecil, but above all she calls on the friendship between herself and Robert Cecil. Lurking behind the letter are the ghosts of Lord Burghley and Sir Nicholas Throckmorton, the old Queen's trusted political fixers through the 1560s. This is the common heritage of young Bess and Robert, but Bess also nods towards the next generation: little Will Cecil had been a 'poor little creature' at the death of his mother, but Bess had taken him in. Now Wat would be a 'poor little creature' if his father was to be taken from him.

Robert Cecil did not listen. Over these weeks, Bess's kinship network evaporated, as friends in happier times lined up to condemn Ralegh, who had been 'deciphered' as 'the ugliest traitor that ever was heard of in England . . .'. Ralegh himself was completely isolated from her in the Tower of London. On 29 November 1603 he watched as two of the conspirators received their punishment. The Catholic priests, Watson and Clarke, were hanged, drawn and quartered beneath his window, a terrifying prequel to his own imminent execution. Last-minute efforts to achieve a pardon were still being made, but to no avail. Instead, more scaffolds were being prepared.

In these final days before his execution, Bess at last received the news that she would be allowed to see her husband. Sir Benjamin Tichborne, his keeper, wrote to the Privy Council that his prisoner 'hath been very importunate with me twice or thrice' of 'his request that you would permit his wife and some others to have access unto him, who are to be accountant to the value of £50,000 (as he saith) and to whom he hath passed certain leases in trust'. At this stage of acute crisis, Bess was at last invited to participate in the business of money and politics, managing the estate conferred in trust to her young son. Officially, on paper, of course, the men sorted it out, since on 4 December 1603 John Shelbury, Ralegh's solicitor, and Thomas Harriot, his long-time friend and adviser, were liaising with the Privy Council negotiating Ralegh's finances. But Ralegh asked for Bess.

Time was running out. Two days later Ralegh saw George Brooke, Cobham's brother, executed. Ralegh would be next. As earlier in the year, he writes to Bess and to her alone this time, his 'dear wife'. The letter she received is a controlled, intense expression of love. The message is simple and passionate: Walter sends his love to Bess, and he asks her to keep it for him, for ever.

He asks his 'dear Bess' to face her grief with her customary strength: 'bear it patiently and with a heart like your self.' He sends her 'all the thanks which my heart can conceive or my words can express for your many travails [that is, efforts or work] and care taken for me, which though they have not taken effect as you wished, yet my debt to you is not the less, but pay it I never shall in this world'. He acknowledges, at last, how much he values the increasingly desperate efforts she has made for him, and that he can do nothing for her 'in this world'.

Yet the message that Bess receives from her condemned husband is more complex than this, and is rooted as much in pragmatism as in the language of romantic love. Sir Walter tells her not to hide herself away after his death. She is on her own now and must work to save herself: 'by your travails seek to help your miserable fortunes and the right of your poor child.' As he says, 'thy mourning cannot avail me: I am but dust'. He has considered her needs but has failed to put his intentions into action. Perhaps the moral advice offered at the end of this section acknowledges his sense of his own failure: 'But if you can live free from want, care for no more: the rest is but vanity.'

In an echo of his earlier letter, written when he attempted to take his own life, Bess is offered God as a substitute husband for her, and father to little Walter: God is, after all, 'a husband and a father which cannot be taken from you'. This time, however, Ralegh does not actively encourage Bess to remarry, but instead warns her that she should take care of herself, and be wary of offers from men. He nevertheless acknowledges that he should not dissuade her 'from marriage, for it will be best for you, both in respect of the world and of God'. In order to convince her of this, he clearly felt the need to make their separation explicit and final. 'As for me, I am no more yours, nor you mine. Death hath cut us asunder and God hath divided me from the world and you from me. Remember your poor child for his father's sake, who chose you and loved you in his happiest times.' In the midst of this farewell, Sir Walter transports them both back imaginatively twelve, thirteen years to a time when anything seemed possible.

Ralegh assures Bess that he is 'a true man, and one who, in his own respect, despises death, and all his misshapen and ugly shapes', offering some comfort in his defiance for the unspeakable horrors of her own dead heart. The letter closes, however, in an almost unbearably poignant way. 'I cannot write much. God knows how hardly I steal this time while others sleep, and it is also high time that I should separate my thoughts from the world.' Bess is 'the world'. She has been his world for so many years, and perhaps only in the months of crisis leading up to his execution did Sir Walter fully appreciate the extent of her commitment to him. 'I can say no more, time and death call me away. My dear wife farewell. Bless my poor boy. Pray for me and let my good God hold you both in his arms. Yours that was, but now not my own, WR.'

6

'Of Liberty Deprived':
The Tower Years

Sir Walter's execution was scheduled for 12 December 1603. Cobham was to die three days earlier, together with co-conspirators Lord Grey and Gervase Markham. Ralegh watched again, on 9 December, the terrible rehearsal for his own death, as one by one the traitors were led to the scaffold. Then something remarkable happened. In each case the condemned man was told at the very last minute that he had been reprieved by his merciful King. Ralegh himself did not go through this charade. King James had played his sadistic little game enough times already, and was content with merely informing Sir Walter that he too was reprieved from immediate death. This act of exquisite psychological torture on the part of the King is hard to explain. Perhaps James belatedly recognized that the judgement was tainted. Perhaps he relished the opportunity to display kingly mercy in a particularly dramatic way. Perhaps he simply wanted to exert his God-given power over his victims. It is certainly true that Lord Cobham, for one, never fully recovered from the psychological trauma of that December day.

Whatever King James's motives, this last-minute reprieve, following on from Ralegh's compelling defence of his own case at Winchester, was the political sensation of the winter. Ralegh, from being the 'best hated man' in England, was now a cause célèbre. Ben Jonson and William Shakespeare, battling it out for theatre audiences on the South Bank of the Thames, both responded to the dramatic potential of the events played out at the Tower of London. Jonson took the character of the noble man of action, doomed to a tragic end when he resists the corrupt leaders of his time, and re-imagined Ralegh as Silius, a tormented Hamlet figure. Unlike Shakespeare's vacillating hero, Silius actually does escape the slings and arrows of outrageous fortune and succeeds in killing himself in Act III of *Sejanus, His Fall*. What is more, his death is celebrated as the meritorious example of a classical end: 'Look upon Silius, and so learn to die.' One William Shakespeare acted in Jonson's play, but clearly thought he could do better with the raw material of Ralegh's trial and almost execution. Shakespeare came up with *Measure for Measure*, performed for the King himself, and by the King's own players, in the Banqueting Hall at Whitehall on St Stephen's Night, 26 December 1604, a year on from the events the play echoes. Shakespeare is at his most topical in *Measure for Measure*, alluding to the plague (which was still wide-spread, leading to the closure of the theatres in the spring of 1604), to the making of a peace (brokered with Spain in August 1604) and to exposure of the Main and Bye Plots that had dominated the previous winter. As Mistress Overdone, the brothel madam in *Measure for Measure*, complains, 'what with the war, what with the sweat, what with the gallows, and what with poverty, I am custom shrunk'. Shakespeare's duke dispenses justice at the end of the play in a theatrical manner which echoes James's tactics with the Main and Bye conspirators, but audiences have always been divided and perplexed by his character, and in particular whether his final act of flamboyant leniency reveals him as a hypocritical tyrant or a benevolent leader. What is certain is that in this very dark comedy, Shakespeare portrays a city (nominally Vienna, actually London) at breaking point. Opinion may be divided as to whether Silius represents Ralegh, or the duke represents King James, but what is certain is that both playwrights vividly depict a society struggling with sleaze, corruption and disease. The dramatic solutions offered by Jonson and Shakespeare, whether honourable suicide or ostentatious displays of princely mercy, leave the social and political problems raised by the plays unsolved.

For Ralegh and Bess, however, King James's princely mercy was extremely welcome, at least at first. Sir Walter's intense relief, despite his brave words of farewell to Bess only a few days earlier, is tangible in his letter of grovelling gratitude to his King. For a short time he entertained hopes that his reprieve would be followed swiftly by a pardon and release. The harsh reality was, however, that Sir Walter may have still been physically alive, but he was now 'legally dead'. As the euphoria occasioned by the stay of execution receded, Sir Walter slid back into deep depression, withdrawing within himself, in no state to support Bess, emotionally, financially or politically.

And it was material considerations that absorbed the Raleghs this first winter in the Tower. Bess actually lived, at least part of the time, with her husband, sharing his imprisonment. Whether she did this out of loyalty, love or necessity is unclear. In the Tower, the Raleghs created a household in miniature. Sir Walter had the constant attendance of three of his own men, and there is nothing to suggest that Bess would have had any fewer women attending to her. Wat was with them, along with his tutors. The Raleghs could not, however, get too settled. They were dependent on the whims of the King, as had been revealed when, after Christmas Day 1603, Ralegh was moved to the Fleet prison for a few weeks. This was not a punitive measure. It was merely that King James needed the Tower for one of his favourite spectator sports, bull-baiting, and the presence of his most celebrated state prisoner might have got in the way of his royal pleasure.

Ralegh was held in the Bloody Tower, originally built to provide superior accommodation for the Constable of the Tower, and deemed suitably spacious to house Sir Walter and his family. In the early years of his imprisonment, improvements were made, including, it seems, the addition of an extra floor to the Tower. The two rooms (which can still be seen at the Tower of London, furnished as they might have appeared during Ralegh's imprisonment) are, however, not large, and the walkway leading from them was only a few metres long. The comparison between the Bloody Tower and the palatial rooms of Durham House or the magnificent parkland of Sherborne must have been a painful one.

Day-to-day life was dominated by bodily concerns, in particular Ralegh's continued illness. He was in a parlous state, both physically and psychologically, claiming to be daily in danger of death 'by the palsy', 'nightly of suffocation by wasted and obstructed lungs'. He feared for his life, begging to be allowed to travel to take the waters at Bath or else he would be 'undone', 'dead or disabled for ever'. Nine months after his reprieve, he suffered a palsy, which left him partially paralysed. In an act of royal largesse, Dr Poe, one of the King's own physicians, was permitted to attend to him.

The visit of any doctor was, however, a mixed blessing for any patient at this stage in medical history. The visit of Leonard Poe, one of the most corrupt and incompetent doctors of his time, was especially unhelpful. The Royal College of Physicians had pronounced him, as early as 1589, as 'completely unlearned and ignorant of medicine in every respect' and forbade him to practise. A year later he was still practising, because the Earl of Essex was offering him protection, as the physician proffered his skills 'in the French disease, in fevers and in rheumatism'. Again, he 'was examined and found to be a completely ignorant man', and again Essex stepped in to protect him.

Putting aside his medical ineptitude, Poe, like many doctors, was savagely satirized for his lecherous activities with his female patients, or with the wives of his incapacitated male patients. If Dr Butler was 'like a Sheffield cutler' with his 'knife in every sheath', then

> you, Doctor Poe,
> Your physick's so so
> You placed not your Glister pipe wrong,
> When you cured Mistress Rich
> of the lecherous itch
> in the absence of spruce Mr Young.[1]

Whether Poe tried to cure Bess of any lecherous itch remains thankfully hidden in the mists of time, but his attempts to alleviate Ralegh's various illnesses had no discernible effect. Sir Walter might have been better taking his own medicine, quite literally. Both he and Bess were known for their skills in the making of remedies, although Bess's speciality was the production of distilled waters, a traditional household task for the aristocratic woman. So a contemporary manuscript has Ralegh's recipe for a pill 'moistened with the syrup of violets' and taken 'in the pulp of an apple', along with two recipes for distilled water that 'his lady makes'. A recipe for 'syrup of violets' appears in many household recipe books of the time, indicating the complex interrelation of cookery and medicine. The cook is instructed to 'first make a thick syrup of sugar and clarify it well, then take blue violets and pick them well from the whites, then put them in the syrup. Let them lie in it 24 hours, keeping it warm in the mean time, then strain these violets out and put in fresh. So do four times, then set them on the fire, let them simper [simmer] a good while but not boil fast. Put in some juice of lemons in the boiling then strain it and keep it for your use.'[2] Various restorative remedies were developed over the years and were recommended to all ages and for a range of conditions, whether for 'old people in fainting fits' or 'to draw poison from the heart'. The quantities varied for each patient: for sucking children, the 'quantity of a great pea' was usually sufficient, while for adults a dose the size of 'the kernel of a filbert' was usually prescribed, although in 'a fit of extremity you may give double or treble as much'. The sick person was instructed to 'take it of a knife's point, or else dissolve it in a spoonful of liquor as you please & wash it down with 2 or 3 spoonfuls of the same liquor'. As so often with medical 'receipts', the large quantities of strong alcohol used to wash down the other more exotic ingredients may have had the greatest impact on the patient.

Ralegh probably discussed and developed his medicines with the help of the South Americans he had brought back with him from the Guiana region. Leonard Ragapo and Harry, both of whom lived in the Tower or nearby, 'frequently visited Ralegh who busied himself with teaching them English and various experiments in medicinal preparations, for which the native drugs *chincona* [quinine] and possibly *coca* were important'.[3] Quinine and coca apart, Ralegh was also, of course, seen as responsible for the introduction of tobacco to English society. In its early days it was the medicinal qualities of the leaf that attracted attention, as one contemporary records:

Sir Walter Ralegh having a strong fever was let blood in both arms and in the next fit following being about noon being in bed and being in a sweat and falling asleep with all upon his back bowing backward his night coif fell from his head and when he awaked he had intolerable pain in his head and taking tobacco it vanished away quickly. The next day about that time the headache came to him again in great extremity & forbearing till it was at the worst he took tobacco again and it came no more.

Tobacco and home-made medicines may have alleviated the symptoms of headaches and palsy, but they could do nothing to offer protection from the plague. The horror of pestilence returned again in 1604. Living in the cramped conditions of the Tower was terrifyingly claustrophobic, as Ralegh's letters testify. Plague reached the next set of rooms to the Raleghs: it came 'next door [. . .] only the narrow passage of the way between'. Young Wat, still only eleven, was particularly vulnerable. He spent fourteen days lying 'next to a woman with a running plague sore and but a paper wall between, and whose child is also this Thursday dead of the plague'. Bess's loyalty to Sir Walter was being tested to its limits in these conditions. Her residence in the Tower, the public sign of her wifely obedience to her husband, was perhaps worth renouncing if Wat's life was at stake. So, taking her son and servants with her, she left Ralegh alone in the Tower. Perhaps she got as far away as Sherborne. Her husband was not happy, writing that 'now my wife and child and others in whom I had comfort have abandoned me, and in what fearful estate the Lord knows'. In economic terms, times were hard, at least in comparison with their lifestyles only the previous year. Ralegh complains that 'I and my wife and my child must proportion our selves. Such a family as we must all live at £4 a week for all our diets, or else we must all go naked.' Whilst four pounds a week was still vastly more than most people lived on at the time, it was a shock for the Raleghs.

Under these circumstances Bess's moves towards independence during the preceding decade stood her in good stead as she adapted to her new life. Her role as trusted mediator became all the more important, as Sir Walter recognizes in a letter to Cecil: 'since the time my wife was last with your lordship,' he writes, 'I have withered in body and mind, by whom [Bess] I perceived a sad change in your lordship's favour towards me, on which all my hopes have ever lived and made me live.' Bess, conscious of the 'sad change' in Cecil's 'favour', was learning to be more assertive in her dealings with the men in power, sensing perhaps her growing strength. Another letter from Ralegh suggests the subtle shifts in power. He writes that it had 'pleased the king to promise my wife her goods and chattels. I have willed her to sue for them. She thinks it to little purpose until she have a bill drawn for them: that she cannot have without a warrant.' On one level, Ralegh acknowledges that Bess herself has been dealing directly with King James, but, on another level, the letter maintains the necessary fiction that Sir Walter was the one in control: 'I have willed her to sue for them.' In the very next sentence, however, it becomes clear that it is Bess who is making the running, since she is the one who 'thinks it to little purpose' to have the promise of the King without a firm commitment in writing (a 'warrant'). Yet another letter from this same period has Ralegh complaining that his 'tenants refuse to pay my wife her rent'. The pronouns here tell the same story – Ralegh still holds on to the idea of *his* tenants, and *his* wife, but in material terms it is *Bess's* rent. In English common law, wives could not hold freehold land (real property) except through their husbands, nor could they alter or dispose of property without their husbands' consent, even if it was their own inheritance, but all women could take on tenancies. Moreover, trusts enabled women to be left freehold land, whose income they might have and which they themselves might bequeath, without being able to dispose of the land itself.

Bess's priority in these months was to salvage what she could from the wreckage of Ralegh's estate. She had to tread carefully, because the Privy Council were still making enquiries into Ralegh's lands and goods, unable to believe that they had confiscated everything and hoping to find a secret source of income: in his Irish dealings, for example. Bess's campaign for Ralegh's movable goods, begun the previous October, paid off, and in February she achieved this, her first aim, although the terms in which the goods and chattels were granted expose her subordinate position as a woman. The grant made by the Crown was to John Shelbury and Robert Smith, who were instructed to use them to pay off debts and for the maintenance of Bess and young Wat. Moreover, many of the very goods and chattels that Bess had worked so hard to have restored to her had indeed been sold off, as Cecil predicted, to fend off ruin. The 'rich hangings' had gone to the Lord Admiral Nottingham for five hundred pounds, the one 'rich bed' had gone to his fellow prisoner Cobham for three hundred pounds. Ralegh's total income per year was assessed at six hundred and sixty-six pounds; of this, sixty-six pounds was allocated to his 'poor wife and child and their servants, which, God knows, will not give them bread and clothes'.

Bess's other, more productive, campaign was to clarify her position with regard to Sherborne. In the months after Ralegh's attainder, Bess wanted the trust to be confirmed in law. She achieved a partial victory in the summer of 1604, when on 30 July an official grant was made to trustees Alexander Brett and George Hall (or Hull). The latter may well have been Sir Walter's brother-in-law, second husband to Margaret Ralegh, while Alexander Brett was a long-time friend and business associate of Bess, as well as the husband of one of her Throckmorton cousins. In this grant of July 1604, a sixty-year lease on Sherborne, 'to Lady Ralegh, her son and her family should Sir Walter so long live', was confirmed, offering some security at least for Bess, and a home away from the Tower.

Ralegh, although implicitly acknowledging his reliance on Bess to achieve some sort of financial recovery, was focused on release. Bess, he wrote, had told him that she had spoken with Robert Cecil 'yesterday about my poor estate and hers'. It had 'pleased' Cecil to 'deal for the assurance of my land unto some feoffees of trust to the use of her and my child, but that for my pardon it could not yet be done'. Bess had indeed done the business with Sherborne (she had the 'use' of the estate), but Ralegh's personal priority, to get a pardon, remained paramount. His ideas as to what he could do once this was achieved ranged from the eminently sensible to the mildly absurd. He could perhaps go down to Sherborne and stay there, or perhaps he could go to Holland, where he would 'by chance get some employment upon the Indies', or, better still, he could manage one of Robert Cecil's parks.

Ralegh may have dreamed of escape to Sherborne, Holland or indeed to the life of a park-keeper, but he remained in the Tower. It was Bess who was constantly moving between Sir Walter and the outside world, attempting to broker deals, bringing letters to, taking letters from, her husband from and to interested parties and, to the consternation of Ralegh's keeper, sending a steady stream of servants between her own house and the Tower. Bess insisted that she should be able to send any 'man or boy' to Ralegh without the need to apply for a special licence. Bess herself was proving wayward. The Governor of the Tower confessed, with some shame, that she (significantly with 'some courtiers') had 'once or twice', finding the gates of the gardens, where Sir Walter was allowed to walk, open, entered and 'complementally' talked with him 'in my presence'. The Governor then locked the garden door, but Bess's claims for freedom of movement did not abate.

Bess was moving between three, possibly four households: Sherborne, the Tower and a rented house in London, probably on Tower Hill. There is one tantalizing reference to suggest that she maintained a house at Mitcham, near her uncle's property at Beddington. One of her letters to the steward at Beddington, John Booth, survives and can be dated to the early years of Ralegh's imprisonment. 'Good friend Booth', she begins, 'I am bold to trouble you with a third trunk which I must desire you to set up with the other.' Lawrence Keymis had 'occasion to go into the west country', no doubt to Sherborne, and, Bess writes, 'I am loath to leave any thing of worth here at Mitcham in all our absence.' The next lines explain why the property at Mitcham will be empty: she feels she must return to Sir Walter 'who hath been lately punished with an extreme cold.' Keymis, in this letter, emerges as a key figure: Bess's right-hand man at Sherborne and, it seems, also at Mitcham.

Bess led this life, moving between her various households, with Wat in tow, as the list of those permitted access ('his Lady and his son and her waiting maid') to Ralegh shows. It is hard to assess the impact of the events of the previous months on a ten-year-old boy. During 1604 Wat had to adjust to the fact that his father was both alive and dead to him, that he had a father and no father. Always close to his mother, physically and emotionally, presumably the relationship between Wat and Bess became even closer at this time. Educational theory had it that the first and best teachers in the household were a child's parents, that children should be kept close to their parents, sleeping in their bedchamber and eating with them at table, since only thus could they fully absorb the moral example of their elders. Bess, long used to being the sole parent when Ralegh had been on his military or exploratory expeditions, presumably continued as the main parent in this respect. During the periods when she was not with Ralegh in the Tower, she was effectively head of the household, and thus responsible for proper governance and discipline. This state of affairs exacerbated some of the problems inherent in the early-modern way of bringing up boys. In general, both boys and girls had to learn obedience, expressed by standing before parents, kneeling for daily blessing or offering deference to those of higher rank and greater age. But as they grew older, boys had to 'make the transition from habits of obedience and internalized self-discipline to those of authority and command'.[4] The move away from obedience to the mother, and towards authority and command over inferiors, which of course included all women, was eased by the cultural belief in the natural deficiency of women: unfinished men, daughters of Eve, passive and weak, women needed men to control them. For Wat, the very person to whom he was expected to show most obedience and respect was, by the nature of her gender, a person who could have no 'natural' authority over him as he grew into manhood. This, allied to the acute uncertainty about his father's health and future, and the constraints of living at least part of his childhood in a prison, ensured that for Wat the transition from boyhood to manhood would not necessarily be an easy one.

Ralegh's first year of imprisonment came and went, however, and some sort of stability, economically and within the family, had been achieved. But at this very point Bess's world was to be shaken by an astonishing development. She was pregnant. Incredibly, she must have conceived this surprise, late baby in the spring of 1604. It is possible that she only told her husband in the autumn and even then, after a fraught year, he was predictably far from delighted as he contemplated, with typical exaggeration, 'utter beggary'. Ralegh does not mention the new baby in his letters (then, again, he did not have a good track record on this) until the winter, and when he writes he is extremely depressed about his prospective fatherhood.

There was, however, a rather puzzling aspect to this startling conception. Bess had not had a child for the previous eleven years. It is just possible that she had become pregnant, one or more times, since 1593 but had miscarried or given birth to a stillborn baby, although the historical record does not make mention of these events. Even if this was the case, it is still remarkable that she was pregnant in 1604, and she appeared to be carrying the baby to term. The eleven childless years suggest the remote possibility that Bess and Sir Walter found a reliable method of contraception (although historians are united in their scepticism about the methods suggested by handbooks of the time – would drinking vast quantities of 'water of honeysuckles', as recommended by *The Jewel of Health*, really 'procure barrenness all the life time'?). It is far more likely that one of them had a fertility problem. A historian of medicine, Deborah Harkness, has no doubt that it was Ralegh who, by the late 1590s probably, and by the early 1600s definitely, would have been impotent, due to the effect of syphilis contracted in the Americas.

This puts a different perspective on the events of 1604: if Ralegh could not have been the father of Bess's late baby, who was? Many years later, and admittedly from the pen of a hostile witness, one speculative version of the affair came out. Bess, the story went, was showing neither loyalty nor love when she moved into the Tower with Ralegh, but instead a ruthless pragmatism. Poor Sir Walter may have been 'friendless' at the time of his 'troubles', as the events of 1603 are described, but Bess had kept the support and friendship of one 'Mr Lessells'. This gentleman was 'my Lady's friend', a man who 'did not leave her'. The innuendo is clear, and the libel was made explicit in the following lines when it was claimed that the only reason that Bess had made a Petition to Robert Cecil 'to visit her Husband, and to be close Prisoner with him' was to cover for her pregnancy. Indeed, it was a close-run thing. She joined Ralegh in the Tower only just in time and then 'suddenly conceived'. Ralegh, having almost lost his life, in the process of losing his estate, had now, it seemed, lost his wife, 'the worst sort of theft, infinitely beyond that of goods', as the preachers said.

Who could this Lessells be, if he indeed was Bess's 'friend' who 'did not leave her'? The strongest candidate is the minor courtier Edmund Lascelles, a man from a similar background to Bess, and moving in the same circles as her, in particular that of Bess of Hardwick, Lady Shrewsbury. While far from a major figure in his time (perhaps Bess had had enough of that for a lifetime), he was nevertheless neither the safest nor the most reliable person to have as a special 'friend'. In

1605 he would be imprisoned for suspected complicity in the Gun-powder Plot, while early in 1606 he was in even bigger trouble, named among the five persons of the Bed Chamber who had sworn to kill the King and Cecil. He later left England to escape his creditors, and by February 1608 was in an appalling position, writing to Cecil that he had failed in all his lawsuits and begging ineffectually for protection and restoration to the King's service. It is impossible to know whether Lascelles was indeed the baby's father, or whether another man was. It is, of course, possible that Sir Walter, despite all the evidence suggesting his poor physical and mental condition in 1604, may have been. What is clear is that no one was coming forward to claim paternity or to support Bess. With absolutely no support from Ralegh, she faced this pregnancy profoundly isolated and under trying physical conditions.

These months were to prove some of the most testing that Bess would ever experience. She faced all the usual fears associated with any pregnancy in her time. These were exacerbated in the first instance by her age. Bess would be forty in the spring of the new year, and as an older woman she was seen, in physiological terms, as at greater risk from the destructive effects of dryness and hardness. It was imperative to counteract these problems with the use of 'hot and moist things which have property to lenify [relax] and supple [make supple], and that both in meat and drink, and also in outward fomentations, bathings, suppositories and anointments'. Advice was given as to precisely what could and should be applied to 'the privy place' and included 'hen's grease, duck's grease, goose grease' as well as olive oil. While being anointed with these oils, Bess would have been encour-aged to drink plenty of 'good ripe wine, mixed with water'. Sage was also highly recommended, often in the form of sage ale. Once again, it appears that much of early-modern life was experienced through a haze of alcohol.

Bess, as a pregnant woman, ought to have been protected from 'sudden fear, affrightments, by fire, lightning, thunder', not to men-tion from 'immoderate joy, sorrow and lamentation'. As autumn turned to winter in 1604 in the Tower, it seems unlikely that she would escape 'affrightments' and 'lamentation'. Perhaps with this pregnancy and birth, she turned to Arthur yet once more, since on 21

November 1604 her brother begged Robert Cecil for permission to visit the Raleghs in the Tower. Arthur's diary for these years does not survive, and there are no other records of Bess's confinement, in both senses of the word, in the Tower. All the usual preparations still needed to be made for the forthcoming birth. A contemporary wrote that 'women will make no other preparation for lying in than what is common, if they only get linen and other necessaries for the child, a nurse, a midwife, entertainment for the women that are called to their labour, a warm convenient chamber'. While male theological writers warned women against spending too much time thinking about the practicalities rather than the spiritual dimensions of their prospective labour, in Bess's case ensuring a 'warm, convenient chamber' in the Tower of London in the middle of winter was probably enough of a challenge.

At last, in the cold and dark of January 1605, Bess gave birth to a son, a brother to the short-lived Damerei and adolescent Wat. In the early stages of labour Bess needed to 'moderately exercise the body in doing some thing, stirring, moving, going, or standing, more than otherwise she was wont to do. These things further the birth and make it the easier.' Women could give birth sitting, in bed, standing being supported by others, or kneeling. Tradition called for the women to remove all rings, laces, knots, fastenings and buckles, as a way of sympathetically easing labour and removing constrictions on the birth, or merely to avoid them getting in the way. Ironically, giving birth in the Tower of London had its positive aspects. Medical opinion argued that the greatest danger to the new baby was cold air: thus, 'royal and aristocratic birthrooms were accordingly hung with arras, the doors guarded, and the windows covered'. If most noble-women gave birth in rooms resembling prisons, then in some ways Bess's experience was archetypal rather than anomalous.[5]

Bess was supported through the birth by her midwife, who in the crisis of labour would in any case have supplanted Sir Walter as the source of support. It was the midwife who took temporary command of the situation and space, and also instructed and comforted the woman, 'not only refreshing her with food, meat and drink, but also with sweet words'. Being in London, Bess had at least a good range of midwives to choose from, and she always had Arthur's undoubted expertise in this area to support her. Out in the country, it was harder for women, as a letter from Joan Thynne at Longleat acknowledges: 'if my sister be in London I pray you entreat her to provide me of a good midwife for me against Easter or a ten or twelve days after, for I think my time will be much thereabout. Here is none worth the having now goody Barber is dead.' It was the midwife who swaddled the child and presented it to the waiting father. Perhaps at this point Ralegh contributed his most famous cordial, with its magnificent list of ingredients (from the flowers of borage and rosemary, marigold and red gilly, saffron and juniper berries, to sassafras of Virginia, pearl and ambergris and musk, all mixed with the syrup of lemons and red roses). The cordial was recommended for years as 'excellent good for women to take as soon as they are delivered, immediately as they lie down'.

A few weeks later the baby was christened. At traditional church baptisms, it was the midwife who carried the infant to the font, proudly displaying the success of her endeavours. So it was presumably Bess's midwife, who had successfully brought mother and child through labour, who carried the swaddled baby to the font in the Chapel Royal of St Peter ad Vincula. St Peter's was Bess's parish church, as it were, lying within the walls of the Tower of London, across the courtyard from the Bloody Tower, her prison home. Close by was the scaffold site where Lady Jane Grey and the Earl of Essex, among other noble prisoners, had been beheaded. Bess's baby was christened Carew on 15 February 1605. The name was possibly a homage to Sir Walter's older brother, Carew Ralegh, but it also creates a link with Bess's own mother, who had been born Anne Carew. This time of birth, traditionally a time of closeness between mothers and daughters, between sister and sister, merely emphasized Bess's aloneness, the only daughter of a long-dead mother. It is impossible to know which, if any, of her female relations cared for her in the Tower, but there is evidence that Mary, the wife of her younger brother Nicholas, sent Bess a wet nurse for the new baby. Young Nick's wife clearly did not have Arthur Throckmorton's talent for choosing good nurses. Bess rejected the woman chosen by Mary as tactfully as possible, writing that she thanks her 'sister for the nurse. I like the woman very well: but that she hath but one breast: and of three children, she hath but one living, all of them she nursed as she sayeth.' Bess, like her contemporaries, believed that lactation involved the transformation of blood into milk by the breasts, and that the nurse's character, eating habits and daily actions all had the potential to affect the child she fed, since, equally obviously, moral qualities as well as physical illnesses were sucked in with the wet nurse's milk. Bess asks Nicholas to say that she had already engaged another nurse, and thus it was not a matter of 'dislike'. Privately, however, she acknowledges to her brother that she fears for the 'healthiness of the woman, though she seems strong having had so lewd a husband', a hint that Bess also had an understanding of the effect that a 'lewd husband' might have on a woman's health.

The dangers of childbirth once again negotiated, Bess could return to being her husband's vital link with the outside world. This, however, carried its own risks. Bess may have come safely through childbirth and plague, as in 1593, but there were yet more challenges to be faced. That year, 1605, was the year of the Gunpowder Plot, when Catholic rebels, led by Guy Fawkes and backed allegedly by Spain, sought to blow up the King and his Parliament. Bess was suspected of involvement on two accounts. The first was plain and simple: her family origins; she was a Throckmorton woman. The Throckmorton family had had a relatively quiet time of it since the mid-1580s, but there was no escaping their involvement in the Gunpowder Plot. It was to the Throckmorton house, Coughton, that Robert Catesby's servant, Bates, rode to tell of the conspiracy's failure. Moreover, although the Throckmorton name may not have featured markedly in the cast of conspirators, a quick glance at the matrilineal family tree reveals the network of Throckmorton women connected to Gunpowder Plotters: for example, Robert Catesby's mother was Anne Throckmorton, and Francis Tresham's mother was Muriel Throckmorton. As a historian of the Plot notes, there was an interlinked group of four crypto-Catholic families at the heart of the assault on James and his Parliament, the group comprising 'Catholic women with conforming husbands and fathers' bonded by intermarriage, and thus creating 'striking networks of closely related wives, sisters and mothers'.[6]

On the one hand, this was precisely the kind of network that Bess was excluded from, on account of her father's rejection of his own family's Catholicism. On the other, her impeccable Protestant and loyal background should have shielded her, as it did her brother, Arthur. He was extremely quick to distance himself from his 'unkind kindred' and was quite happy to act on behalf of the state to punish those of his family who had been involved. (It is nevertheless interesting to note that, although Arthur, as High Sheriff of Northamptonshire, was responsible, in January 1606, for the seizure and safekeeping of conspirator Francis Tresham's goods and chattels – a task for which he would claim payment from the state of a hundred and three pounds – he nevertheless almost immediately returned the goods and chattels to Lady Meryll Tresham.)

But Bess's Protestant pedigree did not shield her as it did her brother. She fell under intense suspicion. It was probably her marriage to Ralegh, and the events with which she had been connected in 1603, that laid her open to charges of conspiring with Spain. The specific charge levelled against Bess was that she had gone down to Sherborne in order to prepare for the imminent Spanish invasion, which would follow swiftly upon the act of terrorism against the King and his Parliament. She had even been seen to be cleaning the armour there. The inquiry into Bess's actions makes fascinating reading. Robert Cecil had got hold of a man, Edward Cotterell, and insinuated him into Bess's household under the new and plausible name of Captain Sampson. (Although there is dispute about this. Some historians argue that the Gunpowder Plot was actually devised and engineered by Robert Cecil and his network of spies in order to further discredit the English Catholics.) Bess paid 'Sampson' the good wage of five shillings a week while all the time he reported back to his real master, Cecil. There was much to report. Ralegh, under the lax regime at the Tower of Sir George Harvey, 'did speak at a window in the wall of the garden' with 'any person that he desired to speak withal' and, possibly even more scandalous, 'Owen a waterman brought him diverse times beer and ale in bottles'. The window was then 'made up', thus preventing Ralegh's communication with the outside world, and presumably the supplies of bottled ale were stopped as well.

Cotterell/Sampson moved from London to Sherborne and back

174

with Bess and reported that in the summer of 1605 all the talk at Sherborne had been 'that Sir Walter Ralegh should be set at liberty at the Parliament, but in what sort he knows not'. Getting on to the subject of Bess and Sherborne, Cotterell alleged that 'the Lady Ralegh was twice there that summer, and about September she did cause all the armour to be scoured as he thinketh because it was rusty. And then she caused also two walks to be made in the garden the furnishing whereof was a great charge unto her, and the house to be dressed up, where before all things lay in disorder.'

What could this mean? Was Bess preparing gleefully for a Spanish invasion – or was she merely being a good housekeeper getting the house 'dressed up'? Cotterell/Sampson was not sure, and hoped to find out more when he travelled back to London to meet up with Bess later in the year. By this stage, however, it appears that she was deeply suspicious of him. He reports that 'as soon as he came to town he met with one William Saunders a servant of the Lady Ralegh'. Together, he, Saunders and another man, Morgan, went to 'the Tower Hill on Thursday' to 'let the Lady Ralegh know that he was brought up about her causes and to see what she would do for him'. To his disappointment, however, 'Morgan and Saunders went into the house, and stayed there a quarter of an hour or thereabouts during which time he walked upon the Tower Hill'. Cotterell/Sampson paced the streets until 'the Lady Ralegh returned him answer that she would have nothing to do with him, and presently upon her coming forth the Lady Ralegh went to the Tower'.

Because of her caution, Cecil had no hard evidence to implicate Bess, although he kept probing, insisting on a further 'examination' of individuals down at Sherborne. All he could come up with was hearsay from a local fair: a witness reported that he had met some unnamed person at 'the fair' and that this unnamed person had said that on 6 November Ralegh would be in danger of his life, but notwithstanding, he would 'escape, and come to greater matters . . .'.

Ralegh, however, was in no fit state to 'come to greater matters'. He was in extremely bad shape, fearful of sudden death or the 'loss of my limbs and sense, being sometime two hours without feeling or motion of my hand and whole arm'. 'I complain not of it . . .' he wrote, disingenuously, but again the doctors were called in. Their report confirmed that 'all his left side is extremely cold, out of sense and motion or numb. His fingers on the same side beginning to be contracted. And his tongue taken in some part, in so much that he speaks weakly and it is to be feared he may utterly lose the use of it.' The doctors' advice was that he should be moved to a warmer room, preferably to a little room which he had built in 'the garden adjoining his still house'.

Although Ralegh remained partially paralysed, and only barely able to speak, Bess, having survived both the birth of Carew and Cecil's best efforts to implicate her in the Gunpowder Plot, was galvanized into challenging her husband. Her words only made Sir Walter's own precarious mental condition worse. In fact, he suggests that she is pushing him towards suicide again: he is made 'more than weary of my life by her [Bess's] crying and bewailing'. He imagines Bess coming back from Sherborne, in post haste as he puts it, when she hears that there is 'nothing done. She hath already brought her eldest son in one hand and her sucking child in another, crying out of her and their destruction, charging me with unnatural negligence and that, having provided for my own life, I am without sense and compassion of their.'

This was, of course, true. No one was looking out for Bess and her two sons. Everything that had been done in any legal or financial sense to improve the situation since 1603 had been done by Bess, while Ralegh merely complained relentlessly that he was near death. A remarkable portrait of Bess survives from the months after Carew's birth, its very existence perhaps celebrating the fact that Bess was still alive. The woman who looks out at the viewer is by no means a conventional beauty, by the standards of her own time or ours. She is certainly not blonde and blue-eyed as some of Ralegh's biographers would have her. Yet her expression is revealing, hovering strangely between a wry smile and stern disdain. She appears canny and, in her fortieth year (although an inscription on the portrait claims she is only thirty-five), strangely confident. The National Gallery of Ireland has painstakingly cleaned the image, revealing new details. Bess wears the sumptuous new fashions of the Jacobean court, with a low-cut dress revealing the blue veins on her pale breasts, the sign of the true noblewoman. Her strangely designed sleeves are cut away at the elbow, and she chooses to wear one sleeve hanging down, the other draped around her wrist. Everywhere there is gold braid, and in her hair is an egret's feather hung with pearls. Amid all this finery, there is one anomaly: the simple, leaf-shaped green jewel suspended from pearls around her neck.

The portrait is a bold image of a woman trying to fight back. In the aftermath of the Gunpowder inquiry, Bess wrote a letter to Robert Cecil, now Lord Viscount Cranborne, making her strongest claim yet for what she believed was due to her. Her argument was that Charles Howard, Lord Admiral, and brother to the Henry Howard who loathed her, had 'taken by strong hand that which his Majesty hath given us for our relief'. The Lord Admiral now had six thousand pounds, and three thousand a year 'by my husband's fall'. Although the letter is not entirely clear in its expression, Bess appears to be arguing that Ralegh's debts were made void 'by a proclamation, before my husband was suspected of any offence'. She is desperate now, because if she was now required to pay those debts, then at least the Lord Admiral could have 'given us something back again' to do so. The debts are 'above three thousand pounds, and the bread and food taken from me and my children will never augment my Lord's table, though it famish us'. This is powerful stuff: what the Lord Admiral Howard takes from Bess he will not even notice. Bess and her children will feel the loss quite desperately. In a remarkable move, this letter is endorsed by eighteen other noblewomen. For one historian, the list of names demonstrates that Bess was 'engaged in collective rather than singular activity'.[7] The list of names gives a tantalizing glimpse of the kinds of networks that Bess was attempting to tap into, although some of the women named remain elusive. Nine out of the eighteen are in some degree Bess's cousins, thus proving the importance of kinship ties. The key families – Carew, Neville, Hastings and Norris – are all connected with Bess's mother rather than her father, and many of these women were engaged in disputes about inheritance. Despite this public demonstration of support, however, there was little that Bess could do against the ascendant Howard family.

Bess, in the same letter quoted above in which she rejects her sister-in-law's choice of a wet nurse, writes at more length about the other legal and financial efforts she is making, indicating her close connections with her younger brother in the early years of the new King's reign, her letter ending with the desire that if Nicholas be 'at leisure', Bess 'would fain speak with' him. She has talked 'this day', she tells Nicholas, with her 'cousin George Throckmorton' who came to her house. George is a suitor for some restitution (Bess has two goes at spelling this word, and ends up with 'restetewsion') and is now 'willing to harken to the statute of ours'. The sum in question is five hundred pounds. Nicholas is out of town. Conveniently, however, Bess can step in. She writes: 'I have chosen Sir Alexander Brett to deal in it for me who *is* in town.' Even so, Bess is dependent on Nicholas to give the go-ahead and urges him forcefully to act:

> I pray neglect not this time with any idle excuses, or sloth, or I know not what. For my cousin George will not be long in Town, but returneth to his charge. He is a proper wise gentleman as he seemeth, and it may be this way we may have some good I pray come about it out of hand.

This, and more, was presumably the tone of voice that Bess was using with her husband. Tired of 'idle excuses, or sloth, or I know not what', Bess was, at last, getting angry. Ralegh was devastated: all he looked for was some 'comfort', but all he got were 'torments and outcries'. Nicholas and Sir Walter were not the only ones receiving the full force of Bess's desire to 'deal' with the financial problems that beset her and her children. The King himself was also in the firing line. Bess's priority was the confirmation of her right to Sherborne, threatened again by a legal challenge to the deed of trust and by James's desire to take the estate from the Raleghs, leaving nothing to them but one 'fee farm' to give them bread. Ralegh's sense of his own powerlessness in the face of this new threat seeps through his apocalyptic vision of Bess and his sons expelled from Sherborne, leaving them with 'no habitation on the face of the earth, the one having no husband, the other no father'.

If Sir Walter was 'no husband' to Bess, what of her wider family, and in particular her two brothers, Arthur and little Nick? Arthur, for one, may have become less close to Bess during these years. His life was increasingly dominated by the conventional concerns of the leading country gentleman, the management of his estate and its perpetuation through the next generation. In the early years of the seventeenth century, he invested huge amounts of money developing the manor at Paulerspury, introducing high-grade horticulture into traditional village farming practices, to the extent that his attempts to bring 'a gentlemanly lifestyle into a district which had previously known different ways' have been noted by historians of the English landscape. In previous generations, the inhabitants of this rural corner of Northamptonshire 'would have been more familiar with forest animals like deer, hares, falcons and wild birds'. Now Arthur planted 'vines, fruit trees and artichokes'. Apparently, the changes were not resisted, and his diary reveals 'supplies of fine foods arriving at the door', including 'a ripe apricot from his own trees in July 1611'.[8] With no sons, Arthur and Anna Throckmorton's prime responsibility as parents therefore was to make good marriages for their four daughters. In 1608 Arthur made a start with the eldest, Mary. Who better for her to marry than the son of his oldest and best friend, Edward Wotton? The arrangements for the wedding of Mary Throckmorton and Thomas Wotton, which took place on 6 June, were highly conventional, both financially and socially. Presumably, Bess attended the wedding of her teenage niece Mary, with Wat, now nearly fifteen, and Carew, just three and a half years old. The younger generation were growing up and moving on, but Arthur's duties as a father continued to preoccupy him. As ever, the task of arranging midwives and nurses fell to him, and so, when Mary approached her first confinement, it was Arthur who arranged for Mistress Mercer the midwife to be sent to his 'daughter Wotton' at Paulerspury. Mary would give birth to her first child at her parents' house, attended by the midwife her father had employed. On 6 December 1608 'my daughter Wotton' entered into labour at five in the morning: a baby girl was born at five in the afternoon the following day. Arthur organized another nurse, known only as 'Nelson's wife', to look after his presumably exhausted daughter. Arthur's little granddaughter was called Kate: her mother was churched just over a month later, in mid-January. The continuation of this practice within the Throckmorton family indicates that Arthur was not the strictest of Protestants. Puritan criticisms of churching focused not only on its dubious theological status but also on the excessive eating, drinking and making merry that accompanied the occasion, festivities from which men were, for once, excluded. Throckmorton women continued to enjoy this important and pleasurable ceremony. There were, however, shadows in this picture of Arthur's prospering estate and family. If the dates of the marriage of Mary and the birth of her baby are placed together, it emerges that she probably married when three months pregnant. Once married, her husband, Thomas, continually applied to her father, Arthur, for money and, typically, he took on his responsibilities in generous fashion, regularly handing out 'loans', although there is never an indication that the moneys were repaid. Some years later, Mary, in a controversial move, would turn away from her father's Protestant religion and return to the Catholicism of the wider Throckmorton family. Despite these undercurrents, however, Arthur's life was fairly settled and increasingly focused on his own children and grand-children: more and more, Bess would turn to her younger brother Nicholas.

His life would change radically during the early years of Ralegh's imprisonment. Some years before, in the closing years of Elizabeth's reign, Bess's little brother Nick had married. His wife was Mary More, daughter of Sir George More, and thus sister to Ann More, the ill-fated wife of the poet John Donne. John and Ann Donne's marriage took place without Sir George's permission and had disastrous impli-cations for Donne's career, leading him to pen the famous epigram: 'John Donne, Ann Donne, Undone.' Sir George may have approved of Nicholas Throckmorton as a son-in-law more than the rebellious, Catholic and far too clever John Donne, but Nick brought to his marriage all the financial problems of the youngest son of a large family. He, like his older brother, had travelled to Italy and, like Arthur, fell in love with the country, even enrolling at the University of Padua in 1590. Young Nick had a good time before his marriage: one of his friends would remember wistfully his 'youthful wenching peccadillios'. His letters to his father-in-law are invariably requests for cash: in one, he exclaims that he has pawned all his plate and used up all his credit. Sir George just has to come through with the money, since 'No less than £200 at Midsummer next can make me show my face in any company'.

The situation would improve dramatically for little Nick, however, and transform him from one of the poorest members of the Throckmorton siblings to the richest. Anne Throckmorton, Bess's mother, had an unmarried brother, Francis Carew. Uncle Francis lived at Beddington in Surrey, in the house where Bess herself had been born. Francis had put a substantial amount of money and energy into developing the property: by 1607 the estate was flourishing with thirty-five servants, the four most senior (including the gardener) receiving the generous sum of fifty shillings a year. Francis lived on his own, and with no heir, in a surprise move, at age eighty-one, he left his entire estate to his youngest nephew, Nicholas. All Nick had to do was change his name from Throckmorton to Throckmorton Carew.

It was easily done. Even before Uncle Francis died at Beddington, other family members started to close in, aware that young Nick was in line for wealth and power, asking for fifty pounds here, a legacy there. Perhaps Bess joined the list of suitors, and was perceived as a threat by one young female relative, Jane Clifford, who was keenly aware of the scramble for precedence. She wrote quickly to Nicholas that she was 'very sorry' for the man she calls her 'good uncle's death', but assures herself that she will be welcome to Beddington still. She hears that there will be a very good funeral, and asks if there are to be any women mourners: 'as I hear my Lady Ralegh is one, I hope you will not forget me as your oldest acquaintance and nearest of blood: others there be that either cannot, or are not, so near but by their husbands'. Nicholas was no doubt besieged by claims, but he quickly consolidated his position, and, unlike Arthur, he would fulfil his duties as a patriarch and produce a number of sons, the first batch with his first wife Mary, more with his second wife Susanna. Only time would tell whether these sons would be worthy of their newly coined Throckmorton-Carew name.

The handover was not entirely without friction. There is evidence that the Darcy side of Anne Throckmorton's family were not happy with the arrangement and there was a serious falling out, with Edward Darcy at loggerheads with Nicholas Throckmorton-Carew. But by 1611 Nicholas had emerged as the key player in the Throckmorton family, as was tacitly acknowledged in a diary entry made by older brother Arthur on 7 October of that year: 'I writ a congratulatory letter to my Lord of Pembroke for his being called to the Council. I sent it to N. Throckmorton for him to deliver.' Arthur recognizes that it is now Nicholas who has the access and influence at court, and he was not the only one to turn to Nicholas as an intermediary. A certain Matthew Bevill wrote from London, asking him to support his desire to 'attend' Sir Walter Ralegh and 'perform him the best service I could', indicating that Nicholas had a direct line to Sir Walter. Indeed, little Nick wrote to his 'Good brother' Sir Walter, reminding him that he was always ready 'to embrace any occasion to show my self respective of you and yours as nature has conjoined us together'. He ends his letter: 'remember me very kindly unto my sister, your wife, & also unto my brother William . . . Your assured loving brother, Nicholas Carew.' This is a rare moment in the historical record, one in which another hidden figure emerges from the shadows, William Throckmorton, Bess's oldest brother, now in his fifties. It appears that he may well have been in the care of the Raleghs, presumably in one of Bess's households, and again there is an indication of some kind of problem which meant that he could not be independent. Thus, while Arthur married off his daughters, and Nicholas became unto the manor born, Bess remained the prime carer not only for her much older and possibly disabled brother but for her two sons.

Separated in age by thirteen years, Bess's sons had very different needs. Wat's educational and social development was the most pressing concern during the early years of his father's imprisonment. Ralegh may have written about the theory of parenting (he advised his nephew John Gilbert to 'Use your fortune wisely in this hard world', having heard that John was 'spending vainly' and, worse, 'carousing'), but it was Bess who did the practice. As with Arthur and his daughter Mary, Bess needed to ensure a good marriage for her son: unlike Arthur and his daughter Mary, Bess also needed to ensure that her son received a good education. With regard to marriage, Wat's prospective union with the immensely wealthy Elizabeth Bassett was being threatened, because others were now claiming that she had been promised in marriage to their son. A legal process was thus executed on Lady Ralegh and John Shelbury, as representatives of Ralegh, over 'the true grantee' of Elizabeth Bassett's 'wardship and marriage which have several claimants'. When the case came to court, Shelbury was examined, but Bess 'would not appear or make answer'. This strategic refusal to engage in the case was highly successful in this instance, and the plaintiffs failed. Elizabeth Bassett remained an elusive prize, however, and the marriage plans were once again put on hold. All attention turned to Wat's education.

In the autumn of 1607 Wat, now nearly fourteen, went up to Corpus Christi College, Oxford, having previously been tutored while in the Tower by one of the Fellows of the College, Gilbert Hawthorn. Wat was developing into a challenging teenager, *avant la lettre*. Stern contemporaries may well have considered him the living proof of the damaging effects of the absence of firm patriarchal control: 'nothing undoeth children more than the fondness of parents when they are young.' Once at Oxford, Wat had increased opportunities to indulge his more wayward traits. One seventeenth-century writer, Anthony Wood, has him given to 'strange company and violent exercises', while another, who was at Oxford with him, described him as 'a handsome, lusty, stout fellow, very bold and apt to affront. Spake Latin very fluently, and was a notable disputant and courser, and would never be out of countenance nor baffled.' He could 'fight lustily and, one time of coursing, put a turd in the box and besmeared it about his antagonist's face'.

This unpleasant little anecdote reveals a lot about Wat and the very male academic culture at Oxford. The 'coursing' alluded to was not hunting, as might be expected, but an activity particular to Oxford and Cambridge: the opposing or challenging of a thesis in the university Schools. As Anthony Wood remembered, 'coursing in the time of Lent, that is the endeavours of one party to run down and confute another in disputations, did commonly end in blows'. Despite Wat's intelligence, wit and ability to speak Latin fluently (his tutors had done their work well), he still, for reasons that remain unclear, felt it necessary to resort to the use of excrement to 'win' his debate. Wat was far from alone in these kinds of activities, however. Most students at Oxford engaged in numerous pursuits alongside their studies, some forgoing their formal education completely: dancing, music-making, fencing and hunting were pursued with all the energy and resources of the irresponsible young and wealthy. Parents may have sent their sons to Oxford in the hope that they would network with the next generation of England's ruling elite, in the hope that their sons would mix with 'such sober and discreet young persons' that their 'Times of Leisure' would be passed 'with Innocence', but there seemed little chance that this would happen in Wat's case.

While it is only possible to speculate about the relationship between Bess and Wat, there is apparently more evidence for the relationship between father and son. It is, however, of a certain kind: public pronouncements on fatherhood. In general, as historians of the period have shown, Ralegh was deeply conventional, urging such routine behaviour as 'love of God and devotion to his service, prudence in speech and action, the avoidance of such dangers to youth as women, taverns and good fellowship' and giving advice on how to manage a wife and household.[9] Bearing in mind Sir Walter's ability to adopt different personae at will, perhaps these pronouncements demonstrate more of Ralegh's image of fatherhood than the reality. So, in a letter to Wat from these years, Sir Walter urges his 'dear and wellbeloved' son 'to awaken' himself 'to industry and rouse up thy spirits for the world'. Ralegh writes eloquently about his own readiness for death ('I have had my part in this world, and now must give place to fresh gamesters'), equally eloquently about the pleasures of life: 'All is vanity and weariness, yet such a weariness and vanity that we shall ever complain of it and love it for all that.' He warns Wat of the dangers that lie ahead of him: 'We are toiled and hazarded with tempests and storms that rise abroad. Public affairs are rocks, private conversations are whirlpools and quicksands.' Despite all this, Ralegh concludes, 'my son, take heart and courage to thee. Thy adventure lies in this troublesome bark.' These are superb words of fatherly advice, combining a sense of the pleasures and possibilities of life with a warning about the many dangers in the 'adventure' of life that lay ahead of young Wat.

There is absolutely no indication, however, that Wat ever read these words (let alone that he responded to them), since all the manuscript evidence suggests that this was a letter designed to be circulated as an example, indeed an exemplum, of the well-known genre of works detailing 'How to be a Good Father and Give Good Advice to your Son'. Ralegh also turned his undoubtedly skilful hand to poetry on the subject, again warning his son of the dangers that lay ahead of him. He cautions Wat that three dangerous things might come together, if his son was not careful, namely the wood, the weed and the wag: that is, the wood of the gallows, the hemp thread of the hangman's bag and 'the wag, my pretty knave, betokens thee'. In the astonishingly bleak final few lines of the poem, Ralegh advises Wat that, although now to the young man the tree appears green, the hemp is still growing in the fields, and the 'wag is wild', when the wood, the weed and the wag come together, 'it chokes the child'. 'God bless the child' the poem ends, but it is a dark, strange, fearful blessing.

Nothing, predictably, survives of Bess's advice to Wat. There were published books of advice written by mothers to sons, but these were quite small in number, despite being very well appreciated if they did appear. One of the most popular was *A Mother's Blessing* written by Dorothy Leigh: not many copies survive, despite many printings, probably because it was read literally to pieces. Typically, nothing is known about the life of its author, and Leigh herself expresses strong reservations about her own writing on the subject of motherhood. The 'usual custom of women', she writes to her sons, would be to 'exhort you by words and admonitions rather than by writing', which is presumably what Bess did. Leigh can only justify her move into writing with the defence that her sons' father is dead, and that she herself might die soon. Interestingly, this particular mother reacts against the prevalent attitude that severity was necessary in the bringing up of children. She desires, entreats and earnestly beseeches both her sons and the reader that they will have their 'children brought up with gentleness and patience'. Her argument is that if a child is treated harshly and perversely, he will in turn learn only harshness and perversity. Alongside published works such as *A Mother's Blessing*, letters also show that mothers maintained close relationships with their adolescent and, indeed, their young adult sons. Some of the anxieties expressed are poignantly timeless: one mother, writing to her son at Corpus Christi, Cambridge, worried about the effects of playing too much tennis in the summer ('If thou lovest my life let me entreat thee to be very careful of thyself for overheating thy blood') and then, in winter, worried about her son being too cold. She urges him to put 'somewhat about thy neck' and even to wear a cape: 'There can be no harm in keeping warm.'[10]

With Wat up at Oxford, Bess could turn her attention to her husband and younger son. In 1607 Bess looked back and said that she had expected her husband to be free during the previous summer. The year had come and gone, however; Wat had gone to university, and still Ralegh remained a prisoner. Both Bess and Sir Walter were learning to accept that his release was not up for negotiation: this may indeed have precipitated Bess's efforts to make sure that Wat would be given the freedom to go to Oxford, to 'go abroad' as the special warrant had it, and begin his own adult life. In terms of day-to-day life, not only was Ralegh not going to be released but there was a new regime at the Tower of London. The investigation into the Gunpowder Plot had thrown up many irregularities and lapses in security there, leading to the replacement of the lenient Sir George Harvey with a far more authoritarian Governor. An order came, in the King's name, that Bess 'resort to her house on Tower Hill or elsewhere with her women and her sons'. She was effectively banished from the Tower of London: allowed to visit from time to time, but no longer allowed to drive up in her coach. She was thus constrained and humiliated, and retreated to the house on Tower Hill to lick her wounds. At these moments in the historical record, there is a brief and tantalizingly unspecific glimpse of Bess's 'women'. There is no way of recovering who these women were, and it is still hard to find out very much, even in general terms, about the lives of servants and female retainers.

Despite the strict new regime, Ralegh had been emerging slowly out of his long-standing depression. In an early sign of recovery, he was reported as walking on the wall of the garden of the Tower of London 'in view of the people' and that 'he stares at them'. This 'indiscreet humour' indicated that the Ralegh pride was beginning to re-emerge. So did his desire for adventure. He still dreamed of a typically grandiose escape route from imprisonment and began touting, to anyone who would listen, his plan to return to Guiana and find the gold that had eluded him in 1595. He started pushing for this in 1607, supporting his request for permission to travel with a challenge: why on earth would he go so far, in his declining years, and 'live from my wife, children and friends in a strange country' unless there was indeed gold to be found? Bess may have asked the same question but in different terms.

No one listened very carefully to Ralegh's plans at this stage. Bess divided her time between Ralegh's quarters in the Tower of London, her rented house in London (probably on Tower Hill), her house in Surrey at Mitcham and her estate at Sherborne, although she presumably had very little spare money to continue the kinds of improvements to the estate begun in previous years. The most difficult times of the year may well have been holidays, such as Christmas, in part because over the twelve days of festivities household expenses doubled, and money was short, but also because the celebrations would have exposed the reality of Bess's disrupted life. Perhaps she still attempted to provide the traditional festival, with extra help being drafted in for the extra work, whether it were travelling up to London in adverse weather conditions to hire more plate and crockery, or scouring the 'vessels', or indeed turning the spit (Widow New earned eight pence for her two days of turning the spit at Beddington one Christmas). The great households of England would send gifts to each other, the servants who brought the gifts (Mistress Quarles's man with anchovies, Nicholas Coke's maid with a pig, Roger Lambert's son for two fat capons, goes the account book at Beddington) rewarded with a few pence. Did these social rituals continue in the Tower? Or at Sherborne without its master? It was not a conventional life, but, with Wat at Oxford and Carew living with her and being tutored at home, it had a kind of precarious stability to it.

This precarious stability was to be rudely disrupted the following year. To understand the chain of events, it is necessary to understand the personality and predilections of King James. The King was bisexual, functioning on a public level as a heterosexual husband and father (he had produced two sons, Henry and Charles, as well as a marriageable daughter, the Princess Elizabeth), but preferring the company of young men, socially, sexually and, most significantly, politically. A historian of sexuality points out the relative tolerance toward homoerotic *private* practice in the Renaissance and that homosexuality 'was neither a separate category of sexuality nor the basis for individual identity that it later became; instead it was understood as one of

187

several forms of debauchery that comprised the disorder in sexual relations that could break out anywhere'.[11] Homoeroticism was specifically condemned because it was understood as most contrary to procreative sex within marriage, but of course James had done his duty in this respect. It was, however, not singled out among the list of allegedly unnatural practices that preoccupied contemporaries: Robert Burton, in his monumental and fascinating prose masterpiece, *The Anatomy of Melancholy*, places sex between men alongside numerous other practices, such as whipping, necrophilia, sex between women, not to mention sex with horses. James's homosexuality was viewed by his contemporaries as a weakness, not necessarily because of its inherent sinfulness but because his actions demonstrated capitulation to his own lust: this in turn was an expression of a 'feminine' lack of self-control, regardless of the desired object of the lust. The same kinds of criticisms had, of course, been levelled at Queen Elizabeth, in the heated debates about her feelings towards men such as the Earl of Leicester or Ralegh himself. The political ramifications of this allegedly 'feminine' lack of self-control was the same for both princes: both James and Elizabeth raised their favourites swiftly to positions of power and wealth.

In this political climate, Bess was both the wrong gender and the wrong age to make any real impact on James. She was also in the wrong faction at court. The Howard family was in the ascendant, and they had their protégé ready for James's attention. Young Robert Carr was their man ('straight-limbed, well-favoured, strong-shouldered and smooth-faced'), and James found him irresistible.

A crisis quickly emerged. James, unable to deny Carr anything, wanted to give him a country estate. Carr wanted Sherborne. At first there were hopes that Robert Cecil might be able to use his power to protect Bess: there was talk that he might yet 'deal extraordinarily well with Sir Walter Ralegh and his'. The King moved to survey the Sherborne property, as the first step to taking it over, and there is evidence that the ever loyal Lawrence Keymis attempted to stall the surveyors in order to buy time. But by the Christmas season of 1608–9, time was running out. Still Bess worked tirelessly to try to keep her beloved, and valuable, Sherborne: the diarist John Chamberlain noted, on 10 January 1609, that 'the Lady Raleigh hath been an importunate suitor all these holy-days in her husband's behalf'. Chamberlain adjudged, however, that 'yet it is past recall'. King James had found that the scribe who had prepared the trust documents in the closing months of Queen Elizabeth's reign had miscopied one word, thus making the deed void. As Carew Ralegh, Bess's son, complained much, much later, the King took away Sherborne 'for want of a word'.

When Bess realized that the situation was indeed 'past recall', and that the King would not be halted in his attempt to give Sherborne to his lover Carr, she then moved to limit the damage and to salvage something for herself. There was no way she was going to let the King take Sherborne 'for want of a word' without some kind of compensation. The deal she eventually achieved testifies to her persistence. In the earliest negotiations, a sum of two thousand pounds was mentioned as compensation for the loss of the estate. At a mid-way stage, the figure of four thousand pounds was being mentioned. Bess would maintain control of one 'fee farm' bestowed on her husband for life, which would provide her and her children a regular income. In an interesting move at this stage of the negotiations, Bess petitioned for the 'fee farm' not to return to the King on Ralegh's death but to be allowed to stay in the Ralegh family: would the King 'allow those poor harmless children to enjoy' the property? This is one of the first indications that as the years went by, Bess was becoming more and more intent on providing some kind of inheritance for her children. Under law, they could inherit nothing by dint of their father's attainder: his blood was irrevocably tainted. This was intolerable, and somehow, with her children in tow and highly visible, Bess made it direct to the King. She demanded to know what James was going to do for her 'poor harmless children'. Her advice to the King was that he should imitate 'the most just and merciful God, who though he punished the fathers yet he gave the land to the guileless and innocent children'. Bess is attempting to flatter and coerce James, calling on all the authority she had as a mother (and, perhaps significantly, distancing herself and her children from her husband). Under pressure from Bess, a beleaguered King James was only too happy to sign the vital document that stated that although, by 'the rigour of law', the fee farm was truly the King's, nevertheless 'all our title and interest may be passed over unto his wife and children, that we be no more troubled with their pitiful cries and complaints for that business'.

Ralegh heard from Bess about the success of the 'cries and complaints' but he was increasingly disconcerted by the emergence of her new authority. Sir Walter ruefully acknowledges that he 'has no property at all in the land in question' and that the King's 'merciful grants both of the land and leases are to the use of my wife and for the present relief of my children, and not to me'. Bess and Wat 'also have divers other leases in their own names', and Ralegh remains bitterly aware that his only interest in all this is 'as a husband during my wife's life'. Worse still, 'there is left in me no other power than my persuasion only, who am but a dead husband to the one and a dead father to the other'. Ironically, the protracted legal battles over Sherborne had 'made them know much of their own strength', and therefore Ralegh is anxious that 'it will not now be easy for me to order them concerning their whole livelihood and estates'. Indeed, Bess had proved remarkably successful in her negotiations for compensation for Sherborne. Astonishingly, by the time the final agreement was drawn up, the original lump sum had quadrupled. Bess would receive eight thousand pounds and an annuity from the Crown of four hundred pounds: even Ralegh admitted that this was 'good usage' on the part of the King. But Sherborne was gone.

A year on, however, the compensation started coming in. First, on 23 December 1609 the eight thousand pounds came from the King, ostensibly to Lawrence Keymis but actually to Bess. Then, on 12 January 1610 Bess received a payment of a hundred and two pounds, one shilling and eight pence for the interest and forbearance of five thousand pounds for interest and estate of the manor of Sherborne, conveyed and passed over unto His Majesty. A few days later, the annuity was drawn up: four hundred pounds per annum, to be granted in trust to Sir Francis Darcy (Bess's maternal uncle) and Sir Nicholas Throckmorton (her younger brother), 'during the life of Elizabeth, Lady Ralegh'. Wat received four hundred pounds for life after Bess's death. Interestingly, a few weeks later, when both the Sherborne process and the annuity were finalized, the trustees had changed: the moneys were now to be paid to Thomas Harriot, John Shelbury and Lawrence Keymis. It is possible that Bess was increasingly comfortable working with male friends (Harriot, Keymis and Shelbury had been long-standing supporters of hers) rather than with her male family members, who could always claim their 'natural' rights over her. She now had the regular income of the annuity, and the lump sum of eight thousand pounds to invest.

A further sign of the shifting balance in the relationship between Bess and her husband came in October 1611. Earlier that year, Ralegh had been punished with a period of solitary confinement, and it was he who begged for Bess to be allowed back to live with him in the Tower. After all, he argued, she had been with him for the six years last past and, 'she being now divided from me and thereby, to my great impoverishing, I am driven to keep two houses' (presumably the second house was the one on Tower Hill). He thus humbly desires that his wife 'may live with me in this unsavoury place'. Behind the rhetoric of parsimony there seems to be a great need to have Bess with him: Ralegh himself was perhaps only partially aware of how dependent he had become on Bess. She was allowed to return, it seems, but there is no evidence that the house on Tower Hill was abandoned.

Over these years, Bess continued to gain experience of the legal world. One of the problems with receiving compensation for the loss of Sherborne was that it encouraged others to sue for debts. The first to crawl out of the woodwork was one of Ralegh's half-brothers, Adrian Gilbert. In 1610 he sued for the huge sum of four thousand, six hundred and fifty-three pounds, a figure he had calculated by going back nearly thirty years to Sir Walter's earliest days at court (when Gilbert apparently lent him ten pounds) but also including a claim for seven hundred pounds that Gilbert claimed to have spent on the Sherborne improvements. Bess contested the case in the Court of Chancery, represented, as ever, by John Shelbury. The judge threw out Gilbert's claim primarily because it was deemed to be 'very old and uncertain' and the debts were set down 'upon old reckoning'. Despite this positive outcome for Bess, the case took three years to progress through the courts, and she should probably have learned a lesson from its speed. But she was clearly someone who could not resist a legal battle, and at the same time that the Gilbert case was dragging on, she instructed John Shelbury and Robert Smith to sue William Sanderson for the return of a massive sixty thousand pounds.

Sanderson was the man with whom Bess had drawn up financial agreements at the start of the 1595 Guiana expedition, and for some reason she believed he owed her this vast sum of money. Sanderson, perhaps understandably, sued Shelbury and Smith in return. This particular fight would drag on for decades, quite literally: the next generation of Raleghs and Sandersons would still be flinging accusations at each other, long after their parents' deaths. Sanderson Senior's fate is shrouded in mystery. It was later claimed that he died in prison as a debtor, but his son claimed that this was untrue and that Sanderson and his wife had been best of friends with Bess and Sir Walter and 'were very often, in visits of civility, and respect to each other' at the Tower, even the night before Ralegh was executed. Bess never received 'her' sixty thousand pounds, but her taste for law would continue throughout her life.

Ralegh, meanwhile, had new hopes for release. He had a new prince to seduce with his undoubtedly powerful rhetoric, the young Prince Henry who was seeking to define himself, in no uncertain terms, against his father, King James. Where James was *rex pacificus*, Henry loved all things military. Where James explored the subtleties of religious and philosophical debate, Henry saw himself as a straightforward, even simplistic, red-hot Protestant warrior, urging the old agenda that England should aid their beleaguered fellow Protestants of Europe. A good way for Henry to challenge his father's authority was to show support for the man he had imprisoned and hated with a vengeance. So Ralegh wrote tracts urging an aggressive policy against Spain, or explaining the true art of building warships, and began his monumental *History of the World*, all with the young Prince in mind as a reader. His writing did not do him much good, however. Robert Cecil and Henry Howard, Earl of Northampton, still implacable enemies to him, were delighted to see that Sir Walter was as 'bold, proud and passionate as ever' and particularly pleased that his 'publication' had 'won little ground'. This may refer either to the registration with the censors of *History of the World* or, in the old sense of publication (simply making something public, circulating it), it could refer to the pieces of advice that Ralegh had been presenting to the young Henry, Prince of Wales.

Ralegh's primary aim remained to gain release, and he did not care where to. One plan was to travel across the Atlantic, perhaps to Virginia. He was quite happy to offer up Bess's life for this ambition. In a letter to Queen Anne, probably written early in 1610, he makes the following grand claim, rediscovering the overblown style that had worked in the old days (sometimes at least) with Queen Elizabeth. Ralegh asserts that, if he went not by a day set, he would forfeit his 'life and estate, that I would leave my wife and two sons pledges for my faith, and that my wife shall yield herself to death if I perform not my duty to the king'. Ralegh also claims that the sailors can 'cast' him 'into the sea', but again it would be interesting to find out precisely how Bess viewed her prospective role as one of the sacrificial victims in this scenario.

Ralegh's pursuit of Queen Anne's favour probably relied on Bess's own influence with the Queen. Anne had not had an easy time of it as Queen of England. Increasingly estranged from her husband, invariably having to communicate with him via his male favourites, she also presided over a court that had its own scandals. Even in the earliest months of her reign, one of the masques in her honour degenerated swiftly into debauchery and, as Anne Clifford remembered it, 'all the Ladies about the Court had gotten such ill names that it was grown a scandalous place, & the Queen herself was much fallen from her former greatness & reputation she had in the world'. What evidence there is suggests that Queen Anne offered Bess what support she could. Perhaps the two women, with their teenage sons and their differently dysfunctional marriages, found experiences in common. It is perhaps no coincidence that Prince Henry's alleged visits to Ralegh in the Tower were in the company of his mother, who may have been quite as interested in the case of Lady Ralegh as she was in that of Sir Walter.

The fates of their two sons, young Wat Ralegh and Henry Stuart, were, however, to be very different. As Wat came to the end of his studies at Oxford, Bess planned for him to complete his gentlemanly education with a tour of Europe, along the lines taken by her brother Arthur decades earlier. John Donne, Bess's brother-in-law and a man with whom she would become increasingly close, may have advised. He had himself travelled widely, most recently on the Continent with his patrons, the Drury family, in the winter of 1611. If Wat was to be sent to Europe, then he needed a companion to supervise and support him. The choice of companion for Wat, already something of a rebel, was perhaps not the wisest. The Raleghs chose Ben Jonson. 'Robust, exuberant and learned', Jonson had emerged from a distinctly non-aristocratic background to become the leading court dramatist of his generation. Jonson's stepfather, whom his mother married shortly after his birth, was a bricklayer, and young Ben followed him into the trade, but only after a superb education at Westminster School. Education and bricklaying aside, Jonson had an extremely wild youth. Typical of his behaviour was the incident when he, while fighting in the Netherlands, challenged a Spanish soldier to single combat in the no man's land between the two armies, killed him and stripped him of his arms and armour all in front of a large audience. He did not calm down in adulthood. Later, in 1598, he murdered the actor Gabriel Spencer, a crime for which he escaped punishment by pleading 'benefit of clergy' (a law that allowed literate criminals a second chance, his education standing him in good stead in this crisis). While in prison, he converted to Catholicism: thus he emerged from prison 'a branded, dispossessed Roman Catholic'. Jonson's track record with women was just as volatile. He had a stormy marriage to one Anne Lewis, which did not stop him from being extremely promiscuous. In 1610 two women, neither married to Jonson, had children for whom he was recorded as the father. This brilliant, violent, licentious man was the one chosen by the Raleghs to escort young Wat around the capital cities of Europe.

Jonson took on the job because, having been one of the most successful – possibly *the* most successful – playwrights of his generation, things by 1611 were not going well for him. It was not entirely that his skills as a playwright were in decline, although some were saying so. More important, King James's financial crisis was becoming more and more acute, and there was simply not enough money to pay for the elaborate court masques that Jonson had been so efficient in churning out over the preceding years.

So in March 1612 the unlikely duo set off for France, a country riven by years of religious wars. Their first stop was Paris, where they were to hear one of Wat's old tutors from Oxford, Daniel Featley, take part in an academic dispute about the Real Presence. Whether Christ was actually present in the bread and wine of Communion was, of course, the crux of the ongoing fight between Catholics and Protestants. Wat, who should really have known better, took the idea of the Real Presence and ran with it, embarking on an escapade deeply offensive to the Catholic majority in Paris. His first action (probably not a difficult one) was to make his governor, Ben Jonson, 'to be drunken, and dead drunk, so that he knew not where he was'. Wat then laid him flat out on a cart, which was then drawn by labourers through the streets of Paris 'at every corner showing them his governor laid out, and telling them, that was a more lively image of the crucifix than any they had'. Wat and Ben beat a hasty retreat from Paris after this episode, and continued on their travels. What is perhaps surprising is that Jonson did not give up the job then and there. Then again, he himself, on his reconversion to Anglicanism the previous year, had attended Communion and drunk the entire chalice of wine: he was no stranger to provocative stunts.

Biographers have been somewhat inconsistent in their attitude towards young Wat. On the one hand, they have been only too aware of his rebelliousness, and on the other, they have admired his spirit. Wat's wildness has been blamed on Bess's indulgence. For example, lacking 'something of his father's cultivated style', Wat, 'with his mother's support', 'played off his tutors one against another and was both unruly and given to practical jokes'. Wat had been 'ungoverned' and was now 'ungovernable'.[13] This kind of verdict is based on Jonson's own reminiscences of the European tour, when he laughed at the memories of the Parisian episode and remembered that 'young Ralegh's mother delighted much' at the 'sport': Bess had said that Wat's 'father young was so inclined'. Jonson also recalled that Sir Walter, 'the father', 'abhorred' his son's behaviour. Without the primary evidence, it remains extremely difficult to assess the relationship between Wat and his mother: all that can be asserted is that it must have been a lively one between two extremely forceful and ebullient individuals.

In April 1613, and just over a year into their travels, Wat and Ben were in Antwerp and skint. Begging letters failed to remedy the situation, and a month or so later Wat was back in England with Bess. As for Ben and Wat, as Isaac Walton suggested later in the seventeenth century, 'they parted I think not in cold blood'. Wat was now almost twenty years old: his gentlemanly education – tutors, Oxford, the Grand Tour – completed.

It was a changed country on his return. For, while Wat drank his way round northern Europe, two deaths, of one old man and one tragically young man, had altered the political landscape in England. On 6 November 1612 Prince Henry died, and with him one of Ralegh's hopes for release, whether real or imagined. Apparently, Henry went for a swim in the Thames, and shortly after became feverish. Every attempt to cure him failed: his mother, Queen Anne, insisted that one of Ralegh's medicines be given to her son. Sir Walter's famous cordial restored the Prince for a short time, but nothing was going to save him. Anne withdrew completely from public life, devastated by the sudden loss. Four months after Henry's death, the Venetian ambassador noted that 'she cannot bear to have it mentioned; nor does she ever recall it without abundant tears and sighs'. Even four years on, Anne could not bear to go to the invest-iture of Henry's younger brother Charles as Prince of Wales in November 1616. The nation went into paroxysms of mourning for their young future King. Fewer tears were shed for the other political figure to die this year. Robert Cecil finally succumbed to the various illnesses that had plagued his life. His end was a sad and painful one, his body tormented by weeping, probably cancerous, tumours. In the spring of 1612, he had 'an ague, a deflation of rheum upon his stomach' and difficulty breathing. It was no surprise that he was 'melancholy and heavy-spirited', but he still made one last effort to take the waters at Bath. In April the waters appeared to 'promise a cure', but it was a false hope. He fell back into illness and decided to leave Bath. On 21 May he and his supporters started on the journey back to London, but Cecil would die three days later, having reached only Marlborough. His death, as he lay attended by Dr Poe, Ralegh's sometime doctor in the Tower, was in the end peaceful: 'though sinking rapidly, he insisted on standing erect with the aid of crutches, while prayers were being offered . . . then, lying with his head on two pillows and his body in a swing, [he] called for Dr Poe's hand, which he gripped hard, when his eyes began to settle, and he sank down without a groan, sigh, or struggle'. His long struggle to reform the economic basis of the monarchy had failed. As for his own estate, he died leaving debts of thirty thousand pounds, enforcing the sale of much of his land and property. As another small, stooped, pain-racked man, Alexander Pope, wrote many years later of his own condition, Robert Cecil was finally released from this 'long disease', his life.

With Henry and Cecil dead, the way was clear for Robert Carr and his supporters. As Simon Schama notes, this was 'a period when the power of the Howard clan was at its peak, and when the King found it virtually impossible to deny Carr anything, not even a wife, for even if the King were a sexually active gay, he seemed completely without jealousy where the heterosexual needs of his young protégés were concerned.'[14] The only problem was that the wife that Carr wanted happened to be married to someone else. She was Frances Howard, the young Countess of Essex, and, ignoring her inconvenient husband's existence, she and Carr began a passionate affair. To marry, however, meant extricating Frances from her marriage to the Earl of Essex. The best strategy seemed to be to seek an annulment on the grounds that Essex was impotent, that the marriage had not been consummated, and that Frances was a virgin: all three of these extremely contentious claims had to be proved, and the scandal-mongers had a field day as the evidence was collected and presented. Their success was ensured by the King's support, and on 3 November Robert Carr was created Earl of Somerset by his loving King, and on 26 December, Lady Essex's marriage having been annulled, the Lady Frances Howard married Carr. Their marriage was celebrated with a flurry of masques from, among others, the newly returned Ben Jonson.

The Howards and their protégé Carr continued to dominate the political world, leaving little hope for such as Bess Ralegh. The court became increasingly characterized by insolvency, sleaze and violence. John Digby (later first Earl of Bristol) may have exposed the scandal that pensions were being paid to courtiers by Spain, but nothing was done to stop the process. Edward Sackville, fourth Earl of Dorset, killed a man in a duel in August 1613, probably over a quarrel concerning Sackville's illicit liaison with Venetia Stanley. Unable to solve his financial problems, and unwilling to prevent the endemic corruption, the King did at least attempt to get to grips with the problem of duelling. A proclamation was issued in February 1614 against the practice, which was re-branded as wilful murder by *rex pacificus* James.

Of course, Wat being Wat, a proclamation against duelling was merely an incitement to do just that. In an echo of his father's exploits in the 1580s, Wat headed to the Netherlands to fight. There is a glimpse here of the undoubted pressure on Wat, living always in the shadow of his renowned father, who had spent his youth in a culture where duelling was not just accepted but almost required, and his adulthood leading military expeditions against the enemies of England. Sir Walter may have been 'legally dead' to Wat, but his legendary status cast a longer shadow over his son with each year of his imprisonment. Whatever Wat's motivations, he was always ready to prove himself in a fight. His opponent in the Netherlands was a gentleman in the service of Lord Thomas Howard, Earl of Suffolk: it can be no coincidence that Wat was taking on someone from the Howard faction. They may well have been fighting over Wat's ambitions with regard to Elizabeth Bassett, the wealthy heiress he had been lined up to marry in the days of his father's success. Elizabeth would marry Lord Thomas Howard's son, and then, on his death, William Cavendish, Duke of Newcastle. She never did become Wat's wife.

Sir Henry Wotton, great friend to John Donne, found out about the two young men's plans and sought to stop the duel. Young Wat was to be hauled up in front of the authorities, but Wotton thinks that this 'will rather defer than prevent this evil, for the difference between them is irreconcilable, Jay having some four or five months since been dangerously hurt by the other in a private chamber, and Ralegh being so far from avoiding the challenge, that (it is thought) he hath only gotten leave to travel for this purpose'. In the end, Sir John Throckmorton, the governor at Flushing, was called in to gather up Wat and send him back to England: perhaps Bess called in a family favour. Wat, as Wotton predicted, was not put off, however, and the following year he was duelling again. This time he wounded one Robert Finet, and then made a hasty retreat to the Netherlands where he was received by Maurice, Prince of Orange.

It did not take long for the shine to wear off the apparent victory of the Carr/Howard alliance. Early in 1615 James became attracted to, and then involved with, a new young man, George Villiers. Carr was soon on the way out. Prompted by someone who wished to cause trouble for him, the Governor of the Tower wrote to the King mentioning that he might just have evidence of a particularly nasty murder connected with the union of Robert Carr and Frances Howard. Sir Thomas Overbury, who had once been a close friend of Carr, had been sent to the Tower by the King in the midst of the negotiations for the Carr/Howard marriage. There, he vomited for three days and was then found dead. The Governor of the Tower now argued that Overbury had been poisoned in order to silence him, and that Carr and Howard were implicated, as was Francis's father, Lord Thomas Howard, Earl of Suffolk. Robert Carr and the Howard family were in deep trouble. Villiers, backed by the old-style Protestant war party, was in the ascendant at last.

7

'God In Mercy Look On Us':
Journey's End

The old-style Protestant war party were now in the ascendant, and their figurehead was the young, handsome and ambitious George Villiers. His rise may have marked a crucial change in the political landscape, but, for Bess, approaching her fiftieth birthday in 1615, life was set in a familiar and reasonably secure pattern, always excepting the latest news about Wat. Well-earned security and calm for Bess, was, however, terrifying stagnancy for Sir Walter. His prison life was killing him slowly, and he felt he must get out at any cost. The crucial challenge was to influence James, and, with the King in grave financial difficulties, influencing James meant offering him money. As even the King recognized, favourites may come and go, but, in his own words, the 'only disease and consumption' that could possibly endanger him was 'this eating canker of want'. So, once again, Ralegh argued that he could lead an expedition to South America and bring back the gold he had failed to find twenty years before. Sir Walter's case was helped by the arrival in the Tower of Robert Carr and Frances Howard: at court George Villiers was pre-eminent, supported by all those who had opposed the Howard faction for much of the previous decade, and all those who itched for a return to the glory days of the 1580s and 1590s.

Many years later, Carew Ralegh reminisced that his father's release was achieved through bribing two eminent courtiers, Sir William St Johns and Sir Edward Villiers (half-brother to George) to the tune of fifteen hundred pounds paid to each. Looking back, Carew believed that if Ralegh had paid seven hundred pounds more he would have received a full pardon and liberty not to go on his voyage. If Carew's version of events is correct, then once again the financial solution (presumably set up by Bess, since she was the financial manager at this stage) went only halfway to solving the problem and came up against the brick wall of Ralegh's ambition and pride. Ralegh may have actually wanted to go on the voyage to Guiana, to prove the sceptics wrong, to live again the life of the adventurer. Others, eager to provoke war with Spain, supported the initiative: the 'Guiana scheme was an excellent weapon for their purposes. It mattered little to them whether a cargo of gold was secured or not; the value of the project lay in the heavy odds which it offered of provoking war. Ralegh might sink or swim, but nothing was better calculated to wreck Anglo-Spanish amity than a pitched battle on the banks of the Orinoco.'[1] It is equally probable, however, that the voyage, and its promise of gold, were the crucial part of the deal with James: as the great historian of this period, S. R. Gardiner, wrote: 'For James there was to be everything to gain. For Ralegh there was to be everything to lose.'[2]

So, on 19 March 1616 Ralegh was 'fully enlarged and delivered' from the Tower of London. He was allowed to 'go abroad', but 'under charge of a keeper', in order to make provision for the proposed voyage to South America. Ralegh, at the time, appeared to believe that he had implicitly been pardoned, because James provided him with a Commission under the Great Seal. Ralegh knew who to thank for his deliverance, writing effusively to George Villiers, who by 'his mediation' had put him 'again in the world'. Bess had been sceptical about Ralegh's quest for El Dorado back in 1595, and desperately anxious for his safe return, so what must she have thought about a second trip in 1616, with Ralegh in his early sixties, weakened by years in the Tower and dangerously out of touch with the real world?

It was a changed world from the one that Ralegh had left in 1603. For a start his son had grown up. An infamous anecdote, recounted by Aubrey later in the century, may not be verifiable but is certainly plausible and can be dated to these months: it has a certain piquancy if Ralegh's recent release from the Tower is factored in to the story. As Aubrey has it:

> Sir Walter Ralegh being invited to dinner to some great person where his son was to go with him, he said to his son: 'Thou art expected to-day at dinner to go along with me, but thou art such a quarrelsome, affronting —, that I am ashamed to have such a bear in my company.

Wat duly 'humbled himself' to Sir Walter and promised to behave very well. It came to the dinner. Wat

> sat next to his father and was very demure at least half dinner time. Then said he, 'I, this morning, not having the fear of God before my eyes but by the instigation of the devil went to a whore. I was very eager of her, kissed her and embraced her, and went to enjoy her, but she thrust me from her and vowed I should not "For your father lay with me but an hour ago".' Sir Walter being so strangely surprised and put out of his countenance at so great a table, gives his son a damned blow over the face. His son, as rude as he was, would not strike his father.

Instead, Wat turned to the gentleman on his other side, hit him in the face and instructed him to pass it on, claiming ''twill come to my father anon'. Meanwhile, on the stage on the South Bank, Ben Jonson offered his own satiric vision of the London of 1616 in his play *The Devil Is an Ass*. The increasingly entrepreneurial, capitalist and hedonistic city life around him is ruthlessly parodied. Jonson mocked schemes to make wine out of raisins or blackberries ('as true a wine as the wines of France'), recipes for skin-cream ('Madam, you take your hen, Plume it, and skin it, cleanse it o' the innards . . . add to four ounces of carmuacins, pipitas, soap of Cyprus . . . three drops preserves from wrinkles, warts, spots, moles, Blemish or sun-burnings') and 'the project of the forks', 'the laudable use of forks' which ought to be brought into 'custom here, as they are in Italy, to the sparing of napkins'. Jonson's London, as ever, was peopled by 'projectors' on the

make, and by young men, their clothes 'all at pawn', cadging money
so that they can carry on consuming

> Pheasant and godwit, here in London! Haunting
> The Globes and the Mermaids! Wedging in with lords
> Still at the table! And affecting lechery
> In velvet!

The life of the London young was exposed as an empty charade by
Jonson. A couple of months after Sir Walter's release from the Tower,
Lady Anne Clifford noted that Wat Ralegh and his 'crew' were up to
no good down on the South Coast: 'At this great meeting at Lewes,
my Lord Compton, my Lord Mordaunt, Tom Nevil, Jo Herbert & all
that crew with Wat Raleigh, Jack Lewice, and a multitude of such
company where there. There was Bowling, Bull baiting, Cards & dice
with such sports to Entertain the time.'[3] Some of these young men
would come on the Guiana voyage, their first chance to show their
mettle on a real expedition, not just in 'sport'. Most significant, Wat
(still out of control) was going along for the ride, captaining his own
ship for the first time.

Whatever Bess may have thought of Ralegh's plans she was loyal to
her husband's dream of South American gold. She threw herself into
organizing the expedition. Ralegh apparently used the lump sum
received in compensation for Sherborne, which he describes as his
wife's eight thousand pounds, to finance his final expedition, although
he admits that he had 'persuaded' his wife, which suggests she may
have had reservations. The eight thousand quickly went: when that
was spent he persuaded 'my wife to sell her house at Mitcham'.
Ralegh's primary aim was, ostensibly, to restore 'my wife and children
their states they had lost', but his method appeared to be to persuade
Bess to venture everything she had worked for during the thirteen
years of his imprisonment. Once she was committed, however, Bess
threw herself into further fund-raising, calling on even the most
obscure relatives, such as the Powis Herbert family, for cash.

Ralegh busied himself spending the money Bess had raised, com-
missioning, on 27 March 1616, Phineas Pett to build a ship of 500
tons for the voyage. Just before the voyage sailed, the final blow to
Bess's hopes of recovering Sherborne came: she had entertained hopes

that, with the fall of Robert Carr, the estate, being returned to the Crown, might yet return to the Ralegh family. But on 17 November 1616, King James found a willing and suitable buyer for Sherborne, Sir John Digby, a rising courtier who had been made a Privy Counsellor earlier in the year. He paid ten thousand pounds for Sherborne, and his descendants are still there. The King had been planning on giving it to George Villiers, but the money from Digby was very, very welcome, and Villiers was satisfied with the gift of five manors in five different counties instead.

What did Bess have to lose now? The winter was spent in London, Bess and Sir Walter living in a house in King Street, or Whitehall as it is now known. The preparation of Ralegh's fleet was watched with interest by the citizens of London and by wary foreign ambassadors. On 16 December 1616 Ralegh's aptly named new boat, *The Destiny*, was launched and these winter months were spent drumming up support for the adventure. Gifts of wine and spirits came in, as did small sums of money from speculators: three hundred pounds from Sir Arthur Ingram, thirty-two gallons of choice aquavitae 'to be presented to Sir Walter Raleigh for his Guiana voyage' from the Earl of Cork, shares of a 'hundred pounds ventured respectively by Richard Calthorp, Thomas Wade and William Gilby, gentlemen of London'. All hoped to get a return on their investments: all hoped that the Guiana gold was really just waiting for Ralegh to find it.

At last the voyage got under way. Seven ships sailed from the Thames, to be joined by three pinnaces at Plymouth and a further four larger ships once they were at sea. All together, a thousand men embarked on the search for El Dorado's gold. But it was a fleet of ramshackle ships and a crew made up of the 'scum of the earth' (as Ralegh would generously describe them). As early as the Thames Estuary there was a riot, when local people 'drove many of Sir Walter's men into the mud of the river', and once in the Atlantic one captain reported 'continual quarrels and fighting amongst our own company with many dangerous hurts'. Bess was left with forty-five pieces of gold and little else. Even this money was quickly called upon when one of the boats returned to London, under the command of Captain John Pennington, sent to get money for bread from Bess. Throughout the voyage, she was a focus for communications from all parties:

ship captains wrote to her, relying on her to convey information, while Sir Walter sent letters to his few powerful supporters via his wife.

One of Bess's letters from this time touches on the everyday, practical issues that still needed to be resolved during these months. Bess had to negotiate the use of horses with her brother, Nicholas, knowing that she will need horses 'to fetch me to London the week after Michaelmas': 'for I must have four mares to drag me home, the ways in this country are so bad, either mine or yours which you will.' Travelling in late autumn through the country roads of England may not have been as demanding as travelling by ship across the Atlantic, but it posed its own challenges. Bess does not say where she is staying (obviously the house at Mitcham was lost to her), but she does say that she is 'here in a very pleasant place as may be, and much made of: yet I must come home afore the term'.

'Home', mentioned twice in this letter, is London. It appears that Bess now moved to a house in Broad Street in the City of London. Her neighbours included the Talbot family, whose London house was also in Broad Street, and Sir William Powlet, the Lord Treasurer. Down the road, the new Merchant Taylors' Hall characterized the up-and-coming nature of the neighbourhood, but this was no Durham House on the Strand, no Sherborne with its vast estate. Instead, Broad Street ran 'down to the little Conduit, called the pissing Conduit', while nearby at 'Skalding Wike' the poulterers scalded the poultry and the air was thick with the smells of inner-city life. But Broad Street was also at the heart of the financial City, and, with both her husband and elder son away at sea, Bess, typically, moved into action on her own behalf. She was in contact at this time with Lady Anne Clifford, who had visited Bess in the Tower during the last months of imprisonment in early 1616, and then stayed in touch. Lady Anne had had her own struggles for financial independence, and she and Bess may well have exchanged thoughts on the subject. Bess's concern was to gain a regular income for herself: the four-hundred-pound annuity from the Exchequer. She wrote to one of the King's ministers, Sir Julius Caesar.

> May it please you to call to mind that when my husband's land was
> taken away from him [. . .] it then pleased the King's Majesty to grant

his Patents to me, and after me to my eldest son [. . .] I then understanding the payments were slow, I desired a covenant of the Lords for performance of that payment, which I had, under their hands and seals, as your Honour knoweth [. . .], being agreeable to His Majesties express commandment that I should receive my payment without molestation or delay [. . .] I have not received one penny from the Exchequer since Sir Walter went.

This is a remarkably assertive letter. Bess is ostensibly extremely confident (writing 'I make no doubt but you will see me satisfied and relieved in this my just desire') and she scores a number of incisive points against various powerful figures. She notes that of the four original men who signed the 'patent' for the payment of the annuity, two have 'performed their covenant with death' (that is, Robert Cecil and the Earl of Northampton), and the other 'being not in case to perform any covenant', a biting allusion to Robert Carr's current imprisonment in the Tower of London. Her barely suppressed bitterness aside, Bess may have felt it would be wise to set up the annuity payments before Ralegh returned from Guiana, just in case, once again, there was crisis in her husband's life.

As Bess pushed for regular annuity payments, Ralegh's fleet made its way towards Guiana's gold, and salvation. The fleet stopped off in Ireland for a few weeks, and Ralegh stayed with Robert Boyle, Earl of Cork, the man who had bought Ralegh's own Irish estates back in the last months of Queen Elizabeth's reign. The conversations and events of this visit would return to haunt Bess years later, but now, in the summer of 1617, these few weeks in southern Ireland offered Ralegh a wonderful antidote to the years of imprisonment in the Tower, days of eating, drinking, business deals and good conversation. When, in late August, the fleet left Ireland with the winds finally propitious for the Atlantic crossing, Sir Walter and Boyle were the best of friends.

Bess waited anxiously for news, writing to her brother Nicholas in the first week of September that 'If you hear any certain news of sir Walter I pray write to me of it'. Even as she writes this request to Nicholas she adds, delightedly: 'I have even now received letters from Sir Walter. He and all his company is well, god be thanked: and was in the ocean when he writ to me.' Bess's love and loyalty towards Sir

Walter, and her anxiety for her son, emerge clearly in this touching letter to her brother, which ends with her prayer 'God bless them'.

This was, however, the last piece of good news for a long time. Another letter followed that of early September. Written in November, it may have been delivered to Bess a month or more later. She read that Ralegh, now in Cayenne, had met up with Harry, the tribal chief, or *cacique*, who had been his companion/servant in the Tower for two years. Sir Walter was gratified at his reception, after his long years of imprisonment, humiliation and legal death in England: 'to tell you that I might be here King of the Indians were a vanity; but my name hath lived among them. There they feed me with fresh meat, and all that country yields; all offer to obey me.' His name had indeed lived among them, in part because the exchange of names was an important token of alliance, and different forms of Ralegh's name (Gualtero, Waterali) were current in the Orinoco region. Yet the fantasy of obedience was indeed a 'vanity' despite the disclaimer. The reality was that the voyage was not going well.

Sir Walter writes to his 'dear heart' Bess of a voyage ravaged by sickness, and that he himself is weak from what he calls 'calenture', a tropical disease causing delirium. The only positive news is that 'your son had never so good health, having no distemper in all the heat under the line [equator]'. Bess is transparently crucial to Ralegh as a point of contact. He reminds her that she should keep in touch with the powerful Lord George Carew and Secretary Winwood, since Sir Walter cannot write to them himself because he 'can write of naught but miseries as yet'. Presumably Bess was being called on to gloss over the realities of the expedition. She was also instructed to pass on Sir Walter's greetings to 'my worthy friends at Lothbury' (presumably Arthur and his family at the Throckmorton Lothbury house), his 'most devoted and humble service to her Majesty' (Queen Anne) and finally his love to his 'poor Carew'.

Although Ralegh felt unable to write directly to the powerful Lords who had seemed to support him, a more public kind of letter appeared at this time. Dated 17 November 1617 but published in a pamphlet early the next year, *Newes of Sir Walter Rauleigh* was hawked around the streets of London and beyond. This news had been 'sent from a Gentleman of his Fleet, to a most especial Friend of his in London, from the River of Caliana, on the Coast of Guiana'. It is quite possible that this 'especial friend' was Bess and that she was already keen to present a positive report on the expedition to the wider public. The spin was starting. Privately, however, Bess knew by this stage that all was not going to plan.

The voyage was proving catastrophic. Many crew members died of disease, among them the young Mordant with whom Wat had partied the previous winter away: others deserted the doomed expedition. Predictably, no gold was found. It was not only England that had changed during Ralegh's imprisonment. The intervening twenty years between the two Guiana voyages 'saw profound changes in native polity and economy which certainly meant that Ralegh had little chance of reconnecting with key native leaders on his return'.[4]

Then, in April 1618, Bess received a further letter from her husband, one which brought devastating news. Their son was dead. Ralegh, the great wordsmith, was lost for words, unable to bring himself to tell Bess that Wat was gone.

> I was loath to write because I know not how to comfort you. And God knows I never knew what sorrow meant till now.

The comfort he does offer is a characteristic of the man.

> Comfort your heart (dear Bess): I shall sorrow for us both and I shall sorrow the less because I have not long to sorrow, because not long to live.

Ralegh will take on all the sorrow of bereavement, but, having taken it to himself, he will shorten the pain (for himself) by his own death. He then refers Bess to the letter he has written to Secretary Winwood 'for my brains are broken and it is a torment for me to write, especially of misery'.

There Bess would have read the stark and perhaps predictable story of Wat's final days. Ralegh had become so ill that he had been forced to send others on to the mainland to search for gold. There, 'the Spaniards began the war and shot at us', wrote Sir Walter. The English were thus forced into attacking the Spanish, and they attempted to storm the settlement of San Thome: Ralegh concludes that 'my son, having more desire of honour than of safety, was slain, and with whom (to say the truth) all respect of the world hath taken end in me'.

So went Ralegh's letter to Secretary Winwood, in which he claims that he does not dare write to Bess, his 'poor wife', in case he renews 'the sorrow for her son'. In any case, 'for a broken mind, a weak body and weak eyes it is a torment to write many letters'. There is a certain fearfulness at work here, although perhaps also a desire to protect Bess from pain for as long as possible, tinged with a desire to protect himself from her expression of her pain. In a cruel irony, however, Ralegh's letter to Winwood was to a dead man: his most powerful political supporter had died during the voyage. Another faction would swiftly rise at court, and it would be one that was deeply hostile to the entire Guiana endeavour.

When Ralegh did bring himself to write to Bess, he closed his letter with two requests. The first was to 'commend me to all at Lothbury' (her family) and the second was more a prayer than a request, that she 'may bear patiently the death of your most valiant son'. Her role model was to be none other than Queen Anne herself, who had stoically borne the loss of Prince Henry. (Of course, Queen Anne had not borne the death of her beloved son with particularly obvious patience, and was still publicly grieving for him five years on.)

Sir Walter added a remarkably touching postscript, able to say at the end of his formal letter what he had been unable to before, writing: 'if I live to return, resolve yourself that it is the care for you that hath strengthened my heart.' Having written these words, Sir Walter's heart seemed already strengthened, and he continued to write. Indeed, his postscript becomes longer than the original letter, revealing more and more of Sir Walter's and Bess's complex relationship. As he says, 'because I think my friends will rather harken after you than any other to know the truth, I did, after the sealing, break open your letter again to let you know in brief the state of that business, which I pray impart to my Lord of Northumberland and Silvanus Skory and to Sir John Leigh'. Ralegh goes on to complain that the Spaniards had been fully briefed about his expedition, and that he has the documentation to prove it. He ends: 'My brains are broken, and I cannot write much. I live yet and I have told you why.' Ralegh lives 'yet' because he cares for Bess. And he knows that his friends will listen to her and believe her, even when they will not listen to and believe him.

The harsh truth that Bess needed to absorb, however, was that Wat was dead, killed, aged only twenty-four, in a rash and unnecessary attack on a Spanish settlement. Bess knew that Wat's final act of empty bravado had not only cut short his own young life but had signed his own father's death warrant, since the most important promise that Ralegh had made to his pro-Spanish King was that no such attack would be made.

There would be yet more casualties of the San Thome attack, most notably Bess's friend, loyal business associate and household steward, Lawrence Keymis. He had been the man entrusted by Ralegh with the task of finding the gold. Keymis had not only found no gold but had also permitted or been unable to prevent the assault on San Thome. Ralegh had had two weeks to ponder this, while Keymis made his way back to the coast, where Sir Walter lay sick in his cabin. On his return, Keymis begged for forgiveness from Sir Walter but to no avail. Ralegh remembered: 'I told him that he had undone me by his obstinacy, and that I would not favour or colour in any sort his former folly.' Keymis replied that he now knew 'what course to take'. Thirty minutes later Keymis was dead, 'having a long knife thrust under his left pap through his heart, and the pistol lying by him . . .'. As one of Ralegh's biographers comments, Sir Walter wrote of his old friend's death 'with a coldness which only gnawing despair can explain, not excuse'.[5]

News of the disastrous progress of the mission filtered back to London, and those who had invested in the expedition started trying to offload their shares in the voyage. Bess was troubleshooting other problems as well. There had been mutiny on the return across the Atlantic, and conflicting accounts of events were coming through to London. On 24 May 1618 one Captain Giles wrote to Bess from Plymouth, enclosing a copy of the letter sent from the captains of Ralegh's fleet to the Lord Admiral. This letter gave Bess the first details of the 'very treacherous' Captain Pennington's betrayal of his leader, Ralegh. Giles sent Bess a 'copy of a letter sent from the Captains to my Lord Admiral', detailing the way in which Pennington had exposed to the other captains the way in which Ralegh had abused them in private, leading, perhaps understandably, to their mutiny.

Giles writes to Bess because she is 'one that utterly detests and abhors all factions and mutinous rebelling against their General'. Meanwhile, the same day, reports came in that 'two of the vessels of Sir Walter Raleigh have returned from the Indies with letters from him to his king, giving account of the failure of his expedition, the whole squadron having been dispersed with much loss of life, including that of his own son, who perished in trying to take some small place defended by the Spaniards'.

The writer of this account, the Venetian ambassador, speculates that Ralegh would turn to piracy. It would be dangerous for him to return, since 'many of the nobles of this court are in despair at such a result, for in the hopes of enriching themselves greatly through the metal which they fancied to exist at St Thomas, they sold their estates to defray the cost of this fleet, on board of which they embarked their own sons and brothers, and thus those who risked their money are utterly ruined whilst many of their kinsmen have lost their lives'. The Venetian ambassador's apocalyptic vision of bankrupted estates – indeed, a lost generation of sons and brothers – was an overstatement, but there was no hiding the disastrous outcome of the expedition, for those who invested in it, for those who travelled with it, and above all for its leader, General Ralegh.

Late in May, Ralegh, with the only two ships that remained loyal to him, reached Ireland again. He was now 'in great need of everything and incapacitated from advancing farther'. This time there was no extended house party, gift giving or business deals made. A few weeks later, in mid-June, a proclamation was published encouraging informers against Sir Walter to come forward and testify, and two days after that, at mid-summer, Ralegh arrived 'at Plymouth from Ireland with a single ship, the others having left him'.

The situation was desperate. The Venetian ambassador watched and noted that Ralegh's 'friends are now endeavouring to obtain a free pardon for him from the king, that he may be at liberty to come to court and not go back to the Tower again'. This was presumably Bess's aim at this stage. She did not stand a chance. The Spanish ambassador, Count Gondomar, had received strict instructions from his own King not to leave London 'until he witness the thorough completion of the punishment of Sir Walter Ralegh'. Gondomar – full name Don Diego Sarmiento de Acuna, the dynamic and charismatic ambassador to the English court from 1613 – was highly influential over James, and now convinced him, if the King needed convincing, of Ralegh's appalling treachery. A price was placed on Sir Walter's head.

Bess went down to the West Country to meet her husband. He was waiting at Plymouth in early July 'but in a bad state of health'. The events of the next few weeks are confused, and Bess's role in them hard to be sure of. Instructions were certainly given for Ralegh to be brought to London for judgement. En route to the capital, the party stopped at Salisbury. There, Ralegh faked illness, inducing vomiting and a rash by means of a patent medicine, in order to buy time to write what became known as his 'Large Apology'. This work is certainly long but not exactly an apology; it is rather an increasingly hysterical justification of his actions. Ralegh mixes humility, in the form of an admission of his failure and his unpardoned status, with aggressive attacks on both the men who failed him in the voyage, the 'very scum of the world', and the 'knaves and liars' who now slander him.

Bess left Ralegh at Salisbury, and it appears that she went on alone to London and that her husband asked for permission to join her in the house in Broad Street 'and for leave to remain there' in custody. Meanwhile, the gossip in London was that Ralegh was expected 'hourly' but that the Spanish were out to track him down wherever they found him. Speculation followed that Ralegh was already in London, but hiding out somewhere. By 10 August he was indeed back in London and, at first, had his wish. He was confined in a 'private house, under the custody of certain persons appointed by the king'.

House arrest did not last long. Ralegh attempted to escape by boat to France. One historian argues that Sir Walter 'allowed himself to be persuaded by the anxious solicitations of Lady Ralegh' to make this last effort to reach safety. It appears that Bess actually went on board the ship that was due to take Ralegh to a secure base in Huguenot France, and that Ralegh, with the one remaining captain loyal to him, was supposed to join her.

This attempt, apart from representing the obvious desire to save

Ralegh's life at any cost, was part of a wider picture, which includes both Bess's long-standing commitment to France and the French Protestant cause and a particular series of negotiations during the latter part of 1616. In the winter of that year the Count of Scarfanassi arrived in England, seeking help for Savoy in its ongoing war with Spain. James had already given Savoy's leader fifteen thousand pounds the previous year, and now there was talk about establishing a Protestant league to defend the small and unprotected state. By December 1616, when Ralegh's ship *The Destiny* was being launched, there was a strong chance of armed intervention and the prospect of an Anglo-Spanish war. Ralegh was thrilled: this would be a far preferable way to justify his 'enlargement' from the Tower and serve his King. He proposed to Scarfanassi that his fleet of ships, being readied for the Guiana voyage, should be supplemented by ships from France and Holland and sent to attack Genoa instead. Ralegh was, in the words of Scarfanassi, keen 'to attack the Spaniards wherever he could, and to spare neither his coasts, his lands, or his vessels, or anything else that depended on Spain, or where he could hope for gain'. King James, in the meantime, however, received assurances of peace from Spain, and so pulled back from this uncharacteristically combative project. Ralegh would go to Guiana: one of the reasons James allowed him to be free of a keeper at the end of January 1617 was so that he could devote himself more fully to the preparations for the voyage.

However, according to government reports later, Ralegh remained drawn to a league with France. He attempted to gain French ships' support for his search for gold. The French would 'displant' the Spaniards at San Thome – in other words, do the dirty work that was forbidden to Ralegh himself. Above all, even before the voyage sailed, Ralegh was concerned that it might fail in its intent, and he therefore attempted to secure permission to enter a French port on his return. As Sir Walter collapsed physically and psychologically in the aftermath of the expedition, it is quite possible that it was Bess who actually put in motion the projected escape to a potential safe haven in France: she would have done anything to keep him alive, as she had done in her appeals to the Star Chamber in 1603.

Astonishingly, however, Ralegh, who climbed into the boat that would have taken him to safety, asked to turn back within half a mile of the English shore. He appeared to have lost the will to live after the death of Wat, or perhaps he wanted one last chance to justify himself to his King and to his friends. Bess's wishes remained unheeded, and he chose to return to English soil and almost certain death. He was sent to the Tower: 'it is expected to go hard with him' reported the ever-watchful Venetian Ambassador.

Unable to persuade Ralegh to save himself, Bess herself became the object of intense suspicion. At first she was 'permitted to keep her own house, with a strict guard set upon her and her little son, which some interpret to be lest she should convey away the wealth and jewels which are thought to be more than perhaps will be found upon the upshot'. Two aspects of this are intriguing. The first is the reference to Carew. Why is a thirteen-year-old boy being described as 'her little son'? It is just possible that Carew was late to develop, as had been his mother, described at seventeen as still little grown. The second is the tantalizing scenario that Bess had access to 'wealth and jewels' that were being concealed at this time: only time would tell if this were the case.

Bess was not allowed to stay in her own house for long, but was soon 'committed to Sir Thomas Lowes'. Lowes was, however, unwilling to take on the responsibility, and excused 'himself upon his many children (which though they be married live with him altogether in one family)'. Lowes may have ducked out of the tricky business of keeping a strict guard on Bess, but others were found to do the job. She was in the custody of a merchant called Mr Wollaston from 20 August to 10 September, but after three weeks of trying to control his prisoner he wrote in desperation to the Privy Council pleading for release from the task in order to attend to his 'many great occasions and affairs'. Another city merchant, Richard Champion, took over with strict instructions that Bess, 'as the King's prisoner', should not be permitted 'any person to have access unto her, save only such as you shall, in your discretion, think fit'. The same set of orders instructed Champion to take three or four unnamed others into custody. At the same time, Bess's furniture and equipment were seized and locked up, forcing her to petition the Privy Council for the use of the most basic necessities of life, even her household linen denied her.

Her husband was lost to her. She was not allowed to visit Sir Walter, even though, by the middle of September his health was deteriorating fast. He was sick of a 'rupture', and blaming his continued illness on the King's physician having applied fomentations 'too strong and too hot'. He was both paranoid and suicidal by this stage, and with good cause. One of the men who would be responsible for Ralegh's fate spared no words in expressing his hatred for him. The new Secretary of State, Sir Robert Naunton, wrote a series of vicious letters in mid-September describing Ralegh to his keeper, Sir Thomas Wilson, in the Tower. Naunton hoped that Wilson would 'every day get ground of that hypocrite, that is so desirous to die' and encourages Wilson to 'work upon that Cripple'. Naunton goes on to give instructions that Ralegh and his keeper be moved into 'the brick tower', where Wilson can keep better control of him, 'and further that the old man of Sir Walter be no longer suffered to attend or come to him, but one of Sir Thomas' servants shall attend and serve him in his place'. Naunton was clearly worried about what could be smuggled in or out of the 'brick tower' and gave order that even Ralegh's 'linen apparel and other necessaries' be searched, and that the physician and surgeon of the Tower be allowed to see Sir Walter only in the presence of reliable witnesses. Wilson did all this and more. He removed Ralegh (whom he calls 'this man') 'to a safer & higher lodging, which though it seems nearer heaven, yet is there no means of escape from thence for him to any place but to Hell'. The move, probably to the Beauchamp Tower, its walls still covered with the chiselled graffiti of condemned prisoners, gave Wilson a chance to do a search of all of Ralegh's remaining possessions: 'I have by this means seen all his trinkets that he hath with him and taken an inventory of everything he hath.' He concludes that 'there is nothing of value', merely 'a sapphire ring which is his seal'. Ralegh, old, sick, bereft of his son, stripped of his possessions, was alone in the Tower, even his old servant denied him.

But Wilson did not rest there. He firmly believed that if Ralegh had nothing, then Bess must have something. His method of finding it was similar to Robert Cecil's back in the years of the Gunpowder Plot. He planted a servant to attend on Ralegh, who would be permitted to go between Sir Walter and Bess. Thus, when on 15 September

Ralegh sent Edwards, his man, to Bess to 'see how she doeth', he presumably did not realize that the man was a spy put in place by Naunton.

All eyes were on Bess. Sir Thomas Wilson was not too worried when Ralegh wanted to send 'a box of spirits and cordials' to Bess, and permitted the delivery, but he was very, very interested to 'observe what came from her'. Every word that Bess wrote was conveyed to the Privy Council by Naunton, a fact of which she was probably starkly aware. When Ralegh wrote a brief note to her, complaining of his sickness and weakness, his constant pain from his swollen side, and hoping that God would comfort them both (it had taken him years to feel comfortable with that plural), Bess wrote back in studiedly neutral and calming terms, perhaps offering the slightest of hints that Sir Thomas Wilson, 'this Knight', was not to be trusted in his apparent 'courtesies':

> I am sorry to hear amongst many discomforts that your health is so ill, tis merely sorrow and grief that with wind hath gathered into your side. I hope your health and comforts will mend and mend us for God. I am glad to hear you have the company and comfort of so good a Keeper. I was somewhat dismayed at the first that you had no servant of your own left you, but I hear this Knight's servants are very necessary. God requite his courtesies, and God in mercy look on us. Yours, E Ralegh 18 October 1618.

As matters became increasingly desperate, Bess cast about for a way through to the monarch himself. She instructed Carew, now thirteen, to write to King James. In his letter, young Carew emphasized his father's loyalty and his years of service to Queen Elizabeth. Carew reminds James that his 'redeeming hand of your princely goodness' has already 'once saved' Ralegh 'from destruction'. He acknowledges that his father's mind is 'despairated' (a wonderful fusion of dispirited and despairing) and that he is 'torn with every misfortune'. All that Carew can ask from James is for mercy, as the 'Image of God', and this he begs with all 'the innocency of a fatherless child'. The words of this 'fatherless child' fell on deaf ears, the father of the English nation unwilling to listen.

Ralegh was indeed 'despairated', but nevertheless managing to fuel the fires of an international crisis. He 'confessed spontaneously' while under 'close examination made for the purpose of passing sentence' (and one wonders exactly what form this 'close examination' took, and quite how spontaneous the confession may have been), that

> when he departed hence for the West Indies, some of the leading ministers and members of the Council, disinclined towards Spain and extremely averse to the alliance with that Crown, amongst whom he mentioned the deceased secretary Winwood, advised and persuaded him to take every opportunity of attacking the fleets or territories of the king of Spain, so as not only to generate distrust between the two crowns, but even to give cause for a rupture. Moreover, M. Desmaretz, the late French ambassador at this Court, promised him not merely positive permission to withdraw to France, but, likewise, in case of nay need, he guaranteed him the protection and favour of his most Christian Majesty.

This was inflammatory stuff. Ralegh had not been acting alone. A French interpreter was brought in and admitted that he had indeed been used in these negotiations.

James, never eager for war, was certainly not looking for a fight with France, and by the end of November a commentator reported that 'his Majesty, with his customary mildness, said [. . .] he asked for nothing from France except they did not approve of what had been done by their minister, which, as your Serenity well knows, was a somewhat ill-advised negotiation'. The French were not going to admit their dealings with Ralegh, and he was left to face his punishment alone.

Arthur emerged from the shadows at this time with his final comment on his complex brother-in-law. He sent Ralegh's 'pleading apology', the work written by Sir Walter at Salisbury to justify himself to his King and his public, to a friend, and he writes:

> I am my self glad (who many ways have been no stranger unto him but have long somewhat inwardly known him and those many excellent parts in him meet for a servant of the mightiest monarch upon earth) that I have seen this answer, the more for the satisfaction of others than for my self, whereby his carriage in this his enterprise of Guyana, are so fully opened, and all unfriendly exceptions answered with such sincerity

and truth as from his aged advised protestations, I do believe that all is true, it being not possible for him to do more.

Arthur muses that the state 'might in my conceit [opinion] have stayed [stopped] this his esteemed golden journey and returned him to his former prison, if such had been his Majesty's pleasure whereby all chances and cases of violence on both sides which adventure of war must of force bring forth, had been prevented'. Typically measured, Arthur regrets that the whole thing has got out of hand, yet again. He hopes that Ralegh 'may live by service to make all whole', but he does not sound convinced that this will happen.

Ralegh himself had, in any case, no desire to live. On 4 October he wrote to Bess, basically handing over to her his accounts and his paperwork. Wat is remembered in passing: 'My son whom I have lost hath also signed that note, inventory and agreement between me and Master Herbert'. He signs himself 'your desolate husband, W R'. As ever, however, there are a series of postscripts. The first instructs Bess to deal with his papers, and would have significance later: 'There is in the bottom of the cedar chest some paper books of mine. I pray make them up altogether and send them me. The title of one of them is *The Art of War by Sea*. The rest are notes belonging unto it.' The second is the now-familiar complaint of physical illness: he has 'grievous looseness' (diarrhoea or dysentery) and wants the powder of steel (that is, iron) and pumice sent to him. Finally, he asks Bess to look after John Talbot's mother. John Talbot had lived with him for eleven years in the Tower and had died on the Guiana voyage: Ralegh worries about his mother 'who, I fear me, her son being dead, will otherwise perish'.

This letter, like all the others, was scrutinized, and Bess was yet again interrogated. She was admitting nothing and denied that she had any writings of her husband apart from articles of agreement about what parts of the goods or treasure acquired on the voyage the adventurers should have: in other words, the financial documentation for the Guiana voyage. Bess claimed that all other papers had already been delivered to an Assistant Secretary of State, and that the chests mentioned by Ralegh had already gone to Alderman Cockayne.

Wilson believed that Ralegh wanted the papers so that he could quickly revise one of his advice papers and dedicate it to the Marquis of Buckingham, the new title for the king's favourite, George Villiers. This was unlikely, given Ralegh's acute depression by this stage, but Wilson had other plans as well. He intended to keep for himself Ralegh's incredible library of books.

Bess had still not given up, however, and was still trying to use her influence at the highest level. At the end of September, it was 'reported in London that the Queen hath begged his life by means of his lady who is great with her', one of the few explicit indications that the vital relationship was between Bess and Anne, rather than between Sir Walter and the Queen. Bess may have been 'great with' Queen Anne, but James was 'great with' his lover, George Villiers. It was through Villiers that even the Queen had to go, and so she wrote to him, begging him, if she 'had any power or credit' with him, to deal 'sincerely and earnestly with the king that Sir Walter Ralegh's life may not be called in question'. The Queen may have called Villiers her 'kind dog', and may have offered to treat him 'extraordinarily kindly' if he intervened, but she was ignored. It is possible, however, that Queen Anne's influence was brought to bear on Bess's predicament. On 15 October 1618 Wilson was discharged as keeper of Sir Walter, and, most important, a postscript to the command set 'Lady Ralegh at liberty'.

But it was a liberty to prepare for the death of her husband. The King and his ministers had a slight problem, in that Ralegh's original conviction for treason back in 1603 had been based on his alleged support for a Spanish invasion, while now in 1618 he was being condemned for authorising an attack on a Spanish settlement. The problem was solved by initiating an arraignment rather than a trial, where Ralegh's recent crimes would be merely related to the few senior officials present, after which the warrant for execution would be signed. King James himself was anxious to ensure that there would be no repeat of the events at Winchester, when Sir Walter had 'by his wit turned the hatred of men into compassion of him': Ralegh would not be allowed to speak. Instead, the presiding judge moralized on the great man's fall: 'Sir Walter Ralegh hath been a statesman, and a man who in regard of his parts and quality is to be pitied. He hath been a star at which the world hath gazed; but stars may fall, nay they must fall when they trouble the sphere wherein they abide.' Ralegh, with a weak voice and racked with sickness, attempted to plead his case. He was interrupted, warned to remember himself, and lectured on how to die well. 'Fear not death too much, nor fear death too little; not too much, lest you fail in your hopes; not too little, lest you die pre-sumptuously.' Ralegh would have little time to contemplate the advice, for seconds later came the words 'Execution is granted'. He would die the next day.

Even at this stage, Ralegh had one last request: that he should not be 'cut off suddenly'. With a flash of his former self he argued: 'I desire I may be heard at the day of my death.' As he was taken back to the Tower, instructions went out to the Sheriff of Middlesex that 'some fit and convenient place or scaffold' be provided at the Palace of Westminster.

Ralegh's final night approached. During this night, Ralegh wrote a short note, allegedly placed in 'his lady's pocket' and put there in case he was not permitted to speak on the scaffold in the morning. He also wrote a testamentary note, once again indicating how important Bess was to him as a financial manager (and indicating his appreciation of the situation of lone, and therefore vulnerable, women, instructing Bess to care for Christopher Hamon's wife and John Talbot's mother: Ralegh was obviously haunted by the image of these women who had lost their husbands and sons). If these instructions are compared with others from men executed for treason, Ralegh's reliance on Bess, and his trust in her abilities, is unmistakable. Chidiock Tichborne, one of the Babington plotters back in 1584, in contrast reassures his wife concerning the payment of his debts that he 'will not that you trouble your self with the performance thereof (mine own heart), but make it known to my Uncles, and desire them for the honour of God to do their best in it'.

Having been kept apart from her husband since late summer, Bess was permitted 'leave to visit him that night'. She found that Ralegh had recovered his poise, now that he truly faced death. It was Bess who, after so many years of being strong when Ralegh seemed broken by events, was most distressed. She had been told that she had 'the disposition of his body', to which Ralegh, allegedly, 'answered smiling, "it is well Bess that thou mayest dispose of it dead, that hadst not always the disposing of it when it was alive": and so dismissed her anon after midnight'. He had only a few hours to live.

8

'Generosa Virago': Creating the Future

'They brought him on foot, surrounded by 60 guards, to the square at Westminster, near the palace, where the scaffold had been erected': so wrote a Spanish diplomat to his King, pleased that the enemy of Spain was at last being brought to account. Spain's enemy was old, sick and broken by the death of his son. He cannot have needed those sixty armed men to guard him on his last journey, the walk to the Palace of Westminster on a chilly late-autumn morning. Again, all Bess could do was look on. Although there is no record of her feelings and reactions, others were profoundly moved by what they saw. From close friends such as Thomas Harriot, who desperately scribbled down his thoughts as he watched events unfold, to young men, such as John Eliot, with no personal connection to the Raleghs but who would remember the day for years to come, the enormous crowds knew they were witnessing something remarkable. Noblemen and noblewomen scrambled for the best views, crowding into the windows of surrounding houses. The courtier Roger Twysden made one of the most detailed accounts of the morning, emphasizing the involvement of this noble audience in the process of execution, as Ralegh enacted an elaborate dance of courtesy and respect with the eminent onlookers: at last, at his death, he was truly 'one of us'. Ralegh looked up to one nobleman's window, 'inclining his body with an observant respect', and asked for the assembled lords to come closer to the scaffold. When they did, he 'reverently saluted, and embraced them'. Ralegh's reason for bringing these men actually on to the scaffold was to use one of them to make a vital point: that his word was indeed his bond, that he was a man of honour. He announced to the crowds that 'this noble Lord [the Earl of Arundel standing by him] can bear me witness', and indeed Arundel did just that, symbolizing the seriousness of the moment by taking off his hat: 'To this the Earl of Arundel taking off his hat, said a Loud it is true Sr Walter Rawleigh, you made such a promise to me then, and I do bear witness you have faithfully performed it.' Ralegh went on to make a remarkable speech, defending his actions in Guiana and since his return. Although he expressed humility towards his King, he never once admitted his own guilt. His speech ended with a highly charged justification of his behaviour towards the Earl of Essex. Still haunted by the public perception of the rivalry between the two men, and in particular by the anecdote that Ralegh had laughed and smoked tobacco as the Earl was executed, Sir Walter expressed both outrage ('What barbarism were it in any man to laugh and be merry at the death of any Christian') and sincere feeling: 'I loved the Earl of Essex so well . . .'. It was in the closing moments of the speech, however, that Ralegh turned to the future, and implicitly to the challenge awaiting Bess. In manuscript after manuscript of the speech (and there were many), it is recorded that he made a request that any defamatory writings, including ballads, should be suppressed after his execution, asking, in the words of Twysden's account, not only that 'no fraudulous writing to defame me, be published after my death' but also 'that those things I have written be not destroyed when I am gone'. Ralegh knew that the battle for his reputation and estate was only just beginning. His own writings, his only legacy, would be vital to the battle. Bess's task was to ensure that they, unlike their author, survived.

Ralegh finished his speech. The Sheriff, solicitous to the last, thought that he might be cold, having talked so long, and asked him to come and warm himself by the fire since he would be 'more able to endure what you are going about'. But he rejected the offer, replying that his 'fit' would come upon him in a few minutes: they had all better get on with it. So the Sheriff issued the proclamation to clear the scaffold. Ralegh threw his hat to one acquaintance, his stitched cap to a 'Mr Smith' (probably Robert Smith, his servant in the Tower) then at last his purse to an old man who stood by him on the scaffold. And then he prayed. Remarkably, he led the crowd in prayer for a full fifteen minutes. Reporters of the event did not only celebrate his religious devotion and his generosity, they applauded his astonishing self-control, his powerful rhetoric, his bravery and above all his humour in the face of death. Touching the blade of the executioner's axe, he joked 'this is a sharp medicine but it is a sure cure for all diseases', while other accounts assert that he was asked which way he wished to lie down in order to be killed. Surely he would like to face the east? 'So the heart be right,' the witty Sir Walter replied, 'it is no matter which way the head lieth.'

This badinage is the stuff of heroic legend, and echoes through most accounts. But Roger Twysden, uniquely, gives the more graphic reality of Ralegh's final moments. Suddenly a far more genuine figure emerges, an old man wilfully shutting out the sight of his impending death, crawling around on his knees, his clothes being ripped from his back by an oblivious executioner. Holding up his hands in devotion, with his 'eyes to heaven', Sir Walter 'kneeled down upon the Execu-tioner's block, being spread of purpose, and grovelling along on his Arms and hands' he attempted 'to reach his neck to the block'. How could Bess bear this? In one of those intolerable details that make the agony of the moment starkly clear, Sir Walter pulled his own nightcap over his eyes and tugged at the executioner's breeches to attempt to tell him what the signal would be for him to strike. The executioner was 'busied a ripping the shirt and waistcoat with a knife, that he might more conveniently bring the Axe to his neck' and did not even notice the tug at his breeches. The executioner now brought the axe conveniently to the neck, twice. After twenty-seven years of marriage, and fifteen years after sentence of death had first been passed, Bess's husband was dead.

There follows a mystery. Account after account records that Ralegh's head was placed in a red bag, and that it and his body, wrapped in his nightgown, were taken away in a 'mourning coach of his Lady's'. But where did Bess take the body of her husband? There are a number of competing theories. A solitary contemporary account suggests that Ralegh's remains were taken to Exeter, to be interred alongside his father and mother, because this is where he had asked to be buried many years earlier. A far more popular theory is that at least his body was buried in St Margaret's Church, the parish church of Westminster. St Margaret's was the closest church to the scaffold, and it may have been the most convenient place to take the body. It may also have been the safest place. Ralegh's performance on the scaffold had stirred up public opinion in his favour, and there were dangers in conveying his corpse any great distance. An addition to this story is that although the body was indeed buried at St Margaret's, the head stayed with Bess. She had it embalmed, and she 'never parted with it while she survived'. One of Ralegh's earliest biographers, writing in 1740, has it as follows: 'His body, as we are told, was buried hard by, in the Chancel of St Margaret's Church, near the Altar; but his head was long preserved in a Case by his Widow, for she survived him twenty-nine Years, as I have found by some Anecdotes remaining in the Family; and after her Death, it was kept also by her Son, Carew, with whom it is said to have been Buried.' Indeed, it may have become something of a relic: a certain Bishop Goodman, who should have known better, said he had kissed it.

There is a third theory, however, based on a short letter from Bess of which only one manuscript copy survives (the copyist, however, keeps her deeply idiosyncratic spelling). Addressed to her 'best brother, Sir Nicholas Carew', dated 29 October, the very day of Sir Walter's execution, Bess's letter is brief and to the point:

> I desire good brother that you will be pleased to let me bury the worthy body of my noble husband Sir Walter Ralegh. The Lords have given me his dead body, though they denied me his life. This night he shall be brought you with two or three of my men. Let me hear presently. God hold me in my wits. E.R.[1]

Could this have happened? It is quite possible that the body was taken to St Margaret's Church during the day and that in the evening ('this night') it was taken by 'two or three' of Bess's men to Beddington for burial. This would then make sense of an epitaph written by Arthur

Throckmorton, dated 31 October, and possibly written for Ralegh's grave in Beddington:

> Behold Brave Raleigh, here interred
> Whose virtue, valour, learning, wit
> Our great rare Queen raised and preserved
> All buried in a place unfit
> Which earth nor envy can make die
> But live with all eternity
> Take this remembrance from thy Brother
> Since he may give thee now no other.

Although it is impossible to be sure of what happened in the hours after the execution at Westminster, this version of events is as plausible as any. Bess had been granted permission to have the body of her husband, and it is quite fitting that she wished to take it to her own family's great house, Beddington, a superb resting place for a man who no longer had an estate of his own. Her brothers, Nicholas and Arthur, loyal in their different ways for so many years, provided the practical support, as their sister's marriage finally came to its terrible end. Arthur recognized in his epitaph that the old Queen had 'raised and preserved' his 'brother': implicit is the acknowledgement that her successor had cast down and destroyed him. Putting eulogy aside, perhaps Arthur had mixed feelings about the effect on Bess of nearly three decades of the qualities in her husband other than his 'virtue, valour, learning, wit': she had suffered again and again from his destructive restlessness, his mendacity and his regular slides into dejection and despair. Ralegh himself wrote his own epitaph, in the final hours of his life. During his last night, Sir Walter's mind had returned to the earliest months of his relationship with Bess. To the last verse of a poem of courtship and seduction, the same poem that had gloried in Bess's eyes 'of light', her 'belly' of the 'softest down', her 'wantonness and wit', Ralegh added two lines of tentative religious hope. These were the lines he wrote into the flyleaf of his Bible, the only book left to him that night.

> Even such is time, which takes in trust
> Our youth, our joys, and all we have,

227

And pays us but with age and dust.
Who, in the dark and silent grave,
When we have wandered all our ways,
Shuts up the story of our days.
And from which earth, and grave, and dust
The Lord shall raise me up, I trust.

Bess chose to remember Ralegh's 'story', and indeed that of her son, as one of valour. Remarkably, her own precious memorial miniatures of Sir Walter and Wat survive, still in their beautiful case.[2] The case was clearly a gift from Sir Walter to his wife in happier times, an oval of gold, about five by twelve centimetres in size, patterned with a floral arabesque, worked in gold cloisons, on a black background with flowers in translucent green. In the centre is a heart-shaped lozenge, under the letter W, while beneath is the monogram ER, all in green translucent enamel. If the case celebrates the love between W and ER, then the images it contains celebrated, unambiguously, the military achievements of Bess's husband and son. Grey-haired Sir Walter is framed by the words Calis and Fial, Cadiz and Fayal – the settings for his greatest naval battles against Spain just over twenty years earlier. A small vignette of a military action at sea shows the attack upon Fayal. The case originally contained a miniature of Wat on the reverse. He too is celebrated as a military hero: his significant battles are given as Guyana and St Tomae, and the image beneath his portrait is of the attack on San Thome in which he lost his life. Bess's posthumous idealization of her warrior husband and son is never clearer than in these miniatures.

Similar iconography is present in an immense portrait commissioned at this time, the use of the relatively new medium of canvas, as opposed to wood panels, permitting the representation of almost life-size figures. The tributes to her son and husband provide a background to a superb study of Bess herself as widow, sitting alongside her surviving son. Young Carew, with his book, at his mother's knee, is dwarfed by the absent presences of his father and brother. When it is remembered that, for different reasons, neither Sir Walter nor Wat had received conventional burials and that neither had been commemorated in any material way, then this portrait becomes their monument: it even appears to be set in a church. Bess's elbow rests on a tomb with Ralegh's coat of arms on it. Bess's other hand guides the viewer's eye to a sword and shield, and a few lines of verse in remembrance of Wat:

> To my eldest son Walter Ralegh
> Guiana's mould interred thy valour's story
> Where thou exchangedst life for martial glory.

'Guiana's mould', the soil in which Wat is interred, may even be represented by the stony rubble seen beneath the armour and inscription. As a whole, the portrait underlines Bess's allegiance to the dead. She is dressed in an unusual and distinctly unfashionable black costume, and wears a veil over her head, appropriately folded into a widow's peak. The only concession to contemporary fashion are the thin black strings around her wrist. In a culture which valued white skin, the black lines draw attention to Bess's aristocratic paleness, but the string also serves a practical function, securing a ring on the fourth finger of Bess's right hand. Bess, more beautiful in late middle age than she had been twenty years earlier, looks out, sadly but steadily, at the viewer.

At the age of fifty-three, she was about to embark on the remarkable closing phase of her life, in which she committed herself passionately to providing a future for her surviving son, developing her legal, financial and political expertise as she went. The maimed funeral rites over, the memorials composed, the real struggle now began. Durham House and Sherborne were long gone, and Bess had spent every penny she had financing the disastrous Guiana expedition. Her possessions had been confiscated in the last weeks of her husband's life, and she was vulnerable politically, since her only royal support in preceding years, Queen Anne, had been losing both her health and influence from the time of Ralegh's execution. Only a week or so after his death, a commentator noted that 'the Queen is still at Hampton Court, and crazy, they say'. By the end of February 1619, the end was near and, as Lady Anne Clifford recorded, on 2 March 'the Queen died at Hampton Court between 2 and 3 in the morning. The King was then at Newmarket. Legge brought me the news of her death about two in the afternoon, I being in the Bedchamber at Knole where I had the first news of my Mother's Death about the same hour.' There was no escape from death or the ensuing necessities. Through the spring of 1619, Bess had to act as executor to the estate of her son, the legal Latin of a document in the Public Records Office at Kew referring in error to her as *Domino ER*, Lord Elizabeth Ralegh, the unconscious error symbolizing vividly her new problematic status as female head of a devastated family that had suddenly lost both father and adult heir.

In the short term Bess believed she could lay claim to two things: Ralegh's ship, *The Destiny*, and his papers. But there were others out to get them first. Thomas Wilson, Ralegh's keeper in the last weeks of his life, had a fair idea of the value of his prisoner's library. Ralegh had asked for a servant to be sent one day 'home to his house', to look in his study for Augustine's *De Civitate Dei* and Holinshed's *Chronicle* 'in searching of which books my man being a scholar tells me he looked over 3 or 400 very fair books of all sorts of learning, especially History, Divinity and Mathematics'. Ralegh's library was indeed superb, and extremely valuable. He had a huge range of books, in English, French, Spanish, Italian and Latin, and they were clearly used by him. Wilson positively salivates over these hundreds of books, and writes to the King, his master, that he knows 'not why those books being now your Majesty's should not be brought into your own library or at least so many as your Majesty shall please to accept, having first caused a catalogue to be taken of them'. Wilson moved in for the kill in the immediate aftermath of Ralegh's execution, and in little over a week he managed to get a warrant to seize books, globes and mathematical instruments 'which can be of small use to his lady and wife surviving'. The insulting terms of the warrant must have merely rubbed salt into his Lady's wounds, reminding her yet again of her inferior status as a woman.

Two days earlier, Ralegh's ship *The Destiny* had been seized by the Crown. Reeling from her double bereavement, Bess's situation was desperate, a matter of clinging on to anything she could keep to support herself and Carew. She fell back, in part, on the familiar strategy of attempting to use her own kinship and patronage networks, writing, in the case of the confiscated books, to Lady Carew, wife of George Carew who had been to see Bess, and knew Wilson well, even giving the man 'good commendations'. Perhaps Lady Carew could intercede on Bess's behalf? The situation was grave. Wilson already had the mathematical instruments. Bess 'was promised them all again' but has 'not received one back'. As for the books, rather than being of 'small use' to her and Carew, Ralegh's library of books is vital to her, 'they being all the land and living which he left to his poor child'. Bess claims that if the books were 'rare, and not to be had elsewhere', then of course Wilson could have them for the King, but she goes on, 'they tell me that Bill the bookbinder or stationer hath the very same'. Bess ends this letter in a state of some exhaustion and despair, as well she might, begging not to be troubled again about the books. She has 'had so many unspeakable losses and troubles' that she really cannot bear that anyone in power should, as she puts it, 'molest' her any further: all she wants is 'comfort and help'.

This was a low point for Bess. And yet even during these earliest days of her widowhood, her energies were concentrated on one aim above all others, an aim alluded to in the letter about the books: 'the land and living left to' Carew. In an attempt to reforge Carew's future, and indeed her own, Bess turned to what we would call spin. This was to be her most important weapon and she used it brilliantly.

Over the days, weeks and months after her husband's execution, a steady stream of 'private' manuscript and printed papers made their way into the public sphere. These papers created and sustained the image of the great hero Ralegh. Public reaction to his performance on the scaffold had been overwhelmingly supportive. As one elegist wrote: 'We died, thou only lived that day . . .'. London, the country, was full of the events played out at Westminster Palace on 29 October. Throughout the country, individuals were collecting what can only be described as Raleghana: putting together accounts of the Guiana voyage, Ralegh's letters of 'apology' to the King and to courtiers, transcriptions of his scaffold speech, complete with witticisms, but absent of any painful moments of incoherence and fear. John Chamberlain, for example, wrote to his friend Dudley Carleton on 7 November with all the news from London, sending him the letter written by Ralegh before he came to Salisbury and some poetry. Chamberlain adds 'a remembrance left with his Lady, written likewise that night, to acquaint the world withal, if perhaps he should not have been suffered to speak at his death, as he was cut off from speaking somewhat he would have said at the Kings Bench: and they had no thanks that suffered him to talk so long on the scaffold, but the fault was laid on the sheriffs and there it rests: his Lady had leave to visit him that night, and told him she had obtained the disposing of his body, to which he answered smiling, it is well Bess that thou may dispose of it dead, that had not always the disposing of it when it was alive: and so dismissed her anon after midnight when he settled himself to sleep for three or four hours'. Bess is everywhere in Chamberlain's letter. It is in her pocket that Ralegh's extra speech is found and, what is more, the story of the last night visit, complete with witty repartee, could only have come from Bess herself.

There was, moreover, an interesting addition to Chamberlain's bundle of papers, one which appears in the vast majority of manuscript collections: Sir Walter's heart-rending letter to Bess which begins 'You shall receive (my dear wife) my last words in these my last lines. My love I send you. . .'. This letter was not written in 1618. It has absolutely nothing to do with the events of that year. It was written in 1603, just prior to Ralegh's scheduled execution, but it did not appear at that time. Suddenly it emerged in the aftermath of Ralegh's actual execution in 1618. The 'publication' of this letter was part of a concerted effort to present a particular version of Ralegh's life and death, focusing on his wonderful marriage to a remarkable woman. Presumably the sleight of historical hand, passing the 1603 letter off as a contemporary document, came from Bess as well. It was a canny response to the potential complete destitution that faced Bess as a traitor's widow, since, looking in detail at this highly charged letter of farewell, it serves her interests astonishingly well. Her husband asserts that 'I meant you all my office of wines, or what I could purchase by selling it, half my stuff and jewels, but some few for the boy . . .' and insists that the Sherborne deal has been conveyed bona fide to the child as Bess 'can witness'. In other words, this letter argues that Bess is the proper owner of the wine licence monopoly, of Ralegh's goods, chattels and jewellery, and, above all, she is the legitimate trustee of Sherborne. No fewer than seventy-four manuscript copies of this letter survive, some of them in a shorter version, and while it may not have had any legal weight, it certainly made an emotional claim for what Bess had been 'meant' to have.

The propaganda battle continued and intensified. Nearly a month after Ralegh's execution, on 21 November, Chamberlain was again writing to his friend Carleton. London was still full of Ralegh: ballads were coming out, being suppressed, and the King was increasingly worried that Sir Walter was emerging as a political martyr, a great military hero destroyed by a vindictive monarch, an exemplary husband to a long-suffering and noble wife. When Sir Lewis Stukeley, Ralegh's keeper in his final weeks, wrote that even Bess had admitted that her husband was a liar under oath, that his 'perjury', wrote Stukeley, 'his Lady hath said, was the cause of all his ruin', that, in other words, Bess herself had admitted that Ralegh deserved everything he got, no one believed him. Instead, he gained the nickname Judas Stukeley.

Stukeley had one more go at Bess, demanding that she be questioned about the allegations of financial corruption made by Ralegh against him: 'his wife if she were put to her oath, can tell whether it were so or no.' Unfortunately for Stukeley, those charges of financial corruption were indeed investigated, and only a few months later he himself was in deep trouble, facing charges that he had been clipping coins for seven years. Ralegh meanwhile, step by step, was being turned into a sacrificial victim to the power of Spain, misjudged by his King, a symbol of a bygone age of English greatness.

Bess's tactics are never more visible than in a marvellous account of her at a London party in the early 1620s. A young Dutchman was doing the rounds of London society, and spent some time in the household of Sir Robert Killigrew. There he met Bess, a 'generosa virago' (noble warrior) whom he addresses in a Latin poem, here loosely translated:

And I cannot remain silent about you too. You, the lady who told stories of the schemes of Elizabeth while she was the reigning queen, of her personality and of the courtship of the bold, insolent Frenchman. You, who were a superb witness of this wonderful epoch and the intrigues of the former court, being both a Throckmorton and the wife (deservedly most highly esteemed) of the hero Ralegh of whom

I remember you speaking often on the edge of tears about the un-
troubled words and the spurred axe of his last moments while I listened
on the edge of tears myself.

Bess, the *grande dame* of Elizabethan politics, is trading on the
memories of her youth, her insider knowledge about the old Queen.
She is also the tragic widow, recounting, 'on the edge of tears',
Ralegh's last moments to all who will listen.

But this tragic widow was having a pretty good time of it in
London. As historians have pointed out, 'the combination of widowhood and old age for wealthier women allowed the exercise of
independence impossible in any other female condition: widowhood
was a time of maximum female autonomy'.[3] Overall, widows' legal
and financial rights were increasing in the later sixteenth century
and beyond, although having wealth was a crucial concomitant to
independence. Widows had far more of a chance to determine their
own next marriage partner, as Bess's mother had done many years
earlier in marrying her second husband, Adrian Stokes. Bess, however,
chose not to remarry, despite having close relationships with her male
friends and associates. Her contemporaries may have been surprised
that she did not marry again. There was of course the small problem
of whom she had been married to, and what had happened to his
head. A common proverb, warning men against marrying widows,
asserted that 'he who marries a widow will often have a dead man's
head in his dish'. This could be quite literally true for any man seeking
to marry Lady Ralegh, if Bess really did keep Sir Walter's embalmed
head with her at all times.

As each year passed, however, there would have been less and less
pressure to remarry. Certainly, in 1628, a preacher could argue that
remarriage after the age of sixty for women was not to be undertaken,
since the two aims of marriage (to create children and to control lust)
were void. There could be no children at that age, and there was no
need to avoid fornication, because the aged should feel no lust: 'the
lecherous old person is hated of God.'[4] There is a curious double
vision at work here. The aged supposedly feel no lust, but at the same
time Bess's contemporaries satirized mercilessly what were perceived
as the rampant sexual appetites of the older, experienced woman: the

oversexed, lustful widow indulging her desires was a stock stage character. As one said, 'widows are seldom slow to put men to it'. Whether Bess was 'seldom slow to put men to it' is impossible to recover, but she was now incontrovertibly an 'old person', since old age began, according to the medical textbooks, with the menopause: women were old 'after their flowers have left them'. Centuries of Ralegh biographies have Bess dwindling into a rather dull widow, if she had not already dwindled into a wife (and if her widowhood is considered at all), reassuring their readers that 'Lady Ralegh's long widowhood was spent in retirement'. Nothing could have been further from the truth.

The legal and financial battles over the failed Guiana expedition were only just beginning, and Bess needed to be ready to fight her corner. Her first priority was to ensure the payment of money owed to her by the Crown, her annuity. Under pressure, Lionel Cranfield, the King's finance minister, paid Bess her pension arrears of four hundred pounds in the Michaelmas term of 1619. Early the next year, Cranfield again acknowledged her persistence: the 'most pressing debts' are those due to Lady Ralegh for *The Destiny*. Bess was due to receive three thousand pounds in 'an extraordinary payment'. Others were clamouring for some sort of compensation for their investment in the Guiana voyage – for example, petitioning for the guns from the expedition – and having far less success. And the legal actions just kept on coming. On 10 October 1621 a Spaniard made a claim for seven hundred pounds against the voyage: his claim was referred to the Court of Admiralty and disappears without trace. Two months later, Lionel Cranfield again notes that Lady Ralegh has been most 'pressing' about money – in this case two hundred pounds – owed to her.

Bess was not merely concerned to salvage what she could in the interest of restoring short-term financial security. In the legal cases that preoccupied her through these years, a pattern emerges, with echoes of the recirculation of the letter of 1603 in 1618. Again and again, Bess returns to the past, fighting legal battles over the events of ten years earlier, twenty years earlier, even, astonishingly, fifty years earlier. There is a sense that, having been forced for decades to tolerate the intolerable, Bess, finally, in widowhood sought to assert control over her past, in some cases to rewrite it.

Many of the legal processes she became involved with are at best complex, at worst incomprehensible. Invariably, if Bess was sued for money, she would immediately sue the complainant in return, and vice versa. So when Sir Peter Van Lore, an immensely wealthy jeweller and banker and the Raleghs' money man for many years, proceeded against Bess in the Court of the King's Bench (the court that dealt with cases concerning great men of the kingdom, or directly affecting the King), Bess quickly sued him in return. The case concerned the fate of 'a chain of pearl' belonging to Bess: were these perhaps the pearls bequeathed to her by her mother Anne, the pearls that even Ralegh, at his most parsimonious in the 1590s, insisted should stay with his wife? Bess claimed that, in the months of crisis immediately after Ralegh's original attainder, she put the pearls in pawn to Van Lore for a thousand pounds. Thirteen witnesses were called, interrogated and made depositions, rehearsing again and again Bess's desperate position back in the earliest months of the King's reign. John Shelbury, ever loyal to Bess, spoke up for his mistress. Ralegh, says Shelbury, persuaded Bess to give 'the jewel of pearls' to Peter Van Lore, because the 'ready money' would be of more use to her than the jewellery. Bess's reluctance to part with her inheritance, her estate, her link with her mother, is tangible. She was tough to persuade, but eventually 'with much difficulty yielded', although remaining 'discontented'. But the necklace had, argued Bess, then been redeemed by the late Countess of Pembroke, who paid one thousand three hundred pounds 'over and above the said thousand pounds', which Van Lore 'most deceitfully, and unjustly he converted to his own use'. Van Lore then covered up the fact that moneys had been paid and discharged.

The problem was, however, that it had taken Bess so long to find out about this irregularity, to find the note that proved she was owed money by Van Lore. As with the touching farewell letter from 1603, it was suspiciously convenient that the vital document only reappeared now. The questions kept coming: 'Was it not lost or laid aside for a long time together so that you did not know what was become thereof? When did you last find the same? When did you make the note first known to the said complainant, what was the reason you did not make the same known unto the said complainant, was not the same note written with the handwriting of the said Sir W R, If yea, then how do you know the same?' The whole case hinged on whether the note was in Sir Walter Ralegh's handwriting. It would be so easy for Bess to forge something now. Despite numerous witnesses to the authenticity of the note, Bess may have sensed that the case was going against her. Anger was the obvious next stage. She railed against 'the senselessness of the bill' against her, which was 'exhibited upon spleen and malice'. Van Lore, 'contrary to his many oaths and protestations', had in fact defrauded her, rather than the other way around. In any case, Van Lore was merely 'a poor stone-cutter, to cut and engrave in seals'. This was perhaps not the most tactful language with which to describe one of the most powerful bankers in London. The judge decided that 'upon consideration', Bess's language was 'partly scandalous and partly impertinent', and she was ordered to pay forty shillings in costs on 19 January 1625.

And yet this apparent defeat was in fact something of a victory. Bess had sued Van Lore in response in the Court of Chancery, one of the leading royal central courts for the resolution of a wide range of disputes between subjects. Chancery, however, had its own distinctive procedures and remedies, some of which were particularly useful to Bess. For a start, a case in Chancery was begun with the submission by the suitor of a bill of complaint in *English* detailing in non-technical language the complainant's situation and asking for appropriate relief. (Elsewhere in the legal system, the litigant had to purchase a specific writ in Latin in order to initiate a particular action.) This use of English made the court particularly accessible for women. But in Bess's case Chancery was valuable in a more important way. The Court had the power to issue an injunction against the defendant, which could bar the defendant from continuing an ongoing action in another court. So if Van Lore was suing Bess, as he was doing in the King's Bench, the best way to get him to drop that case, or at least to halt it in its tracks, was to sue him in Chancery. In the meantime the complainant could put pressure on an opponent to compromise or to settle a dispute by the threat of expense and delay of judicial proceedings. The worst that could happen to a complainant was to have the bill formally dismissed (a dismission). Chancery would not actually issue a decree against him or her. Van Lore's claim against Bess in the Court of the King's Bench had been neutralized for month after month, indeed year after year, by the Chancery proceedings against him.

If the case with Van Lore went back twenty years, to the period 1603–5, Bess's other great legal battle of the early 1620s went back, astonishingly, to the issue of her inheritance from her father, fifty years on. She initiated a new investigation into the debt contracted between her mother and the Earl of Huntingdon. On 8 July 1622 the official inquiry took place, and later that month the Privy Council ordered that seven hundred and fifty pounds be paid to Bess in compensation. The case dragged on, however: in August 1623 the Earl of Cork was writing about the efforts to recover 'my Lady Raleigh's dower'.

It is hard to believe that Bess was solely motivated by the desire to recover the actual sum loaned to the Earl of Huntingdon. Consciously or unconsciously, these legal cases reveal a passionate commitment to righting the wrongs of the past; they reveal a need to bring justice where there had been injustice. The loss of her inheritance when she was seven, the loss of her estate when she was thirty-eight, the loss of her husband when she was fifty-three, all these losses were being reinterpreted, relived in the early years of her widowhood. In social and financial terms, Bess knew that, as a widow, whatever she managed to salvage was at last hers and hers alone. But in psychological terms, whether she recovered what she felt had been lost almost becomes irrelevant: the struggle to achieve restitution was the thing. This struggle kept her in London, always busy, and separated her more and more from the traditional family structures that had dominated her earlier years. Bess's excitement about, her commitment to, her legal cases bubbles over into a brief note to her brother, Nicholas, written one Sunday in June 1620:

> Good Brother, I beseech you pardon me that I cannot keep promise to see Beddington this week. I have such occasions this term that till it be done I cannot stir. But next week following I will God willing see you. In the mean time I pray you commend my love to my sister. And so I commit you to God. Your loving sister. E Ralegh

The 'occasions this term' were Bess's legal cases: these were her opportunities, her causes, her business in life. Till they were 'done' she 'cannot stir'.

Sadly, there is nothing in the historical record to show whether Bess remained close to Arthur as they both reached old age. In the summer of 1626, approaching his seventieth birthday, Arthur died, and on 1 August he was laid to rest at his estate in Northamptonshire, at Paulerspury. He was buried alongside the 'three little children' of the man he called 'my son Wotton'. This father/son–in–law relationship had been of great importance to Arthur, the marriage of his daughter Mary to the son of the friend of his youth, Edward Wotton, perhaps the most significant moment in his life. His marriage, however, was also a great joy as well as a great burden to him. The relationship between Anna Lucas and Arthur Throckmorton, forged in those far-off days of musk codpieces, is commemorated in a wonderful, and possibly unique, tomb still in the church at Paulerspury. Two portly, middle-aged figures lean on their arms and gaze at each other: it is the most unsentimental, yet touching, celebration of a long and companionable marriage. Arthur had been a loyal husband, an anxious and loving father and a remarkable brother to Bess. With him gone, there was only little Nick.

There are hints in the archives that Nicholas did not quite know what to make of his older sister in her widowhood. His life was now one of patriarchal wealth and domestic stability. When one wife died, he swiftly married another, Susanna. This second marriage would be commemorated in the church at Beddington, where the perfect family is carved in stone. Nicholas clearly worried about, and discussed, his more wayward sister with his male relatives, perhaps troubled by the prospect of this loose female cannon in their midst. Nicholas' brother-in-law, John Poyntz, clearly felt there was a problem to be solved but did not have much idea of a way forward: 'what you will do with my Lady Ralegh I must leave to you.' The next few lines of his letter are almost illegible, but there is mention of a 'case' and questions as to how it 'standeth'. Poyntz carries on to write, rather ominously, that 'they say that Beddington house is not fortunate to women'. A later letter asks Sir Nicholas what further 'proceeding hath been between the widow and you or whether it wholly pleases'.

These hints of friction, or perhaps merely bemusement, did not stop Bess visiting Beddington regularly. The house was still magnificent, an inventory of the time giving a vivid description of the best bed in the house, the bed that Queen Elizabeth herself had slept in when she visited the property. The bedstead itself was worth only a few shillings, but a 'down featherbed with a bolster and two down pillows' added another five pounds to the value, and this was then doubled by the 'two blankets and a counterpane of tapestry'. The opulence of the furnishings was epitomized, however, by the lavish hangings: 'five curtains of crimson worsted and one valance of needlework with crimson silk fringe.' It is not surprising that Bess enjoyed visiting Beddington, the house of her earliest memories, and she made sure to thank Nicholas 'for my good cheer when I was with you'. A rare glimpse of the day-to-day practical issues of household management discussed by brother and sister comes in a letter from this time. Nicholas had obviously asked his older sister for the loan of a still, and Bess in reply apologizes that she has only a tin one 'here': she has not done any distilling since Joan left, Joan presumably being a particularly able distiller. Bess is keen to help, though, and plans to send for a 'glass body' in London, which she will deliver to Beddington with Samuel King, who 'will come and set it up for you'. Alternatively, Nicholas can send his fruit to Bess and 'we will set up one here and distill them for you', or rather Mistress Q (her full name is illegible, but may read Quarslesse) will. What is frustrating is that it is not entirely clear where Bess is living when she writes this letter, although there is certainly a sense of a woman moving between different households, perhaps a house near Mitcham, a place in London and her brother's house at Beddington, but also a woman who retained loyal servants: Captain King had been one of the few sea captains from the Guiana voyage who had remained steadfast to Sir Walter and to Bess in the last months of Ralegh's life.

In many respects, Bess fulfilled the socially acceptable role of the elderly matriarch within the extended family. She was eloquent on the opportunities and dangers in store for the next generation, and traded on her insider knowledge of London society. 'I being yesterday at my lord of Dorset', she writes to Nicholas, 'he showed me his brave and rich apparel and his pages' clothes', a matter of some excitement because Dorset was fitting out an expedition to France and had not appointed all his pages yet. Bess immediately asked him if he would accept one of Nicholas's sons, and Dorset 'said he would and should think it an honour' (or 'thinker hit a nonnar' as Bess has it). Bess has no doubts about the value of the position for her nephew: 'it will do the boy much good to see France, and the greatest assembly of nobles in this journey that any young man hath seen or shalt see in an age.' This was the world, of grand embassies to France, of assemblies of nobles, that Bess was born into and clearly relished. She had equally strong opinions about prospective marriage partners for her nieces. She wrote to Nicholas that she had been entreated by her 'cousin', or kinsman, Clavel

> to further his suit to you for my niece Mary. But I am very far from that mind: I told him I thought he would lose his labour, for you would not yet think of a husband for her. He and his needy Uncle would fain finger some money and that is the end. But I know you too wise to harken to him: but dispatch him with good words.

Bess adds that she will tell Nicholas 'more of this youth' when she sees him, and asks her brother to burn her letter. Bess's judgement was astute, if this letter refers to John Clavel, the nephew of Sir William Clavel. Born in 1603, John was indeed 'needy', so needy that he became a highwayman out of allegedly great necessity in the later 1620s. Another suitor had a more favourable assessment from Bess (no mention now of niece Mary being too young to marry), and was indeed sent down to Beddington with a letter of introduction from her. This young man was not 'fain' to 'finger some money', instead he brought his own money with him. 'This gentleman', Bess writes, is 'desirous to see and to be seen. He is in my opinion worthy of a welcome being a proper gentleman, and his father's heir and his uncle's, which is rich and was never married. God must give the success, and to God I recommend you and yours.' God would determine the outcome, the 'success' in its old sense, but Bess was going to give every encouragement to a very wealthy young man to see and be seen by her nieces.

There was good reason to search out wealthy husbands, because behind the façade of the perfect family at Beddington there was a huge financial crisis lurking. Young Francis Carew, Nicholas's oldest son, was causing his father much grief. He 'hath run him self so far in debt, that I never could know, nor as yet do know, the certainty of them, although I have paid at several times far above one thousand pounds of them, and fearing if I should make him my executor my whole estate would be dissipated and my intent and meaning wholly frustrated', writes Nicholas despairingly. The solution in the long term was to settle the estate on the young son of Francis, little Nicholas, as is done in old Nicholas's will, but in the short term the Carew money was running through Francis' fingers like sand.

As Bess became more confident and experienced in her business dealings, and as she became more wealthy and independent, her relationship with her younger brother became increasingly stormy. Sometimes it is a matter of a perceived lack of respect. She was furious with Nicholas when he failed to 'put a man to my son' (although she immediately points out that Carew had nevertheless found a 'very honest one' of which she is very glad): 'yet hit had bin but a nordinari curtisi.' A letter to her brother of 8 July 1629 gives a glimpse not only of how Bess worked as a businesswoman but also of her burgeoning frustration with a system that systematically excludes women from the financial world. Nicholas has complained to her that he is being importuned for the principal and interest on a loan (in Bess's name) due since 9 June. Immediately, and angrily, Bess writes back. She rages that she has not left town in six months, so why on earth do people not trust her? In any case, she is only a month behind in her payments and, as she knows only too well, the King himself falls behind six weeks in his interest payments. Her dramatic solution is to pay the entire amount off immediately, but in reality she is simply going to shift the loan somewhere else. Three sentences at the end of the letter expose her curious and complex position as a woman transacting business. First she has to ask her brother to organize the transfer of the bond: 'if you please to change the bond to Mr Bloar.' To do so she must send one of her men and one of Mr Bloar's: 'for which my man and his shall wait on you.' Bess claims, with some disingenuity, that she finds 'no pleasure or profit to pay so much interest' and ends by beseeching her brother to 'be not troubled about it: for I will bear all'. She clearly has a sense of her own aims (pleasure and profit) and a sense of her self-sufficiency ('I will bear all') but has, always, to be represented by a male family member or one of her own men. The same frustration is apparent in an attack on her brother for 'the selling of my house' and then leasing it to one Sir John Leigh. 'Brother', she writes,

> as yet ever since I knew you it hath been your destiny, power or mind, never to do me the least favour or courtesy more than to strangers: and therefore I pray be not mistaken. I looked for no more in this matter concerning the selling of my house and taking Bloar's lease. You could not have lost by it, but have gotten more than you shall by his letting his lease alone. And although my purse is far short of Sur Jhoon Lises [sic] yet your gain should have been never the less I assure you: and I know he may do you favours in court as I can not yet the fines would have been very favourable in your purse.

Here Bess ruefully acknowledges both her lack of money and her lack of courtly influence, her permanent exclusion from certain male worlds. But she is quick to rally. 'But what shall I say? If it be your destiny never to do me any favour I must be contented: a friend is much more worthy than a brother god bless you.'

And Bess had some pretty good friends in these years. As soon as she had enough income, she moved from her lodgings near Austin Friars to a large house in Broad Street, perhaps the very house she had lived in during Ralegh's last years. Broad Street was a busy and prestigious address, regularly visited by King James and his continuing favourite, George Villiers, a street of wealthy mansions and their owners' coaches. The usual dangers of crowded city life were never far away, whether a child killed by a runaway coach in the street outside, or the ever-present threat of fire. In November 1623 a fire in Broad Street 'terrified all this town, for the wind was so high and sat in such a corner that it threatened much harm, and withal the fire was so furious that the flakes and coals were carried far and near some into the Thames and some beyond the cross in Cheap: and surely but for the good order and great care there had been great danger, but by the diligence of good people (whereof divers were maimed and hurt)' only four or five houses were 'quite burned and some dozen pulled down and defaced'. The writer of this panicky letter, John Chamberlain, tots up that one Broad Street resident has lost ten thousand pounds, while Holingshead, his neighbour, has lost six thousand pounds 'besides the housing and a world of household stuff and other goods lost and purloined in that confusion'. One of the houses pulled down was the Lady Ralegh's: again Bess lost her home. Her response was, of course, to write to a rich and powerful friend and ask for money. Lord Buckhurst at Knole received a letter explaining that, unfortunately, her house had been burned down, and could she possibly have two hundred pounds from him? His reply does not survive. Another member of the nobility, the Earl of Pembroke, head of the Sidney family, presented young Carew, now eighteen years old, to King James. The King apparently found him too much like the ghost of his father. If any question marks hung over Carew's paternity, this strong reaction from James may have helped to convince onlookers that Sir Walter was in fact father of the son.

It is perhaps no surprise that Lady Ralegh, daughter of Nicholas Throckmorton, widow of Sir Walter Ralegh, found her friends in the elite houses of the country. What is more intriguing is that in her widowhood she developed close friendships with two of the great writers of her time, John Donne and Ben Jonson. The latter has been linked to Sir Walter Ralegh in terms of their shared interest in writing, and had of course accompanied Wat around the hostelries of northern Europe. But with Sir Walter and Wat long gone, Bess and Ben continued their friendship. Jonson was one of the witnesses called to support Bess's case against the jeweller Van Lore in 1623, and in his testimony avers that he 'very well knoweth' Bess. (His deposition has excited Jonson scholars because it gives his age, '50 years and upwards', and also informs the court that he is 'of Gresham College'.) Although Jonson had, rather abruptly, left London in the autumn of 1618 (he travelled to Scotland to undertake a walking tour, a strange choice of leisure activity in his own time, and the more strange for an extremely overweight, hard-drinking forty-five-year-old) and thus missed Ralegh's execution, he returned to the capital, to a late and not always successful flurry of literary activity and to renew his friendship with Bess.

John Donne also became an increasingly important figure in Bess's life in her widowhood. There were, of course, already connections between the two, not least that they were brother- and sister-in-law, and there were good practical reasons for Bess and Donne to share travel arrangements, as they both moved between London and Beddington, the family base. Bess's brother-in-law, now the Dean of St Paul's, was not always the most reliable travel companion, particularly if the lure of the court beckoned. Bess recognized this in a letter to her brother Nicholas apologizing for the fact that she may not make it down to Beddington in the near future:

> Brother – if I could have had the Dean of Pauls' company, I had visited [Bess writes wisseted] you this holidays. But he must be at Court he sayeth. After he will return from court by his brother Grimes, and visit you, but I know not the day else I would meet him.

The connections between Donne and Bess had lain dormant during Ralegh's lifetime, in part because John Donne did not have a high opinion of Sir Walter's character or abilities. Bess, moving between the Tower, her London house, her uncle's property at Beddington and her own house at Mitcham, would have had plenty of opportunity to engage with her brother-in-law, living as he did close by at Mitcham. In the winter of 1612–13, the ever-increasing Donne family moved to Drury Lane, to Drury House, a 'brick house in the tenure of Mr Doctor Dunn with a little passage and a small Court to the same belonging'. Lady Drury, of the same family that had shown such interest in Bess's early marriage to Bassingbourne Gawdy, lent Donne's family items to furnish the house there. Through these years in London, Donne would rise and rise in reputation as a preacher: by 26 July 1617 he was preaching at Knole, and in October 1621 he was appointed Dean of St Paul's. By the time he and Bess became close, after Ralegh's execution, he was the most fashionable and influential preacher in London, the fêted author of best-selling sermons. Bess herself was partial to a good funeral. She describes in one letter staying with Lady Dorset, who, being invited to some great lady's funeral, brought Bess along as well. All the best people were there, and there was a 'great banquet and a sermon that, but for our blessed lady, never was there such a woman': Bess is being, it seems, a shade ironical at this point, and it is pleasing to imagine her and John Donne sharing their opinions of the latest London sermons and fashions on their carriage journeys between the city and London, and at the house parties thrown by their mutual friends, such as the Killigrew and Drury families.

As Christmas approached in 1623, Bess wrote to her brother, Nicholas, from Boswell Court, her new temporary London home in the aftermath of the Broad Street fire:

> 21 December:
> Brother I will be very glad to hear of your perfect health as I hope I shall by this bearer, and must entreat you, that you will remember me of some venison this Christmas, that I may eat with my true neighbours for more than two I have not in this Court, which is Mr Chamely and Mr Pym. I pray, commend me to my sister, and when the weather is finer I will see you. Thus wishing you and yours as to mind . . ., I remain, your loving sister, E Ralegh.

Bess may have been old, and she may have been widowed, but she is startlingly full of confidence and vitality. Her letter to her brother asking for some Christmas venison is that of a woman relishing her independence and able to enjoy the good things of life. But the two men mentioned in this letter offer a clue to her abiding ambition. It was no coincidence that the 'true neighbours' who were going to share her Christmas venison were Francis Pym and William Cholmeley, a couple of the new young breed of aggressive Parliament men. Pym would later be one of the leading figures in the colonization of the Island of Providence in Central America, and of Connecticut, but as a young man in England he already had a reputation as a great speaker (Chamberlain commended him for his 'neat speech' back in December 1621) and as something of a trouble-maker: early in 1622 he was accused, at the instigation of Count Gondomar, still highly influential as he had been in the year of Ralegh's execution, of 'having forgotten the duty of a servant, the duty of a counsellor, and as might be thought the duty of a subject'. These young men were representative of the character of the 1621 Parliament, which urged their pacifist King to act against Spain, 'once our scorn, now our terror'. Too young to have lived the reality, these men idealized the glory days of the 1580s and 1590s, when England took on the might of Catholic Europe. Bess was in a superb position to influence them, with her vivid memories of those years, and as widow to the increasingly iconized Sir Walter, scourge of Catholic Spain.

She had continued the process of transforming her husband into a national hero through these years. King James, already worried in the aftermath of Ralegh's execution, asked for a pamphlet to be prepared which would expose him as a liar and a cheat. The *Declaration (of the true motives and inducements which occasioned His Majesty to Proceed in doing Justice upon him as hath been done)*, when it was finally published, did not do much good, in part because Bess continued to get 'private' works out to a wider readership. From works such as Ralegh's moving farewell letter to her, or his Large and Small Apologies for the Guiana voyage, she moved on to the circulation of Ralegh's more general treatises on politics, and in particular his discussion of the rights of Parliament. (A manuscript copy of one of Ralegh's political works which survives in the Folger Shakespeare Library has been annotated by its owner, Sir Roger Twysden, with the date 1622: 'The Lady Raleigh did assure me this was her husband's doing', he notes). She was working towards her most ambitious aim yet: to have Ralegh's charge of treason reversed in retrospect, his 'attainder' revoked, through an Act of Parliament. If successful, Carew Ralegh would be able to inherit not merely the wealth that Bess herself was starting to accumulate but would be able to lay claim to the lands owned by his father prior to his attainder. As such, as one of the Parliamentary debaters would later point out, it was 'an unusual bill, not only of restitution of blood, but to be restored to lands'. Sherborne would return to the Ralegh family. Yet it would not be the Sherborne Lodge that Bess remembered. Digby, its current owner, according to one architectural historian, had 'transformed' Sherborne 'from a disgraced courtier's place of temporary retreat into a permanent seat of the aristocracy'. Enlargement had been deemed necessary. Wings had been thrown out beyond the towers, thus 'retaining the four original external elevations but doubling its accommodation. Probably only the contemporary fashion for curious planning would have accepted so bizarre a solution.'[5] The original compact square house, with its four hexagonal corner towers, had been transformed into a building in its present H-shape. Sherborne may have been larger and considerably uglier than it had been in Bess's time there, but she still wanted it back. For Digby, now the Earl of Bristol, 1624 would be a testing year. Already under house arrest at Sherborne for his opposition to George Villiers, Duke of Buckingham, he now faced the prospect of the loss of his estate. He may have been struggling politically, but he nevertheless insisted that a proviso be added to the Parliamentary bill, stipulating that Carew Ralegh, if restored in blood, would be able to inherit land, any land, but *not* Sherborne. The House of Commons considered the bill in its session in April 1624. Bess knew that she might have to lose the battle for Sherborne in order to win the war for restitution in blood, and to her delight, a month later, the Act was passed, complete with the Earl's proviso about Sherborne. There was only one final obstacle in Bess's path: the bill needed to be signed by the King.

This James refused to do. In the face of this defeat, Bess, sixty in the spring of 1625, merely redoubled her efforts. Through another summer of plague in London, when men and women were 'buried like dogs' in the open fields, she worked tirelessly. She would have been safer out of the city, a place of 'dirt, corruption, and disease', where plague spread unchecked through the crowded streets. But London was also a place 'whose sheer size and amorphousness was felt to undermine the traditional social order', which 'rendered social identity dangerously fluid': as such, it could be a place of great potential for a woman attempting to overturn the social order that she had been forced to obey for decades.[6] More than 40,000 people would die in London alone in this epidemic, one in eight of the city's population, but for Bess these thousands were irrelevant. There was only one death that year that counted. On 27 March 1625 King James I of England at last departed this life. Bess's 'brother', John Donne, preached to the court at Denmark House for the King's lying in state. He asked the assembled courtiers to consider the hand 'that signed to one of you a Patent for Title, another for Pension, to another for Pardon, to another for Dispensation, Dead'. For Bess, these words had particular resonance: James's hand had refused to sign the Bill of Restitution. Would his son, the new Charles I, be any more willing?

Early the next year, Bess's Bill of Restitution was presented again to parliament. On 13 February the Earl of Bristol went again through the arguments as to why a proviso should exclude Sherborne. Nothing was done. The debate came round again in May. This time Digby petitioned the Attorney-General. He pointed out that the late king James 'had compounded with Sir Walter Ralegh for all pretences, and given him £8,000 and to his wife and eldest son £400 per annum for their lives'. Bess, argued Digby, had already been compensated for Sherborne, fair and square, and thus she had no claim upon the property. He had a point. But still nothing was done.

Bess was learning to be patient. She kept a watchful eye on political and military developments, and in the closing months of 1626 saw an opportunity for action. There were some fertile tensions at court focusing on the wife of the new King Charles, the French Catholic Henrietta Maria. Henrietta Maria, sister to Louis XIII, had been the eventual choice of bride for young Prince Charles after the repeated failures to secure a match with a Spanish princess, but she brought her own nation's internal religious conflicts with her. To celebrate the Anglo-French alliance epitomized by the marriage of Charles and Henrietta Maria, English ships were commanded to join in a French attack on Spain. But the political leader in France, Cardinal Richelieu, had his own agenda, and used the English ships to launch an attack on the Huguenot enclave of La Rochelle: Protestant opinion in England was outraged at this subversion of purpose for English forces. Diplomatic relations between England and France worsened still further when in November of 1626 the Governor of Guienne seized a fleet of about 200 English ships laden with wine from Bordeaux, which in turn led to English reprisals against French ships. A few months later, in the spring of 1627, English ships were authorized to seize any French ships wherever they were found, and the king's chief minister and Lord Admiral, the Duke of Buckingham, started making plans for an expedition to relieve the Huguenots of La Rochelle. A few days after mid-summer, the military expedition to the Île de Ré (an island off La Rochelle) set off from England, arriving there on 10 July 1627. Buckingham travelled with 100 ships, 6,000 soldiers and 100 horsemen. The expedition was, however, a complete fiasco. By the middle of November, the fleet were back in England, in disarray, and there was a public outcry about the disaster. Buckingham chose not to listen: he wanted to try again.

On 30 January 1628 the writs were ordered for a Parliament to meet on 17 March to finance another expedition to relieve La Rochelle. This Parliament was to be vital to Bess, in that once again she was to press for the Act of Restitution to be passed. This time she had a new strategy, which becomes clear in a financial memo concerning payments received to fight the war in France. On 31 May 1628 King Charles admitted that he was extremely financially 'streightned' and thus needed to get money from somewhere or someone. He wanted between eighteen and twenty thousand pounds. Charles received a thousand pounds from one courtier, a few thousand more from the sale of woods (Rockingham forest and Leicester Chase), but his greatest single donation to the cause came from one person: Lady Ralegh paid up four thousand pounds.

Her income over the previous years, according to the documentary evidence, was measured in hundreds, not thousands, of pounds. She risked everything she had to get the four thousand together, calling on her brother Nicholas to stand as surety as she borrowed money at exhorbitant rates of interest. (One banker's docket shows that she borrowed one thousand and forty pounds on 6 June 1628, promising to repay two thousand pounds if she defaulted on the repayment of the loan. Bess used her regular bankers, the Plummer family of Gray's Inn.) She was astute enough to demand, explicitly, some short-term financial return for her generous donation to the war cause. She expected either a lump sum or repeated payments 'due unto her and in arrearage from his Majesty by pension or otherwise'. It appears that Bess, unsurprisingly given the parlous nature of King James's finances and their corrupt and inefficient administration, had never actually received her lump sum for Sherborne. All she had received as income from the Crown, since 1610, were regular payments of a few hundred pounds 'for the interest and forbearance'. Forbearance money (such as the hundred and two pounds, one shilling and eight pence she received on 12 January 1610) was money paid to a creditor (in addition to the interest) for allowing the repayment of money beyond the stipulated time. The financial bond of 1628 reminded the King that Bess at best expected to get her lump sum, at worst expected the irregular forbearance payments to become more regular. Above all, however, Bess's donation of four thousand pounds signified her continued loyalty to the aggressive foreign policy of her husband, her father and, from time to time, of the old Queen. It demonstrated to King Charles that he had a loyal and generous subject in Lady Elizabeth Ralegh. Whether it would be enough to ensure royal approval for Carew's restitution in blood would remain to be seen.

She was playing for high stakes, and her opponents knew it. The Earl of Bristol carefully collected together all the documentation he had to show his lawful entitlement to Sherborne: his dossier of manuscripts still survives at the estate. By the time the 1628 Parliament was called, it was not only the Earl of Bristol who was worried about the implications of a reversal of Ralegh's attainder. Robert Boyle, Earl of Cork, was now involved. Bess was pushing for compensation for what she viewed as the gross undervaluation of Ralegh's Irish lands in the last months of Queen Elizabeth's reign. The buyer of the Irish lands, at a knockdown price, was Robert Boyle, Earl of Cork. He had benefited from Ralegh's attainder, and now Bess wanted the financial record set straight. 'Ralegh's widow and surviving son considered that in view of the benefit which had accrued to him Cork should be compelled, in equity if not in justice, to make some reparation to them for the unwise sale made by Ralegh.'[7] Cork's letters and diaries tell a complex legal story, of claims and counterclaims, some of which centre on yet another figure from the past, John Meers. The case rested on Cork's dealings with Sir Walter Ralegh back in the closing years of Queen Elizabeth's reign and, as with the legal cases of the early 1620s, unverifiable memories of the past were dredged up to sanction the actions of the present. Cork remembered Ralegh stopping off in Ireland and receiving supplies, gifts and money. And he conveniently recalled Sir Walter's precise words to his son:

Wat – you see how nobly my Lord Boyle has entertained and supplied me and my friends, and therefore I charge you upon my blessing, if it please God that you outlive me and return, that you never question the Lord Boyle for any thing that I have sold him. For I do lay my curse upon my wife and children if they ever question any of the

251

purchases his lordship hath made to me, for if he had not bought any Irish land of me, by my fall it would have come to the crown, and then one Scot or other would have begged it from whom neither I nor mine would have had any thing for it, not such courtesies as now I have received.

Cork clearly believed that Bess could be warned off with this image of being cursed by her husband, but, as one historian points out, it 'did not produce the required result'.[8] Bess had been invoked in so many ways, at so many times, by her husband and others that it is doubtful whether she put much belief in any of these rhetorical claims or curses upon her future. More threatening were the attacks that Cork was making on Bess's own business dealings, accusing her, in an echo of Van Lore's claims from the early 1620s, of forgery. She in turn was involved in yet further Chancery proceedings, this time against John Meers, who had been her servant and steward in the 1590s. This case is, like so many, extremely complex, but it appears that Meers, a known forger of documents, was being sued by Bess in her attempt to prove that many of the documents which had ratified various earlier agreements (presumably those that she believed were not in her interests) were forgeries. Meers went to the Earl of Cork. Meanwhile, Cork had got hold of a bond for three thousand pounds (signed by Bess, her son Carew and Elizabeth Meers, daughter of John), 'which bond for assuring of a sixth part of what they shall recover by the testimony of John Meers proves their combination'. Cork was trying to prove that Bess and Carew had got to Elizabeth Meers and were using her to expose her own father's dealings: the three of them would then share out the profits if Meers was indeed exposed as a crook. Cork, in contrast, was determined that Meers should win his case, and thus prove that the documents concerning the Irish lands would be valid, and gave 'Mr John Meers of Sherbourne towards his charges in London, about his suit in Chancery with the Lady Raleigh and her son Mr Carew Raleigh, 40 shillings'.

Just as Bess knew that she had to pay out her four thousand pounds to demonstrate her support for her King, the Earl of Cork knew what he had to do to protect his own interests: he needed to bribe people. So on 19 May 1628 he noted in his diary: 'I gave his Majesty's

Attorney General £10 sterling: to be of counsel with me in the cause of Mr Carew Raleigh's bill in parliament for restitution of his blood, to have a proviso inserted of saving my right to the lands I purchased of Sir Walter Raleigh, Mr Staynes having formerly given him another £5.' A week later, Cork is bribing one Heneage Finch with the sum of ten pounds, 'the bill being now in the upper house of parliament with the Lords of England', and he continues to throw out ten shillings here, a horse there, in his attempts to maintain support for his defence of his right to his lands. Finally, on 4 June 1628 Cork notes in his diary that his man paid the officers of the upper House of Parliament twenty-seven pounds 'for entering a proviso in Mr Carew Ralegh's act of restitution of his blood, that he & his heirs shall be liable to all such bonds, covenants, & warranties as his father had entered into unto me'. If he could also prove Meers to be an honourable gentleman in his Chancery Case, then those 'bonds, covenants, & warranties' might stand unchallenged. The Meers case was still unresolved at the time of 1628 Parliament. Bess and Carew claimed they could not 'set forth the truth' and present the relative documents because 'the Lady Ralegh has a suit in Chancery' against Meers, and has 'cause to suspect that the Earl of Cork has secretly obtained all or the most part of those writings from Meers'.

At last, in mid-June, Parliament considered the case. The Earl of Cork, for one, was in a frenzy of anxiety about what he called the 'great hearing'. He bemoaned bitterly the 'fees' he had paid out 'to council and officers': he was the poorer by 'one hundred pounds sterling'. Of those who debated it, few can have not had their pockets lined by one party or another. Many of the speakers knew the individuals involved personally: Francis Pym insisted, for example, that the House was 'bound in conscience to consider' the case. The venison of Christmas 1623 had paid off. The case that Parliament was bound to consider in conscience went as follows:

An act for Carew Ralegh to be restored: Whereas Sir Walter Ralegh was attainted of high treason and so this petitioner is corrupt in blood to the blemish of his family; and for that this petitioner was born since that attainder, and being sensible how ill he stands to the eye of the law: be it enacted that Carew Ralegh shall be restored in blood as if no attainder had been, and that this petitioner may have and demand such lands, etc., as if the same attainder had not been.

If Carew Ralegh was, as he hoped, restored in blood, he would be enabled to take 'by descent what his father had'. Cork had paid out his money, and Digby had his dossier: both men kept their estates, for it was ruled that 'the son shall not take advantage of the attainder of the father'.

But the Act itself was passed. All that was needed was the approval of King Charles. This time, the King approved Parliament's decision, swayed by Bess's donation to his war fund. Mr Carew Ralegh was to be restored to his blood. He could 'have and demand such lands as if no attainder had been'. Bess had rewritten the history books: the terrible events of 1603 and 1618 were erased, as if they had never been.

Epilogue

—————>❍<—————

Bess's campaign had finally, ten years after Sir Walter's execution, twenty-five years after his attainder, succeeded. Yet from her house in Drury Lane just west of the City of London, she continued to fight the old battles into the next decade, unwilling despite or indeed because of her age to retire into inactivity. In the summer of 1631, the second Guiana voyage was again the subject of a lawsuit. At mid-summer the boat builder Phineas Pett petitioned the Lords of the Admiralty in an attempt to claim repayment on the losses he suffered in building Ralegh's ship, *The Destiny*. He was desperate, unable to pay his debts, and asked for seven hundred pounds. Bess had her own ideas about *The Destiny*: it was her boat. She thought that she was owed six hundred since that was the sum (the 'composition') she had invested in the boat which had been 'seized into his Majesty's hands upon the attainder of Sir Walter Ralegh and afterwards found not to belong to him but to the said Lady'. The Irish question continued to rumble away through until 1638, with the Earl of Cork unable to shake Bess off his tail but never really threatened by her. In one of those moments that epitomizes the male world of the great estate owners, the world from which Bess was excluded, the Earl of Cork visited his good friend the 'Earl of Bristol at Sherborne'. Cork liked what he saw and planned to build an imitation of the Sherborne courtyard at his house at Stallbridge.

Although she never recovered Sherborne, Bess did amass a considerable fortune in her years of widowhood. The records suggest that she believed it was worthwhile to give up her royal pension in return for immediate and regular interest payments on the loans she was making to King Charles. She cannot have believed she would ever see the capital again, but presumably the interest payments were more reliable than a pension (and in particular a pension that was still paid to her via her male family members). In an irony presumably not wasted on Bess, the money paid out to her came from the royal income from the sale of tobacco. Back in 1627, King Charles, as keen as his father to raise money, had 'granted a monopoly for the sale of tobacco, which will yield him a considerable sum' (according to the Venetian ambassador). Now Bess was going to receive some of the income from the emergent tobacco industry, or as the dry terms of the official documentation expressed the deal:

> 25 July 1631 – Warrant to allow to Lady Ralegh the interest of £3000 at 8%, received by her out of the impositions upon tobacco, such £3000 being part of £4000 advanced by her to his Majesty by way of loan.

These documents of July 1631 are, however, the last documents I have found which mention Bess directly. If, as the earliest biographers of her husband suggest (without any evidence, unfortunately), she survived until 1647 or even 1648, and died at the great age of eighty-two, then she still had many more years of life ahead of her. All that can be known for sure is that well into her sixties she was acting as a businesswoman investing her capital and accruing interest. She was no longer reliant on a royal pension, no longer dependent on male family members to act as financial conduits or mediators.

And yet everything she did, everything she had done, was to restore her son in blood and to provide an inheritance for him. Her loyalty to family did not stop at her son: a remarkable document, lying unnoticed in the British Library, shows that by 5 August 1629 Bess was in effect supporting Nicholas Throckmorton-Carew to the tune of ten thousand pounds. There is something of a mystery here. Was it not rather convenient that, within a few months of its being possible for her son to inherit, Bess became immensely wealthy? Where did this money come from? It is just possible that the suspicions that surrounded Bess in the weeks before and after Sir Walter's execution were well founded. Back in 1618 she had been 'permitted to keep her own house, with a strict guard set upon her and her little son, which some interpret to be lest she should convey away the wealth and jewels which are thought to be more than perhaps will be found upon the upshot'. There is the odd, inconclusive clue that she did indeed 'convey away' at least some things. A few years after the second Guiana voyage, Carew Ralegh donated a valuable illuminated manuscript to the fledgling Bodleian Library of Oxford University. Intriguingly, this manuscript was, it seems, part of the booty from the voyage, once the property of the Governor of San Thome in 1617–18. Could Bess have concealed her wealth and jewels for a decade, waiting for the moment she could acknowledge them openly? It is quite possible.

The rediscovered wealth was being spent, however, on keeping the family finances together, as Francis Throckmorton-Carew, Nicholas's son, went through his family's wealth. Bess's injection of money did not solve the fundamental problem: Francis's inability to live within his means. Surviving letters between father and son make painful reading. Francis was sent off to France, his father advising him to live privately, cut his hair, be wary of Jesuits. It did no good. A few months later, one Thomas Goodman, who had foolishly stood as surety for Francis's debts, came to Nicholas 'weeping': he would rather go to prison than act as guarantor again. Nicholas does not even know the full enormity of the situation: 'I am very sorry I never could, nor I think never shall know the certainty of your debts', he wrote to his son. Worse was to come. Francis sent over to England for his trunk and clothes. His father was furious. How dare his son ask his wife to send 'your uncut velvet cloak, and your cloth suit, with two new beaver hats and two pair of boots, with such linen as she could conveniently send you, as though all Paris and France had not sufficient to furnish your proud and vain mind'.

Bess's boy Carew was proving altogether more satisfactory as a son and heir. Shortly after being restored in blood, Carew, aged only twenty-three, married Philippa, a rich young widow. This marriage has often been dismissed by Ralegh's biographers as Carew's acquiescence to his father's cynical advice to marry for money, advice that Sir Walter, allegedly, completely failed to follow in his own life. But Philippa's political pedigree was far more important to Carew than her wealth (although the latter was presumably welcome).

Her first husband had been the much older Sir Anthony Ashley, once the companion of Arthur Throckmorton back in 1596 at Cadiz, and thus a man of Bess's generation. Ashley's final years had been dogged with problems: he was nearly cashiered in 1609, over some unspecified 'foul matters', and was then indeed imprisoned for corruption. John Chamberlain commented on one of his last acts of foolishness on 4 January 1622: 'On Thursday night last, Sir Anthony Ashley in his dotage married Mistress Shelton a young gentlewoman of the kindred, by whom he hath promise or expectation to become some great man.' Ashley had great expectations because young Philippa, daughter of Thomas Shelton (or Sheldon), was a cousin of George Villiers, Duke of Buckingham. As such she was absolutely at the heart of the court, part of a small group of women closely related to the Duke (his wife, his mother, his sister-in-law, and his sister) who in turn 'became the king's surrogate family'.[1] Carew's marriage to Lady Philippa Ashley, née Sheldon, cousin to the all-powerful Duke of Buckingham, brought not merely wealth but a superb opportunity to join the royal household.

Despite the assassination of the Duke of Buckingham only months after Carew married Philippa, Bess's son went from strength to strength politically and socially. In a deeply symbolic moment, he became, in 1635, a Gentleman of the Privy Chamber. Bess may have never regained her position, but, forty-three years later, her son became one of the most trusted servants to Charles I.

An anecdote from the late 1630s, with strong echoes of the world Carew's father had inhabited in the court of the 1580s, has him involved in a trivial argument with another courtier. A letter-writer of the time describes the incident, along with the vital news that the King, 'troubled with a bile in his posteriors, is interrupted in his hunting the stag'. (The King's bodily functions remained, as ever, a topic of public interest.) Carew, now nearly thirty-four years of age, was in attendance upon the King at Oatlands, when a stag was shot.

Carew claimed that the deer had two or three horns, while another courtier (Sir William St Ravee) said it had four or five. Carew in the presence of 'divers' others in the 'outer court' at Oatlands drew his sword on Ravee, and was promptly sent to the Fleet prison for a 'sennight'. Having had a week to think about his actions, he was released, but not before paying a bond of a thousand pounds and giving two sureties for good behaviour. If this was not enough to remind Bess of her own youth at court, then there was Carew's participation in the court masque, *Love's Triumph through Callipolis*, forty years on from the days in which his mother would have performed in Queen Elizabeth's courtly entertainments. Appropriately enough, *Love's Triumph* marked a final return to favour for Ben Jonson, who had been sidelined as court dramatist in the early years of King Charles's reign. In the winter of 1630, he was asked to provide the masque for the Twelfth Night celebrations, with his old masquing co-author, Inigo Jones. The editor of Jonson's dramatic works does not think much of the piece his author produced (apparently it shows 'but a faint reflection' of Jonson's earlier genius in the genre), and this was indeed to be Jonson's final masque at court, yet to produce it at all was a kind of triumph. Two years earlier, in the year of Carew's restitution in blood, Jonson had suffered a severe stroke: he would spend the last years of his life paralysed and confined to his chamber. That he continued to write, as he did, was a remarkable achievement.[2]

The piece, which went down well at the time, represented the various 'depravities of love' in typically hyper-stylized fashion. A group of 'sordid and illiberal' lovers are seen off by the power of Queen Henrietta Maria, 'best judge of perfection', and presides over a world where 'love is mutual', a world where she is herself the embodiment of 'Heroic love'. The message was underlined by some exquisite dancing, then 'the Revels', and finally a scene change engineered by Jonson's collaborator, Jones: 'the throne disappears: in place of which, there shooteth up a Palm tree with an imperial crown on the top, from the root whereof, Lilies and Roses, twining together, and embracing the stem, flourish through the Crown.' The symbolism suggested that everything was perfect in this perfect world.

Carew Ralegh was, however, participating in a royal world that was increasingly alien to, and alienated from, the political life of the nation. The year of his altercation over stag antlers, 1639, was one of the last years when this kind of court pettiness mattered to anyone.

For, as Bess reached advanced old age, and as her friends and family died (Donne in 1631, Jonson in 1637, Nicholas in 1644), around her England was descending into civil war. Parliament raised its battle standard, and forces loyal to King Charles gathered in response. Her son Carew sold, at a loss, his estate in Surrey, but he then disappears from sight, re-emerging only when the civil wars ended with the execution of the King. It has proved impossible to track the movements of his mother, as she fades from the historical record.[3]

It is possible to catch glimpses of the places she had lived and the impact of war upon them. London was under mob rule, Throckmorton fought Throckmorton in Warwickshire and Northamptonshire. Coughton Court was occupied then sacked by Parliamentary troops, the house on the front line of the war between Parliamentarians and Royalists. In the neighbouring counties, the devastation continued as the decisive battles were fought: Ripple Field on 13 April 1643; Lansdown Hill on 5 July 1643; Cropredy Bridge on 29 June 1644. Sherborne too, that symbol of Bess's years of wealth and power, was under siege, in flames, and then deserted. Lord Hertford, loyal to King Charles I, had been forced to take refuge at the castle. Once there, he dug in, and thus began the infamous siege of Sherborne, which ended only in 1645, when the great parliamentarian general, Lord Fairfax, stormed the Royalist garrison there. Digby, Earl of Bristol, a Royalist, had been sent to the Tower on the orders of Parliament in 1642: he later retreated to exile in France. One of the new Members of the Parliament of 1642 was Carew Ralegh, MP for Haslemere: no longer a royal servant, Carew had come out in support of the Parliamentarian cause. He had, at last, his revenge on Digby, and years later he was quite sure of the reason for the defeat of the King and his supporters. Joining a long list of men who had created an image of Bess either cursing or being cursed, he described how his mother fell to her knees, begging God for justice, demanding the punishment of those who had brought her to 'Ruin and Beggary'. Carew went on, complacently: 'What hath happened since to that Royal Family, is too sad and disastrous for me to repeat, and yet too visible not to be discerned.' The execution, in 1649, of King Charles I himself, indeed the downfall of the monarchy in England, is reinterpreted as God's belated (and indeed posthumous – Bess died before Charles was executed) response to the injustices suffered by Bess at the hands of King Charles's father.

In the midst of these wars, the last of Bess's brothers died. Young Nick Throckmorton, now Sir Nicholas Carew of Beddington, passed away on 25 February 1644. If she was still alive, Bess was now the only survivor of her generation. That same year, her husband's famous farewell letter was finally published in print form: it was popular enough to go into a second edition almost immediately. The letter was now entitled 'To day a man, to morrow none'. The Ralegh name was thriving; the image continued to be forged. The letter's appearance may have represented Bess's farewell to the public world, a last gesture of her loyalty to Sir Walter, a last remembrance of his loyalty to her, a memorial to a world that was now vanishing in the flames of civil war.

Ralegh had his 'dear Bess' to help forge his reputation, make sure his name lived on. Long after his mother's death, Carew continued her work, pursuing, astonishingly and without success, his claim on Sherborne well into the 1650s, and disseminating his father's writings, sending out 'verscs and discourses of several kinds'. Bess, the complex, formidable, passionate, resilient survivor, had no one to keep her name alive, no one to tell her story, no one even to record her passing. I have searched archive after archive, parish record after parish record, for a clue as to her final resting place. It is merely a sentimental hope that it was at Beddington, the place she herself did 'desiar to be berred'. With no one to write her epitaph, perhaps her own motto should be allowed to express a life lived with such courage, endurance and spirit: 'laisse tomber le monde.'

Notes and References

—————❦—————

Introduction (pages 1–11)

1 Susan Brigden, *New Worlds, Lost Worlds*, 2000, pp. 101–2.
2 The historian A. L. Rowse noted the similarities between Sir Nicholas Throckmorton and Sir Walter: both men shared Machiavellian political views and espoused aggressive foreign policies. Quoting Sir Nicholas, Rowse comments that it might 'be the voice of Ralegh speaking'. *Ralegh and the Throckmortons*, 1962, pp. 336–7.
3 Paul E. J. Hammer, *The Polarisation of Elizabethan Politics*, 1999, p. 288. When in 1591 Adrian Stokes's brother William died (he who had inherited Beaumanor), it was the Earl of Essex who got the property. He sold it immediately, but it was another connection with the Throckmorton family.
4 Hammer, p. 86
5 Sylvia Freedman, *Poor Penelope: Lady Penelope Rich, An Elizabethan Woman*, 1983, p. 5.
6 Hammer, p. 95

Chapter 1: 'My One and Only Daughter: Growing Up Under Elizabeth (pages 13–56)

1 *Marriage with My Kingdom: The Courtships of Elizabeth I*, 1977, p. 160, quoted in Susan Doran, *Monarchy and Matrimony: The Courtships of Elizabeth I*, 1996, p. 4.

2 Susan Brigden, p. 197.
3 Op. cit., p. 198.
4 Doran, p. 60.
5 Antonia Fraser, *Mary Queen of Scots*, 1969 (2001), p. 317.
6 Op. cit., p. 319.
7 Op. cit., p. 317.
8 Danielle Clark, *The Politics of Early Modern Women's Writing*, 2001, pp. 20–21.
9 Doran, p. 1
10 Doran, p. 158.
11 Doran, p. 160.
12 Doran, p. 162.
13 Hilary Spurling, *Elinor Fettiplace's Receipt Book: Elizabethan Country House Cooking*, 1986, p. 98.
14 Brigden, p. 200.
15 Brigden, p. 289.
16 One biographer of Ralegh (Pierre Lefranc, *Sir Walter Ralegh Ecrivain*, 1968) has argued for a marriage date of 20 February 1588, calculated from a much later legal document which asserts that 'on 20 February in the 30th year of Elizabeth's reign [i.e. 1588] or round about this said date Elizabeth married Sir Walter Ralegh, soldier'.
17 Charlotte Merton, *The Women who served Queen Mary and Queen Elizabeth*, 1992, p. 36.

Chapter 2: 'True Within Ourselves': Bess and Sir Walter (pages 57–76)

1 Paul E. J. Hammer, p. 399.
2 *The Reign of Elizabeth I: Court and Culture in the Last Decade*, ed. John Guy, 1995, p. 3.
3 Susan Doran, p. 6.

Chapter 3: 'Him That I Am': Building a Life at Sherborne (pages 77–102)

1 David Cressy, *Birth, Marriage and Death: Ritual, Religion and the Life-Cycle in Tudor and Stuart England*, 1997, p. 45.
2 Quoted in Cressy, p. 55.
3 Cressy, p. 83.
4 Hilary Spurling, p. 223.
5 'Lady Ralegh was worried. The tranquillity of the little world she and

Walter had built themselves at Sherborne was being broken in upon by this strange tropical obsession. Her husband was off whipping up support in London among prospective investors and partners. He had less and less time for her and their baby son Wat', writes Robert Lacey, *Sir Walter Ralegh*, 1973, p. 228.

6 Susan Brigden, 2000, p. 298.
7 Anonymous review, *The Times Literary Supplement*, 12 September 1968, p. 971.
8 A. L. Rowse reads this as 'venia a casa mia'. *Ralegh and the Throckmortons*, 1962, p. 197.

Chapter 4: 'A Most Dangerous Woman': The Return to Power (pages 103–138)

1 Paul E. J. Hammer, *The Reign of Elizabeth I: Court and Culture in the last decade*, ed John Guy, 1995, p. 83.
2 Robert Lacey, *Sir Walter Ralegh*, 1973, pp. 278 and 283.
3 I am indebted to Karen Robertson for this reference.
4 Roy Strong, *Gloriana: The Portraits of Queen Elizabeth I*, 1987, p. 147.
5 Paul E. J. Hammer, 1999, pp. 389 and 394.
6 *Hilary Spurling, p. 96.*
7 *Felicity Heal and Clive Holmes, The Gentry in England and Wales, 1994, pp. 80–81.*
8 P. M. Handover, *The Second Cecil: The Rise to Power 1563–1604*, 1959, p. 218.
9 Handover, p. 276.

Chapter 5: 'My Dead Heart': The Traitor's Wife (pages 139–158)

1 See Mark Nicholls, 'Sir Walter Ralegh's treason: a prosecution document', *The English Historical Review* vol. 110, 1995, pp. 902–25.

Chapter 6: 'Of Liberty Deprived': The Tower Years (pages 159–199)

1 British Library MS 241, John Sanderson's Diary and Commonplace book, 1560–1610, with thanks to Deborah Harkness for sharing her research on Poe.
2 Hilary Spurling, p. 98
3 *The Discovery of Guiana*, ed. Neil Whitehead, 1997, pp. 30–31. Whitehead argues (p. 57) that Ralegh's researches 'seem very much in tune

with current hopes that the biodiversity of the rain forest may eventually reveal many useful medicines'.

4 Felicity Heal and Clive Holmes, *The Gentry in England and Wales 1500–1700*, 1994, p. 250.

5 See David Cressy, pp. 52–3.

6 Pauline Croft, 'The Catholic Gentry, the Earl of Salisbury and the Baronets of 1611', in *Conformity and Orthodoxy in the English Church c. 1560–1660*, eds. Peter Lake and Michael Questier, 2000, pp. 262–81.

7 Karen Robertson, 'Tracing Women's Connections from a Letter by Elizabeth Ralegh', in *Maids and Mistresses, Cousins and Queens: Women's Alliances in Early Modern England*, eds. Susan Frye and Karen Robertson, 1999, pp. 149–50, 158.

8 Joan Thirsk, in *Material London ca. 1600*, ed. Lena Cowen Orlin, 2000, p. 99.

9 Heal and Holmes, p. 247

10 Quoted in Anne Laurence, *Women in England: A Social History 1500–1760*, 1994, p. 87.

11 Mark Breitenberg, *Anxious Masculinities in Early Modern England*, 1996, pp. 58–9.

12 See the introduction to Ben Jonson, *The Alchemist and other plays*, ed. Gordon Campbell, 1995.

13 Rosalind Miles, *Ben Jonson: His Life and Work*, 1986, p. 148.

14 Simon Schama, *A History of Britain 1603–1776*, 2001, p. 49.

Chapter 7: 'God In Mercy Look On Us': Journey's End (pages 200–221)

1 V. T. Harlow, *Ralegh's Last Voyage*, 1932, p. 23.

2 S. R. Gardiner, *History of England 1603–1642*, Vol. III, p. 43.

3 *The Diary of Anne Clifford, 1616–1619: A Critical Edition*, Katherine O. Acheson, 1995, p. 51.

4 *The Discovery of Guiana*, ed. Neil Whitehead, 1997, p. 46.

5 William Stebbing, *Sir Walter Ralegh: A Biography*, 1899, p. 325.

Chapter 8: '*Generosa Virago*': Creating the Future (pages 222–253)

1 In original spelling: 'I desiar good brother that you will pleased to let my beari the worthi boddi of my nobill hosban Sur Walter Ralegh. The

Lordes have geven me his ded boddi, thought they denied me his life. This nit hee shall be brought you with two or three of my men. Let me here presently. God hold me in my wites. E.R.'

2 Now at Belvoir Castle, the property of the Duke of Rutland.
3 Sara Mendelson and Patricia Crawford, *Women in Early Modern England*, 1998, p. 180.
4 Op. cit., p. 69.
5 Nicholas Cooper, *Houses of the Gentry 1480–1680*, 1999, p. 121.
6 Michael Neill, *Issues of Death*, 1997, p. 24.
7 Linda Levy Peck, *The Mental World of the Jacobean Court*, 1991, p. 20.
8 Op. cit., p. 21.

Epilogue (pages 255–261)

1 Helen Payne, 'Aristocratic Women, Power, Patronage and Family Networks at the Jacobean Court 1603–1625', Reading University Conference Paper, 17 July 2001, p. 7, privately communicated.
2 Ben Jonson, *Works*, eds C. H. Herford and Percy and Evelyn Simpson, vol. II, 1925–52, p. 330.
3 Carew did well for himself during the years of Oliver Cromwell's rule, buying the estate of West Horsley (an imposing red-brick building in Surrey, now the home of the Dowager Duchess of Roxburgh) in 1656. Various local myths link Sir Walter Ralegh to the building, including the story that an old servant had 'discovered an earthen pot or urn, in which it was supposed the bowels of Sir Walter Raleigh were contained'. There is, however, only one verifiable reference linking Carew to the place in the parish records at West Horsley for these years (on 23 May 1660, Henrietta Ralegh was baptized, although no parents' names are given). Probably the family remained based in Gloucestershire at Churchdown, and kept a house at St Martin in the Fields in London. Carew's political career centred on his management of the increasingly powerful navy: not an active soldier and sailor like his father, he was, however, a superb administrator. What is certain is that Carew was buried in St Margaret's Westminster, on 1 January 1666, six years after the restoration of King Charles II, although how he died remains yet another mystery. The Parish Register reads: '1 January 1666 Carey Rawleigh esq. Kild. M. Chancel'. Was he, at the age of sixty-one, killed in a fight, like his older

brother? And did his burial at St Margaret's signify that he believed he was going to share a grave with his father? There is a long-standing story that he had his father's head buried with him. Carew's last act was to leave everything he had to his wife, Philippa. Lady Ashley, already a rich widow when she married Carew, became wealthier still.

Appendix

To Lady Ralegh [from Winchester, 4–8 December 1603]

A FAREWELL IN EXPECTATION OF DEATH

[*headed*] The Coppy of a Letter written by Sir Walter Raleigh to his wife the night before he expected to be putt to death att Winchester in 1603

You shall nowe receive (my deare wife) my last words in these my last lynes. My love I send you, that you may keepe itt when I am dead, and my counsell, that you may remember itt when I am no more. I would not by my will present you with sorrowes (dear Besse). Lett them goe into the grave with mee and bee buried in the dust. And seeing itt is not the will of God that I shall see you any more in this life, beare itt patiently and with an heart like thy selfe.

First I send you all the thankes which my heart can conceive or my words can express for your many travailes [= *labours*] and care taken for mee, which though they have not taken effect as you wished, yett my debt to you is not the lessse, but pay itt I never shall in this world.

269

Secondly, I beseech you, for the love you bare mee liveing, doe not hide your selfe many dayes after my death but but by your travailes seeke to help your miserable fortunes and the right of your poore child. Thy mourninge cannot availe mee: I am but dust.

Thirdly you shall understand that my land was conveyed *bona fide* to my childe. The writeings weere drawne att Misomner twelve monthes. My honest cosen Brett can testifie soe much, and Dalberrie too can remember somewhat therein. And I trust that my blood will quench the malice that have thus cruelly murthered mee, and that they will not seeke alsoe to kill thee and thine with extreame povertie. To what freind to direct thee I knowe not, for all mine have left mee in the true tyme of triall. And I plainely perceive that my death was determyned from the first day.

Most sorrie I am (God knowes) that being thus surprised with death I can leave you in noe better estate. God is my wittnesse I meant you [*to have*] all my office [= *grant*] of wynes, or all that I could have purchased by selling itt, halfe my stuffe and all my jewells, but some on't for the boy. But God hath prevented all my resolutions and even that great God that ruleth all in all. But if you can live free from want, care for noe more: the rest is but vanitie.

Love God and beginn betymes to repose yourselfe on him, and therein shall you finde true and lasting riches, and endlesse comfort. For the rest, when you have travailled and wearied all your thoughts over all sorts of wordly cogitations, you shall but sitt downe by sorrowe in the end. Teache your sonne alsoe to love and feare God whilst hee is yett younge, that the feare of God may growe upp with him, and the same God will bee a husband to you and a father to him, a husband and a father which cannot bee taken from you.

Baylie oweth me 200*li* and Adrian Gilbert 600*li*. In Jersey I have alsoe much monye oweinge mee besides. The arrerages of the wynes will pay my debts. And howsoever you doe, for my soules sake, pay all poore men. When I am gone no doubt you shall bee sought by many, for the world thinks that I was very rich. But take heed of the pretences of men, and theire affections, for they last not, but in honest and worthie men, and noe greater misery can befall you in this life then to become a prey and afterwards to bee despised. I speake not this (God knowes) to disswade you from marriage, for it will bee best for you, both in respect of the world and of God.

As for mee, I am noe more yours, nor you mine. Death hath cutt us a sunder and God hath devided mee from the worlde and you from mee. Remember your poore child for his fathers sake, who chose you and loved you in his happiest tymes.

Gett those letters (if it bee possible) which I writt to the lords [*Letter 171*] wherein I sued for my life. God is my wittnesse, itt was for you and yours I desired life. But itt is true that I disdaine my selfe for begging it. For knowe it (deare wife) that your sonne is the sonne of a true man, and one who, in his owne respect, dispiseth death, and all his mishapen and ouglye shapes.

I cannot write much. God hee knowes how hardly I steale this tyme while others sleepe, and itt is alsoe high tyme that I should separate my thoughts from the world. Begg my dead body which liveinge was denyed thee and either laye it att Shirbourne (if the land continue) or in Excester church by my mother and father. I can say noe more, tyme and death call mee away.

The everlasting, powerfull, infinite and omnipotent God, that Almighti God whoe is goodnesse itt selfe, the true life and true light, keepe thee and thine. Have mercy on mee and teach mee to forgive my persecutors and accusers, and send us to meete in his glorious kingdome.

My deare wife farewell. Blesse my poore boye. Pray for mee and lett my good God hold you both in his armes. Written with the dyeing hand of sometyme thy husand but now (alasse) overthrowne.

      Wa Raleigh

   Yours that was but nowe not my own

      W R

Note on Methodology

—————>❈<—————

When I set out to write this book, my first aim was to take the moments when Bess appeared in traditional biographies of Ralegh (the innocent Maid of Honour, deflowered by the virile Sir Walter; the devoted wife providing a haven of domesticity away from the public world; the loyal widow, keeping her husband's embalmed head with her at all times) and re-examine them from her perspective. I always sensed, however, that Bess might have her own untold story and, as each new research trip uncovered further small pieces of evidence, a remarkably full image of a fascinating and courageous life emerged. There remain significant moments that are still obscure, either because those at the time sought to conceal the true version of events (Bess's marriage is a case in point) or because contemporaries did not see an event as significant (did Bess bear other children who were either stillborn or died young, for example?). Particularly frustrating are the occasions where it is clear that those in charge of keeping and then cataloguing documents have simply ignored or, worse, destroyed materials that were deemed irrelevant to the traditional understanding of history. So, for example, a series of letters ascribed to Arthur Throckmorton in the British Library catalogues turned out, on closer examination, to be written by his mother, Anne – a pattern of misattribution that occurs with disturbing frequency. In another

273

archive, while Arthur's formal covering letter survives, Bess's own letter, originally enclosed with it, sadly does not. When the direct evidence is missing I have therefore turned to the diaries, letters and records that describe other women's lives: for example, when describing the birth of Bess's children or discussing the educational possibilities open to girls.

As for the text itself, all spelling and orthography have been modernized (except for the retention of the verb ending 'th'). Punctuation has been supplied according to current practice in order to make it easier to follow a writer's sense, and all dates have been changed to the modern style (during Bess's lifetime the new year was usually calculated from March). Endnotes have been kept to a minimum but interested readers wishing to enjoy letters and other documents in their early-modern format should turn to the bibliography, where works such as Latham's 1999 edition of Ralegh's letters are listed along with other excellent scholarly studies of the period. Finally, I have attempted to make the vexed issue of names and titles as simple as possible by continuing to refer to an individual by the name and title used when he or she was first introduced. Robert Cecil, for example, is referred to by his name throughout, rather than by the series of titles conferred on him over the years.

Annotated Bibliography

―――⟶●◀―――

I have consulted all of the following books for background information, and recommend them to the reader who seeks further information.

Letters and Diaries

Acheson, Katherine O. 1995. *The Diary of Anne Clifford, 1616–1619: A Critical Edition*. New York: London: Garland, 1995.
Clifford, D. J. H., ed. 1990. *The Diaries of Lady Anne Clifford*, Sutton Publishing.
Two editions of Anne Clifford's fascinating diaries and reminiscences.

Latham, Agnes, ed. 1999. *The Letters of Sir Walter Ralegh*. University of Exeter Press.
The most recent edition, in original spelling, of the letters.

Moody, Joanna. 2001. *The Private Life of an Elizabethan Lady: the Diary of Lady Margaret Hoby, 1599–1605*. Sutton Publishing.
A real insight into day-to-day life for one of Bess's contemporaries. Hoby's journal is brought to life by an excellent introduction from Joanna Moody.

Whitehead, Neil, L., 1997. *The Discovery of the Large, Rich and Beautiful Empire of Guiana*. Manchester University Press.

Ralegh's own, compelling account of his expedition in search of gold in 1595, prefaced by an anthropologist's intriguing introduction.

Social History

Arnold, Janet. 1988. *Queen Elizabeth's Wardrobe Unlocked*. Maney Publishing.
Beautifully illustrated and packed with intriguing details, this is a groundbreaking study in the history of dress.

Cooper, Nicholas. 1999. *Houses of the Gentry 1480–1680*. Yale University Press.
Airs, Malcolm. 1998. *The Tudor and Jacobean Country House: A Building History*. Bramley.
Mowl, Timothy. 1993. *Elizabethan and Jacobean Style*. Phaidon Press.
Three excellent recent architectural and social histories.

Cressy, David. 1997. *Birth, Marriage and Death: Ritual, Religion and the Life-Cycle in Tudor and Stuart England*. Oxford University Press.
Scholarly yet accessible, this is a superb study of ordinary human lives during Bess's lifetime.

Heal, Felicity and Clive Holmes. 1994. *The Gentry in England and Wales*. Macmillan.
A highly respected overview of the gentry as a social class.

Houlbrooke, Ralph. 1984. *The English Family 1450–1700*. Longman.
One of the leading reference books for the history of the family.

Spurling, Hilary. 1986. *Elinor Fettiplace's Receipt Book: Elizabethan Country House Cooking*. Viking Salamander.
This fascinating insight into the Elizabethan culinary year enables the reader to recreate the foods of the past.

The Arts

Briggs, Julia. 1997. *This Stage-Play World*. 2nd ed. Oxford University Press.
A superb introduction to the literature of the time, Briggs is both authoritative and readable.

May, Steven, ed. 1991. *The Elizabethan Courtier Poets: The Poems and Their Contexts*. University of Missouri Press.

ANNOTATED BIBLIOGRAPHY

This wide-ranging work includes all the poems ascribed to the Earl of Essex.

Rudick, Michael, ed. 1999. *The Poems of Sir Walter Ralegh*. Arizona Center for Medieval and Renaissance Studies in conjunction with the Renaissance English Text Society.
A scholarly edition of the poetry, in original spelling and giving all the variant forms for each poem.

Strong, Roy. 1987. *Gloriana: The Portraits of Queen Elizabeth*. Thames and Hudson.
Beautifully illustrated study of the Queen's changing image.

Political History

Beer, Anna. 1997. *Sir Walter Ralegh and His Readers in the Seventeenth Century: Speaking to the People*. Macmillan.
My academic study of Ralegh's political writing, with chapters on his execution and posthumous reputation.

Brigden, Susan. 2000. *New Worlds, Lost Worlds*. Penguin.
A fascinating narrative of the entire Tudor period from an eminent historian.

Doran, Susan. 1996. *Monarchy and Matrimony: The Courtships of Elizabeth I*. Routledge.
The most convincing academic study of Queen Elizabeth's marital negotiations.

Hammer, Paul E. J. 1999. *The Polarisation of Elizabethan Politics: The Political Career of Robert Devereux, 2nd Earl of Essex, 1585–1597*. Cambridge University Press.
An impeccably researched reevaluation of the Earl of Essex's political career.

Nicholls, Mark. Sir Walter Ralegh's treason: A prosecution document. *English Historical Review* 100: 902–25.
A groundbreaking analysis of the evidence for Ralegh's treason charge.

Schama, Simon. 2001. *A History of Britain: The British Wars 1603–1776*. BBC.

277

Based on the television series, Schama offers a lucid narrative of British history from the accession of James I.

Biographical Studies

Bald, R. C. 1970. *John Donne: A Life*. Clarendon Press.
The standard biography of Donne.

Barroll, Leeds. 2001. *Anne of Denmark: Queen of England*. University of Philadelphia Press.
Not so much a biography as an analysis of court culture, Barroll nevertheless includes some interesting details concerning this neglected queen's life.

Edwards, Edward. 1868. *The Life of Sir Walter Ralegh*, 2 vols. Macmillan.
Redolent with Victorian values, Edwards remains one of Ralegh's most thorough biographers. Some of Bess's letters appear in an appendix.

Fraser, Antonia. 1969, 2001. *Mary Queen of Scots*. Phoenix Press.
A compelling account of the life of this complex figure.

Handover, P. M. 1959. *The Second Cecil: The Rise to Power 1563–1604*. Eyre & Spottiswoode.
Haynes, Alan. 1989. *Robert Cecil, 1st Earl of Salisbury: Servant of Two Sovereigns*. Owen.
Two biographies of Robert Cecil, the former less scholarly but perhaps more pleasing to read.

Harlow, V. T. 1932. *Ralegh's Last Voyage*. Argonaut Press.
Harlow's analyses may sound old-fashioned now, but his collection of the documents connected with Ralegh's final voyage is nevertheless still the best available.

Lacey, Robert. 1973. *Sir Walter Ralegh*. Weidenfeld & Nicholson.
The most engaging biography of Ralegh in recent years (and recently reissued).

Lindley, David. 1993. *The Trials of Frances Howard: Fact and Fiction at the Court of King James*. Routledge.
Lindley offers both a study of Frances Howard and the culture she lived in. A valuable contribution to the history of aristocratic women.

Rowse, A. L. 1962. *Ralegh and the Throckmortons*. Macmillan.
Rowse offers an extremely entertaining version of the life and times of Arthur Throckmorton.

Women's History

Aughterson, Kate, ed. 1995. *Renaissance Woman: Constructions of Femininity in England*. UCL Press.
Packed with well-chosen primary texts, supplemented by helpful notes from the editor, this book demonstrates vividly the ways in which women were expected to lead their lives.

Clark, Danielle. 2001. *The Politics of Early Modern Women's Writing*. Longman.
A scholarly and densely written study, with an excellent section on education.

Eales, Jacqueline. 1998. *Women in Early Modern England, 1500–1700*.
A textbook setting out some of the data and debates in women's history.

Frye, Susan, and Karen Robertson, eds. 1999. *Maids and Mistresses, Cousins and Queens: Women's Alliances in Early Modern England*. Oxford University Press.
A collection of academic essays, including Karen Robertson's analysis of one of Bess's letters.

Mendelson, Sara, and Patricia Crawford. 1998. *Women in Early Modern England*. Clarendon Press.
Laurence, Anne. 1994. *Women in England 1500–1760: A Social History*. Weidenfeld & Nicholson.
Two highly readable reviews of all aspects of women's lives.

Merton, Charlotte. 1992. *The Women who Served Queen Mary and Queen Elizabeth*, D. Phil. dissertation, Trinity College, University of Cambridge.
Merton's doctoral thesis remains unpublished but is full of fascinating details of women's lives at court.

Index

Accession Day Tilt 48, 103
Acuna, Don Diego Sarmiento de
  212–13, 245
Anjou, Francis, Duke of, and Elizabeth
  I 33–4, 37–8
Anne of Denmark, Queen 53, 141,
  142, 193, 196, 220, 229
Arden, Mary 67
Aremberg, Count of 142–3, 144, 153
Arnold, William 79
Arundel, Earl of 224
Ashby, William 53
Ashley, Sir Anthony 258
Ashley, Philippa 258
Aubrey, John 78, 201–2

Babington Plot 51
Bacon, Anne 109–10
Bacon, Anthony 70
Bassett, Elizabeth 182–3, 198
Bassett, William 126
Batty, Bartholomew 36
Beaumanor (house) 29, 36, 42
Beddington (house) 23–4, 227, 240
Bess of Hardwick (Lady Shrewsbury)
  115, 135, 169
Bevill, Matthew 182

Biron, Duc de 129–30
Blount, Charles 10, 63
Boleyn, Anne 13, 14
Booth, John 167
Bothwell, Earl of 24
Boyle, Robert (Earl of Cork) 205,
  206, 237, 251–3, 255–6
Brett, Alexander 99, 114, 148, 166,
  178
Bridges, Elizabeth 9
Brigden, Susan 16
Bristol, Earl of, see Digby, John
Brooke, Elizabeth 107
Brooke, George 143, 156
Brooke, Henry, see Cobham, Lord
Buckhurst, Lord 244
Buckingham, Duke of, see Villiers,
  George
Burghley, Lord (William Cecil) 20, 39,
  40, 58, 59, 74
Burton, Robert 188

Cadiz expedition 105, 106
Caesar, Sir Julius 51, 206–7
Calthorp, Richard 205
Camden, William 25
Carew, Francis 23, 29, 35, 41, 181

Carew, Lord George 4, 65, 110, 114, 130, 131–2, 135, 136, 208
Carew, Nicholas 14, 23
Carleton, Dudley 230, 232
Carr, Robert 197, 199, 201, 205
  and James I 188
  marriage 197
  and Sherborne 188–9
Catesby, Robert 173
Cavendish, Mistress 4
Cayoworaco 123–4
Cecil, Robert 58, 61, 70, 71, 72, 74, 79, 92, 100, 131–2, 139, 171, 192
  acquires Durham House 141
  and Bess 75, 86–8, 97–8, 107, 109, 128–9, 132–3, 136, 151, 154, 156, 174–5
  death of 196–7
  and distribution of Ralegh's property 151
  and Essex 106, 107, 120
  and James I 131, 141
  and Ralegh 75, 107, 109, 132, 136–7, 140–3
Cecil, Will, and Ralegh 127
Cecil, William, see Burghley, Lord
Chamberlain, John 188–9, 231–2, 233, 244, 258
Champion, Richard 214
Charles I 196, 249, 250, 251, 256, 261
children, in Tudor England 31–2
Cholmeley, William 245
Christmas 84–6
Civil War, English 260–1
Clarence, George, Duke of 21
Clavel, John 241
Clavel, Sir William 241
Clifford, Lady Anne 35, 44, 81, 90, 91, 139–42, 193, 204, 206, 229
Clifford, Jane 181
Cobham, Lord (Henry Brooke) 42, 118, 127, 132, 142, 153, 159
  and Bess 128
  interrogation of 143
  and Ralegh 152

Coke, Edward 152, 153
Coke, Nicholas 187
Collingwood, Goody 82
Cork, Earl of, see Boyle, Robert
Cotterell, Robert 174–5
Cranborne, Lord Viscount, see Cecil, Robert
Cranfield, Lionel 235
Cromwell, Thomas 14, 26

Daniel, Samuel 134
Darcy, Edward 35, 150, 181
Darcy, Sir Francis 4, 190
Darcy, Lady Mary 49, 50
Darnley, Lord 24
Dee, John 104
Dekker, Thomas 117, 144
Derby, Countess 9
Devereux, Penelope (née Rich) 6, 63, 146
  character 10
  sexual relationships 8
  and Sir Philip Sidney 9–10
Devereux, Robert, see Essex, Earl of
Digby, John (Earl of Bristol) 197, 205, 248, 249, 251, 255–6, 260
Donne, John 115, 180, 193, 198, 244–5, 248–9, 260
Doran, Susan 33, 69
Drury, Lady 42, 50
Drury, Lord 42
Dudley, Catherine 21, 22, 27
Dudley, Guilford 16, 21
Dudley, Robert, see Leicester, Earl of
Dumaresq, Daniel 113
Durham House 41, 66, 80, 81, 122–3, 136, 141

Edward VI 16
El Dorado expedition 96, 97, 101–2
Eliot, John 223
Eliot, Sir Thomas 125–6
Elizabeth I 2, 3, 4, 20–1, 46, 51, 119
  death of 138, 139
  and Essex 6, 9, 120
  and Francis, Duke of Anjou 33–4, 37–8

and Leicester 21
and Mary, Queen of Scots 51–2
portraits of 119–20
and Ralegh 3, 65
succeeds to English throne 18
and Thomas Seymour 15
Elizabeth, Princess 142
Essex, Earl of (Robert Devereux) 8, 9,
    58, 60, 63, 103, 115, 224
    attempted coup 121
    and Elizabeth I 6, 9
    execution 121
    and Ralegh 6–7, 107, 108–9
    and Robert Cecil 106, 107, 120
    secret marriage 8–9

Fairfax, Lord 261
famine 77, 125
Fawkes, Guy 173
Featley, Daniel 194–5
Finch, Heneage 253
Finch, Sir Moyle 72
Finet, Robert 198
FitzJames, John 112
Frobisher, Sir Martin 65
Fuller, Thomas 23

Gardiner, S. R. 201
Gawdy, Bassingbourne 42, 43
Gilbert, Adrian 62, 130, 191
Gilbert, Humphrey 40
Gilbert, John 59, 123
Gilby, William 205
Gondomar, Count, see Acuna, Don
    Diego Sarmiento de
Goodman, Thomas 257
Gorges, Arthur 113
Gorges, Sir Ferdinando 120–1
Gould, Alice 4
Grenville, Sir Richard 3
Grey, Lord 159
Grey, Lady Catherine 17, 18–19, 21
Grey, Lady Jane 15, 16–17
Grey, Lady Mary 18, 19–20, 29–30
Gunpowder Plot 170, 173–4, 186

Hall, George 166
Hamon, Christopher 221

Harcourt, Dorothy 50
Harington, John 67
Harkness, Deborah 169
Harriot, Thomas 113, 114, 148, 156,
    190, 223
Harris, Christopher 91
Harvey, Sir George 174, 186
Hastings, Henry, see Huntingdon,
    Earl of
Hawkins, Sir John 74
Hawthorn, Gilbert 183
Heneage, Elizabeth 72
Heneage, Thomas 40, 66, 72, 75, 77,
    115
Heneage-Finch, Elizabeth 130
Henrietta Maria, Queen 249
Henry, Prince 192, 193, 196
Henry IV, King of France 7
Henry VIII 14
Herbert, Henry 17
Hertford, Earl of, see Seymour, Edward
Hill, John 124
Hilliard, Nicholas 119–20
Hoby, Edward 40
Hoby, Margaret 27, 122, 139
Holbein, Hans 2
homosexuality 187–8
Hooker, John 64
Howard, Charles 127–8, 177
Howard, Frances, Countess of Essex
    141, 197, 199, 201
Howard, Lord Henry 133, 192
    attack on Bess 144–6
    attacks the Raleghs 134–5
Howard, Lord Thomas (Duke of
    Suffolk) 199
Huguenots 22
Hull, Mistress 91
humours, theory of 130–1
Hunsdon, Lord 77
Huntingdon, Earl of (Henry Hastings)
    21–2, 26–7, 99, 101, 110, 237

Ingram, Sir Arthur 205
Islands Expedition 107, 108–9

James I (James VI of Scotland) 53,
    131, 139, 197–8, 218, 247
  death of 248
  and George Villiers 198–9
  homosexuality of 187–8
  and Ralegh 159, 220
  and Robert Carr 188, 197
  and Robert Cecil 141
  and Sherborne 189, 205
  succeeds to English throne 139
Jones, Inigo 259
Jones, John 83
Jonson, Ben 112, 160, 194, 195,
    203–4, 244–5, 259, 260

Katharine of Aragon 14
Keyes, Thomas 20, 30
Keymis, Lawrence 111, 167, 188, 190,
    211
Kildare, Lady 127–8, 132–3, 136, 151
Killigrew, Sir Thomas 21, 25, 233
Killigrew, Sir William 150
King, Samuel 240
Kingsmill, Bridget 110
Knollys, Lettice 33, 37
Knollys, Sir William 48

Lacey, Robert 5, 108
Laighton, Thomas 91
Lambert, Roger 187
Lascelles, Edmund 169–70
Latham, Agnes 95
Leicester, Earl of (Robert Dudley) 6,
    20, 27, 33, 34
  and Elizabeth I 21
  marries Lettice Knollys 37
Leigh, Dorothy, A Mother's Blessing
    185
Leigh, Sir John 210, 243
Lennox, Duke of 134
Lewis, Anne 194
love, attitudes to 92
Lowes, Sir Thomas 215
Lucas, Anna, see Throckmorton, Anna

Manners, Bridget 44, 69, 72
Markham, Gervase 159
Marlowe, Christopher 89, 115

marriage, attitudes to 92–3
Mary, Queen of Scots 20, 21, 24, 37
  Babington Plot 51
  execution 52
  marriage to Darnley 24–5
Mary Tudor, Queen 16–17, 18
medicine 162–4
Meers, Elizabeth 252
Meers, John 110, 251, 252
More, Ann 180
More, Sir George 180
More, Mary 180

Naunton, Sir Robert 216, 217
Norfolk, Duke of 25
Norris, Sir John 7
Northumberland, Earl of 16

Orsini, Virginio 127
Overbury, Sir Thomas 199
Oxford, Earl of 34, 38, 49

Parr, Catherine 15
Pembroke, Countess of 236
Pembroke, Earl of 244
Pennington, John 205, 211
Pett, Phineas 204, 255
Philip II, King of Spain 19
plague 73, 75, 94, 144, 152, 164
Plowden, Alison 13
Poe, Leonard 162, 196
Pope, Alexander 197
Powlet, Sir William 206
Poyntz, John 239–40
Price, Robert 42
Puckering, Sir John 99, 100, 101
Pym, Francis 246, 253

Ragapo, Leonard 163
Ralegh, Bess (Elizabeth) 1–2, 47
  arrested 66, 214
  attacks on 132–5, 144–6
  birth 13, 23
  character 97, 248
  at court 1–2, 5, 11, 32, 33–5, 38,
    47–8, 51, 64–5
  education 27–8
  financial affairs 26–7, 86, 95,

98–101, 110–11, 113–14, 137–8,
165–6, 177–8, 206–7, 229–31,
235, 238, 242–3, 250–1, 256–7
friends 75, 156, 244–6
and Gunpowder Plot 173–4
health 130, 131
her children 62–4, 75, 83–4, 126,
172, 209, 211
and her mother 25, 55
increasing authority of 111–12, 118,
122, 132, 164–5, 190
interrogated 219
legal cases 191–2, 234–8, 251–3,
255
marriage 4, 42–3, 59, 65–8
medicinal skills 162–3
obtains Bill of Restitution 247–50,
253–4, 255
portraits of 65, 133–4, 176–7,
228–9
pregnancies 3–4, 56–7, 60–1, 81–4,
168–72
and Queen Anne 141–2, 193, 220
and Ralegh's burial 225–7
Ralegh's escape attempt 213–15
and Ralegh's execution 221–3
and Ralegh's expeditions 96–7,
204–9, 211, 213
and Ralegh's posthumous reputation
231–4, 247
and Ralegh's suicide letter 147–9
and Ralegh's trial 150–2
relationship with Ralegh 6, 10,
55–6, 93–4, 96, 131, 156–8, 176,
178
and Robert Cecil 86–8, 97–8, 107,
109, 128–9, 136, 154–6, 164–5
and Sherborne 77–80, 84–6, 89–91,
124–5, 166, 189–91
social life 35–7, 115–18
spied on 216–17
Tower of London 70–1, 77, 161,
164, 186
writings of 28–9, 109–10
Ralegh, Carew 189, 202, 215, 217,
244, 247, 252, 254–5, 257, 261
birth and christening 172

enters Parliament 260
Gentleman of the Privy Chamber
258–9
marriage 257–8
restitution in blood 252–3, 255
Ralegh, Damerei 63–4, 66
birth of 62
death of 75
Ralegh, Sir John de 64
Ralegh, Margaret 166
Ralegh, Walter
appearance 2, 5, 117
arrested 38, 66
and Bess's pregnancy 56, 57
burial 225–7
character 2, 5, 96, 123
condemned to death 150, 221
depression 96, 104, 161, 219, 220
early years 30–1
and Elizabeth I 2–3, 4, 39–40, 65,
71–2, 80–1, 135
epitaph 227–8
escape attempt 213–15
and Essex 6–7, 107–9, 121, 224
execution 221–5
expeditions 40, 49, 60–1, 65, 96–7,
101–2, 104–9, 202, 204–13
financial ruin and eviction 140–1
governor of Jersey 125
health 130–1, 161–2, 175–6, 216
illegitimate daughter 4, 113, 147
marriage 4, 59, 65–6, 66–8, 92
medicinal skills 162–3
poetry 2–3, 7, 35, 71–2, 115–16
portrait of 228
relationship with Bess 5, 10–11,
55–6, 61–2, 80, 88, 94–6,
111–12, 118, 190–1
religious beliefs 89
reprieved by King James 159
and Robert Cecil 69–70, 88, 107,
109, 132, 136–7, 148
and Sherborne 67, 124–5, 137
suicide attempt 147–50
and tobacco 163–4
in Tower of London 70–1, 143,
147, 161, 202, 215

and treason 143–6, 154, 219–20
trial of 152–4
urges Bess to remarry 147–9
and Wat Ralegh 83, 94–5, 126, 184–5, 203, 209–10
wealth of 52, 55
will of 95, 113
writes from condemned cell 156–8
Ralegh, Walter ('Wat') 88–9, 198, 204
birth 83
character 195
death of 209–10
education 125–6
and his father 113–14, 167–8, 184–5, 203
marriage plans for 182–3
portrait of 228
tours Europe 193–5
at university 183–4
Rich, Lord 9, 10, 63
Rich, Penelope, see Devereux, Penelope
Richelieu, Cardinal 249
Roanoke 40, 49
Robsart, Amy 21, 37
Russell, Elizabeth 9

Sackville, Edward 197
St Johns, Sir William 202
St Ravee, Sir William 259
Sanderson, William 96–7, 191–2
Saunders, William 175
Scarfanassi, Count of 214
Schama, Simon 197
Seymour, Edward (Earl of Hertford) 18, 20
Seymour, Jane 13, 14
Seymour, Lord Thomas 15
Shakespeare, William 116, 160
Shelbury, John 156, 165, 182–3, 190, 191, 236
Sheldon, Philippa 258
Shelton, Mary 69
Sherborne 77–80, 84–6, 89–91, 114–15, 124–5, 166, 188–9, 204–5, 247–8, 251, 256, 260
Shrewsbury, Lady, see Bess of Hardwick
Sidney, Lady Barbara 112

Sidney, Sir Philip 8, 9–10, 38, 53
Sidney, Sir Robert 107
Simier, Jean de 33
Skory, Silvanus 210
Smith, Robert 165, 191, 225
Smythson, Robert 115
Somerset, Earl of, see Carr, Robert
Southwell, Elizabeth 9
Spencer, Gabriel 194
Stafford, Lord 54
Stafford, Sir Edward 70
Stanley, Venetia 197
Star Chamber 151
Stokes, Adrian 18, 19, 29, 30, 35, 42, 49, 55, 234
Stokes, William 42
Strong, Roy 119
Stuart, Arabella 121, 135, 144
Stukeley, Sir Lewis 233
Suffolk, Duke of 17
Suffolk, Frances, Duchess of 16, 17, 18–19

Talbot, George 34
Talbot, John 219, 221
theatre 116–17, 160
Throckmorton, Anna (née Lucas) 50, 54, 62, 63, 82, 239
Throckmorton, Anne (née Carew) 13, 17–18, 22–3, 25–6, 42, 46–7, 52, 181
ambitions for Bess 31–2, 42–4
and Bess's inheritance 26–7, 52
death of 54
marriages 14, 16, 29
Throckmorton, Arthur 13, 18, 25, 29, 31, 39, 43, 46–7, 49, 50, 52–3, 63, 66–7, 75, 77, 82, 97, 104, 114, 146–8, 170–1, 218–19, 227
and Bess's inheritance 99–100
and Bess's marriage 58–9, 100–1
as country gentleman 178–9
death of 239
and Essex 58, 121–2
as father 179–80
and Gunpowder Plot 174
as head of family 41, 54–5

health 130, 131
knighted 106
marriage 50
and Ralegh 105–6
visits Sherborne 88–9, 91
and Walsingham 53, 54
Throckmorton, Francis 32, 34–5, 45–7
Throckmorton, George 14, 178
Throckmorton, Job 7
Throckmorton, Sir John 198
Throckmorton, Mary 82
Throckmorton, Muriel 173
Throckmorton, Sir Nicholas (father)
    13, 14, 15, 21–2
  acquitted of treason 17
  death 25
  and Elizabeth I 20–1
  imprisoned 17, 25
  marriage 16
  and Mary, Queen of Scots 20, 24
Throckmorton, Nicholas (brother) 55,
    104, 173, 178, 180–1, 190, 206,
    226, 238–9
  and Bess 233–40, 242–3, 256–7
  death of 260, 261
  financial crisis 242
  growing role of 181–2
  marriage 180
  and Ralegh 182
Throckmorton, Robert 18, 55
Throckmorton, Thomas 55
Throckmorton, William 17, 25,
    99–100, 182
Throckmorton-Carew, Francis 257
Throckmorton-Carew, Nicholas, see
    Throckmorton, Nicholas (brother)
Thynne, Joan 172
Thynne, Maria 122
Tichborne, Benjamin 156
Tichborne, Chidiock 221
tobacco 163–4
Tresham, Francis 173, 174
Tresham, Lady Meryll 174

Troyes, Treaty of (1564) 22
Twysden, Roger 223–4, 225, 247

Van Lore, Sir Peter 236–8
Vavasour, Anne 38
Vavasour, Thomas 9
Villiers, Sir Edward 202
Villiers, George (Duke of Buckingham)
    198–201, 205, 220, 243, 248–50,
    258

Wade, Thomas 205
Walsingham, Lady 110
Walsingham, Sir Francis 8, 27, 34, 38,
    39, 45, 51, 52, 53, 54
Walsingham-Sidney, Francis 8–9
Walton, Isaac 195–6
Wentworth, Peter 80
Willoughby, Lord 54
Wilson, Sir Thomas 216–17, 220, 230
Wiltshire, Marquis of 129
women
  advice to sons 185–6
  churching of 84
  and education 27–8
  and marriage 92–3, 234–5
  political opportunities for 44–5
  political role of 26
  and pregnancy 81–3, 170–1
  and property 101, 165
  prospects for 26
  and sex 112–13
  social freedom of 93
  and theatre 117
  widowhood 234
Wood, Anthony 183
Wotton, Edward 52, 53, 67, 154, 179,
    239
Wotton, Sir Henry 198
Wotton, Thomas 179, 180
Wyatt, Sir Thomas 35